Mometrix
TEST PREPARATION

I0866888

Florida

Grade 8 Science Test Prep Guide

DEAR FUTURE EXAM SUCCESS STORY

First of all, **THANK YOU** for purchasing Mometrix study materials!

Second, congratulations! You are one of the few determined test-takers who are committed to doing whatever it takes to excel on your exam. **You have come to the right place.** We developed these study materials with one goal in mind: to deliver you the information you need in a format that's concise and easy to use.

In addition to optimizing your guide for the content of the test, we've outlined our recommended steps for breaking down the preparation process into small, attainable goals so you can make sure you stay on track.

We've also analyzed the entire test-taking process, identifying the most common pitfalls and showing how you can overcome them and be ready for any curveball the test throws you.

Standardized testing is one of the biggest obstacles on your road to success, which only increases the importance of doing well in the high-pressure, high-stakes environment of test day. Your results on this test could have a significant impact on your future, and this guide provides the information and practical advice to help you achieve your full potential on test day.

Your success is our success

We would love to hear from you! If you would like to share the story of your exam success or if you have any questions or comments in regard to our products, please contact us at **800-673-8175** or **support@mometrix.com**.

Thanks again for your business and we wish you continued success!

Sincerely,
The Mometrix Test Preparation Team

Written and edited by the Mometrix Exam Secrets Test Prep Team
Printed in the United States of America

TABLE OF CONTENTS

Introduction

Thank you for purchasing this resource! You have made the choice to prepare yourself for a test that could have a huge impact on your future, and this guide is designed to help you be fully ready for test day. Obviously, it's important to have a solid understanding of the test material, but you also need to be prepared for the unique environment and stressors of the test, so that you can perform to the best of your abilities.

For this purpose, the first section that appears in this guide is the **Secret Keys**. We've devoted countless hours to meticulously researching what works and what doesn't, and we've boiled down our findings to the five most impactful steps you can take to improve your performance on the test. We start at the beginning with study planning and move through the preparation process, all the way to the testing strategies that will help you get the most out of what you know when you're finally sitting in front of the test.

We recommend that you start preparing for your test as far in advance as possible. However, if you've bought this guide as a last-minute study resource and only have a few days before your test, we recommend that you skip over the first two Secret Keys since they address a long-term study plan.

If you struggle with **test anxiety**, we strongly encourage you to check out our recommendations for how you can overcome it. Test anxiety is a formidable foe, but it can be beaten, and we want to make sure you have the tools you need to defeat it.

Secret Key #1 – Plan Big, Study Small

There's a lot riding on your performance. If you want to ace this test, you're going to need to keep your skills sharp and the material fresh in your mind. You need a plan that lets you review everything you need to know while still fitting in your schedule. We'll break this strategy down into three categories.

Information Organization

Start with the information you already have: the official test outline. From this, you can make a complete list of all the concepts you need to cover before the test. Organize these concepts into groups that can be studied together, and create a list of any related vocabulary you need to learn so you can brush up on any difficult terms. You'll want to keep this vocabulary list handy once you actually start studying since you may need to add to it along the way.

Time Management

Once you have your set of study concepts, decide how to spread them out over the time you have left before the test. Break your study plan into small, clear goals so you have a manageable task for each day and know exactly what you're doing. Then just focus on one small step at a time. When you manage your time this way, you don't need to spend hours at a time studying. Studying a small block of content for a short period each day helps you retain information better and avoid stressing over how much you have left to do. You can relax knowing that you have a plan to cover everything in time. In order for this strategy to be effective though, you have to start studying early and stick to your schedule. Avoid the exhaustion and futility that comes from last-minute cramming!

Study Environment

The environment you study in has a big impact on your learning. Studying in a coffee shop, while probably more enjoyable, is not likely to be as fruitful as studying in a quiet room. It's important to keep distractions to a minimum. You're only planning to study for a short block of time, so make the most of it. Don't pause to check your phone or get up to find a snack. It's also important to **avoid multitasking**. Research has consistently shown that multitasking will make your studying dramatically less effective. Your study area should also be comfortable and well-lit so you don't have the distraction of straining your eyes or sitting on an uncomfortable chair.

The time of day you study is also important. You want to be rested and alert. Don't wait until just before bedtime. Study when you'll be most likely to comprehend and remember. Even better, if you know what time of day your test will be, set that time aside for study. That way your brain will be used to working on that subject at that specific time and you'll have a better chance of recalling information.

Finally, it can be helpful to team up with others who are studying for the same test. Your actual studying should be done in as isolated an environment as possible, but the work of organizing the information and setting up the study plan can be divided up. In between study sessions, you can discuss with your teammates the concepts that you're all studying and quiz each other on the details. Just be sure that your teammates are as serious about the test as you are. If you find that your study time is being replaced with social time, you might need to find a new team.

Secret Key #2 – Make Your Studying Count

You're devoting a lot of time and effort to preparing for this test, so you want to be absolutely certain it will pay off. This means doing more than just reading the content and hoping you can remember it on test day. It's important to make every minute of study count. There are two main areas you can focus on to make your studying count.

Retention

It doesn't matter how much time you study if you can't remember the material. You need to make sure you are retaining the concepts. To check your retention of the information you're learning, try recalling it at later times with minimal prompting. Try carrying around flashcards and glance at one or two from time to time or ask a friend who's also studying for the test to quiz you.

To enhance your retention, look for ways to put the information into practice so that you can apply it rather than simply recalling it. If you're using the information in practical ways, it will be much easier to remember. Similarly, it helps to solidify a concept in your mind if you're not only reading it to yourself but also explaining it to someone else. Ask a friend to let you teach them about a concept you're a little shaky on (or speak aloud to an imaginary audience if necessary). As you try to summarize, define, give examples, and answer your friend's questions, you'll understand the concepts better and they will stay with you longer. Finally, step back for a big picture view and ask yourself how each piece of information fits with the whole subject. When you link the different concepts together and see them working together as a whole, it's easier to remember the individual components.

Finally, practice showing your work on any multi-step problems, even if you're just studying. Writing out each step you take to solve a problem will help solidify the process in your mind, and you'll be more likely to remember it during the test.

Modality

Modality simply refers to the means or method by which you study. Choosing a study modality that fits your own individual learning style is crucial. No two people learn best in exactly the same way, so it's important to know your strengths and use them to your advantage.

For example, if you learn best by visualization, focus on visualizing a concept in your mind and draw an image or a diagram. Try color-coding your notes, illustrating them, or creating symbols that will trigger your mind to recall a learned concept. If you learn best by hearing or discussing information, find a study partner who learns the same way or read aloud to yourself. Think about how to put the information in your own words. Imagine that you are giving a lecture on the topic and record yourself so you can listen to it later.

For any learning style, flashcards can be helpful. Organize the information so you can take advantage of spare moments to review. Underline key words or phrases. Use different colors for different categories. Mnemonic devices (such as creating a short list in which every item starts with the same letter) can also help with retention. Find what works best for you and use it to store the information in your mind most effectively and easily.

Secret Key #3 – Practice the Right Way

Your success on test day depends not only on how many hours you put into preparing, but also on whether you prepared the right way. It's good to check along the way to see if your studying is paying off. One of the most effective ways to do this is by taking practice tests to evaluate your progress. Practice tests are useful because they show exactly where you need to improve. Every time you take a practice test, pay special attention to these three groups of questions:

- The questions you got wrong
- The questions you had to guess on, even if you guessed right
- The questions you found difficult or slow to work through

This will show you exactly what your weak areas are, and where you need to devote more study time. Ask yourself why each of these questions gave you trouble. Was it because you didn't understand the material? Was it because you didn't remember the vocabulary? Do you need more repetitions on this type of question to build speed and confidence? Dig into those questions and figure out how you can strengthen your weak areas as you go back to review the material.

Additionally, many practice tests have a section explaining the answer choices. It can be tempting to read the explanation and think that you now have a good understanding of the concept. However, an explanation likely only covers part of the question's broader context. Even if the explanation makes perfect sense, **go back and investigate** every concept related to the question until you're positive you have a thorough understanding.

As you go along, keep in mind that the practice test is just that: practice. Memorizing these questions and answers will not be very helpful on the actual test because it is unlikely to have any of the same exact questions. If you only know the right answers to the sample questions, you won't be prepared for the real thing. **Study the concepts** until you understand them fully, and then you'll be able to answer any question that shows up on the test.

It's important to wait on the practice tests until you're ready. If you take a test on your first day of study, you may be overwhelmed by the amount of material covered and how much you need to learn. Work up to it gradually.

On test day, you'll need to be prepared for answering questions, managing your time, and using the test-taking strategies you've learned. It's a lot to balance, like a mental marathon that will have a big impact on your future. Like training for a marathon, you'll need to start slowly and work your way up. When test day arrives, you'll be ready.

Start with the strategies you've read in the first two Secret Keys—plan your course and study in the way that works best for you. If you have time, consider using multiple study resources to get different approaches to the same concepts. It can be helpful to see difficult concepts from more than one angle. Then find a good source for practice tests. Many times, the test website will suggest potential study resources or provide sample tests.

Practice Test Strategy

If you're able to find at least three practice tests, we recommend this strategy:

Untimed and Open-Book Practice

Take the first test with no time constraints and with your notes and study guide handy. Take your time and focus on applying the strategies you've learned.

Timed and Open-Book Practice

Take the second practice test open-book as well, but set a timer and practice pacing yourself to finish in time.

Timed and Closed-Book Practice

Take any other practice tests as if it were test day. Set a timer and put away your study materials. Sit at a table or desk in a quiet room, imagine yourself at the testing center, and answer questions as quickly and accurately as possible.

Keep repeating timed and closed-book tests on a regular basis until you run out of practice tests or it's time for the actual test. Your mind will be ready for the schedule and stress of test day, and you'll be able to focus on recalling the material you've learned.

Secret Key #4 – Pace Yourself

Once you're fully prepared for the material on the test, your biggest challenge on test day will be managing your time. Just knowing that the clock is ticking can make you panic even if you have plenty of time left. Work on pacing yourself so you can build confidence against the time constraints of the exam. Pacing is a difficult skill to master, especially in a high-pressure environment, so **practice is vital**.

Set time expectations for your pace based on how much time is available. For example, if a section has 60 questions and the time limit is 30 minutes, you know you have to average 30 seconds or less per question in order to answer them all. Although 30 seconds is the hard limit, set 25 seconds per question as your goal, so you reserve extra time to spend on harder questions. When you budget extra time for the harder questions, you no longer have any reason to stress when those questions take longer to answer.

Don't let this time expectation distract you from working through the test at a calm, steady pace, but keep it in mind so you don't spend too much time on any one question. Recognize that taking extra time on one question you don't understand may keep you from answering two that you do understand later in the test. If your time limit for a question is up and you're still not sure of the answer, mark it and move on, and come back to it later if the time and the test format allow. If the testing format doesn't allow you to return to earlier questions, just make an educated guess; then put it out of your mind and move on.

On the easier questions, be careful not to rush. It may seem wise to hurry through them so you have more time for the challenging ones, but it's not worth missing one if you know the concept and just didn't take the time to read the question fully. Work efficiently but make sure you understand the question and have looked at all of the answer choices, since more than one may seem right at first.

Even if you're paying attention to the time, you may find yourself a little behind at some point. You should speed up to get back on track, but do so wisely. Don't panic; just take a few seconds less on each question until you're caught up. Don't guess without thinking, but do look through the answer choices and eliminate any you know are wrong. If you can get down to two choices, it is often worthwhile to guess from those. Once you've chosen an answer, move on and don't dwell on any that you skipped or had to hurry through. If a question was taking too long, chances are it was one of the harder ones, so you weren't as likely to get it right anyway.

On the other hand, if you find yourself getting ahead of schedule, it may be beneficial to slow down a little. The more quickly you work, the more likely you are to make a careless mistake that will affect your score. You've budgeted time for each question, so don't be afraid to spend that time. Practice an efficient but careful pace to get the most out of the time you have.

Secret Key #5 – Have a Plan for Guessing

When you're taking the test, you may find yourself stuck on a question. Some of the answer choices seem better than others, but you don't see the one answer choice that is obviously correct. What do you do?

The scenario described above is very common, yet most test takers have not effectively prepared for it. Developing and practicing a plan for guessing may be one of the single most effective uses of your time as you get ready for the exam.

In developing your plan for guessing, there are three questions to address:

- When should you start the guessing process?
- How should you narrow down the choices?
- Which answer should you choose?

When to Start the Guessing Process

Unless your plan for guessing is to select C every time (which, despite its merits, is not what we recommend), you need to leave yourself enough time to apply your answer elimination strategies. Since you have a limited amount of time for each question, that means that if you're going to give yourself the best shot at guessing correctly, you have to decide quickly whether or not you will guess.

Of course, the best-case scenario is that you don't have to guess at all, so first, see if you can answer the question based on your knowledge of the subject and basic reasoning skills. Focus on the key words in the question and try to jog your memory of related topics. Give yourself a chance to bring the knowledge to mind, but once you realize that you don't have (or you can't access) the knowledge you need to answer the question, it's time to start the guessing process.

It's almost always better to start the guessing process too early than too late. It only takes a few seconds to remember something and answer the question from knowledge. Carefully eliminating wrong answer choices takes longer. Plus, going through the process of eliminating answer choices can actually help jog your memory.

Summary: Start the guessing process as soon as you decide that you can't answer the question based on your knowledge.

How to Narrow Down the Choices

The next chapter in this book (**Test-Taking Strategies**) includes a wide range of strategies for how to approach questions and how to look for answer choices to eliminate. You will definitely want to read those carefully, practice them, and figure out which ones work best for you. Here though, we're going to address a mindset rather than a particular strategy.

Your odds of guessing an answer correctly depend on how many options you are choosing from.

Number of options left	5	4	3	2	1
Odds of guessing correctly	20%	25%	33%	50%	100%

You can see from this chart just how valuable it is to be able to eliminate incorrect answers and make an educated guess, but there are two things that many test takers do that cause them to miss out on the benefits of guessing:

- Accidentally eliminating the correct answer
- Selecting an answer based on an impression

We'll look at the first one here, and the second one in the next section.

To avoid accidentally eliminating the correct answer, we recommend a thought exercise called **the $5 challenge**. In this challenge, you only eliminate an answer choice from contention if you are willing to bet $5 on it being wrong. Why $5? Five dollars is a small but not insignificant amount of money. It's an amount you could afford to lose but wouldn't want to throw away. And while losing $5 once might not hurt too much, doing it twenty times will set you back $100. In the same way, each small decision you make—eliminating a choice here, guessing on a question there—won't by itself impact your score very much, but when you put them all together, they can make a big difference. By holding each answer choice elimination decision to a higher standard, you can reduce the risk of accidentally eliminating the correct answer.

The $5 challenge can also be applied in a positive sense: If you are willing to bet $5 that an answer choice *is* correct, go ahead and mark it as correct.

Summary: Only eliminate an answer choice if you are willing to bet $5 that it is wrong.

Which Answer to Choose

You're taking the test. You've run into a hard question and decided you'll have to guess. You've eliminated all the answer choices you're willing to bet $5 on. Now you have to pick an answer. Why do we even need to talk about this? Why can't you just pick whichever one you feel like when the time comes?

The answer to these questions is that if you don't come into the test with a plan, you'll rely on your impression to select an answer choice, and if you do that, you risk falling into a trap. The test writers know that everyone who takes their test will be guessing on some of the questions, so they intentionally write wrong answer choices to seem plausible. You still have to pick an answer though, and if the wrong answer choices are designed to look right, how can you ever be sure that you're not falling for their trap? The best solution we've found to this dilemma is to take the decision out of your hands entirely. Here is the process we recommend:

Once you've eliminated any choices that you are confident (willing to bet $5) are wrong, select the first remaining choice as your answer.

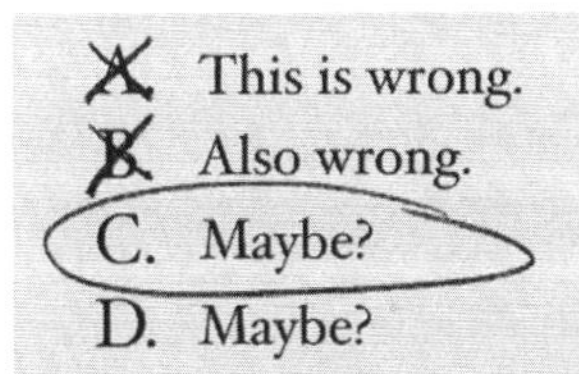

Whether you choose to select the first remaining choice, the second, or the last, the important thing is that you use some preselected standard. Using this approach guarantees that you will not be enticed into selecting an answer choice that looks right, because you are not basing your decision on how the answer choices look.

This is not meant to make you question your knowledge. Instead, it is to help you recognize the difference between your knowledge and your impressions. There's a huge difference between thinking an answer is right because of what you know, and thinking an answer is right because it looks or sounds like it should be right.

Summary: To ensure that your selection is appropriately random, make a predetermined selection from among all answer choices you have not eliminated.

Test-Taking Strategies

This section contains a list of test-taking strategies that you may find helpful as you work through the test. By taking what you know and applying logical thought, you can maximize your chances of answering any question correctly!

It is very important to realize that every question is different and every person is different: no single strategy will work on every question, and no single strategy will work for every person. That's why we've included all of them here, so you can try them out and determine which ones work best for different types of questions and which ones work best for you.

Question Strategies

Read Carefully

Read the question and the answer choices carefully. Don't miss the question because you misread the terms. You have plenty of time to read each question thoroughly and make sure you understand what is being asked. Yet a happy medium must be attained, so don't waste too much time. You must read carefully and efficiently.

Contextual Clues

Look for contextual clues. If the question includes a word you are not familiar with, look at the immediate context for some indication of what the word might mean. Contextual clues can often give you all the information you need to decipher the meaning of an unfamiliar word. Even if you can't determine the meaning, you may be able to narrow down the possibilities enough to make a solid guess at the answer to the question.

Prefixes

If you're having trouble with a word in the question or answer choices, try dissecting it. Take advantage of every clue that the word might include. Prefixes can be a huge help. Usually, they allow you to determine a basic meaning. *Pre-* means before, *post-* means after, *pro-* is positive, *de-* is negative. From prefixes, you can get an idea of the general meaning of the word and try to put it into context.

Hedge Words

Watch out for critical hedge words, such as *likely, may, can, often, almost, mostly, usually, generally, rarely*, and *sometimes*. Question writers insert these hedge phrases to cover every possibility. Often an answer choice will be wrong simply because it leaves no room for exception. Be on guard for answer choices that have definitive words such as *exactly* and *always*.

Switchback Words

Stay alert for *switchbacks*. These are the words and phrases frequently used to alert you to shifts in thought. The most common switchback words are *but*, *although*, and *however*. Others include *nevertheless, on the other hand, even though, while, in spite of, despite*, and *regardless of*. Switchback words are important to catch because they can change the direction of the question or an answer choice.

☑ Face Value

When in doubt, use common sense. Accept the situation in the problem at face value. Don't read too much into it. These problems will not require you to make wild assumptions. If you have to go beyond creativity and warp time or space in order to have an answer choice fit the question, then you should move on and consider the other answer choices. These are normal problems rooted in reality. The applicable relationship or explanation may not be readily apparent, but it is there for you to figure out. Use your common sense to interpret anything that isn't clear.

Answer Choice Strategies

☑ Answer Selection

The most thorough way to pick an answer choice is to identify and eliminate wrong answers until only one is left, then confirm it is the correct answer. Sometimes an answer choice may immediately seem right, but be careful. The test writers will usually put more than one reasonable answer choice on each question, so take a second to read all of them and make sure that the other choices are not equally obvious. As long as you have time left, it is better to read every answer choice than to pick the first one that looks right without checking the others.

☑ Answer Choice Families

An answer choice family consists of two (in rare cases, three) answer choices that are very similar in construction and cannot all be true at the same time. If you see two answer choices that are direct opposites or parallels, one of them is usually the correct answer. For instance, if one answer choice says that quantity *x* increases and another either says that quantity *x* decreases (opposite) or says that quantity *y* increases (parallel), then those answer choices would fall into the same family. An answer choice that doesn't match the construction of the answer choice family is more likely to be incorrect. Most questions will not have answer choice families, but when they do appear, you should be prepared to recognize them.

☑ Eliminate Answers

Eliminate answer choices as soon as you realize they are wrong, but make sure you consider all possibilities. If you are eliminating answer choices and realize that the last one you are left with is also wrong, don't panic. Start over and consider each choice again. There may be something you missed the first time that you will realize on the second pass.

☑ Avoid Fact Traps

Don't be distracted by an answer choice that is factually true but doesn't answer the question. You are looking for the choice that answers the question. Stay focused on what the question is asking for so you don't accidentally pick an answer that is true but incorrect. Always go back to the question and make sure the answer choice you've selected actually answers the question and is not merely a true statement.

☑ Extreme Statements

In general, you should avoid answers that put forth extreme actions as standard practice or proclaim controversial ideas as established fact. An answer choice that states the "process should be used in certain situations, if..." is much more likely to be correct than one that states the "process should be discontinued completely." The first is a calm rational statement and doesn't even make a definitive, uncompromising stance, using a hedge word *if* to provide wiggle room, whereas the second choice is far more extreme.

⊘ Benchmark

As you read through the answer choices and you come across one that seems to answer the question well, mentally select that answer choice. This is not your final answer, but it's the one that will help you evaluate the other answer choices. The one that you selected is your benchmark or standard for judging each of the other answer choices. Every other answer choice must be compared to your benchmark. That choice is correct until proven otherwise by another answer choice beating it. If you find a better answer, then that one becomes your new benchmark. Once you've decided that no other choice answers the question as well as your benchmark, you have your final answer.

⊘ Predict the Answer

Before you even start looking at the answer choices, it is often best to try to predict the answer. When you come up with the answer on your own, it is easier to avoid distractions and traps because you will know exactly what to look for. The right answer choice is unlikely to be word-for-word what you came up with, but it should be a close match. Even if you are confident that you have the right answer, you should still take the time to read each option before moving on.

General Strategies

⊘ Tough Questions

If you are stumped on a problem or it appears too hard or too difficult, don't waste time. Move on! Remember though, if you can quickly check for obviously incorrect answer choices, your chances of guessing correctly are greatly improved. Before you completely give up, at least try to knock out a couple of possible answers. Eliminate what you can and then guess at the remaining answer choices before moving on.

⊘ Check Your Work

Since you will probably not know every term listed and the answer to every question, it is important that you get credit for the ones that you do know. Don't miss any questions through careless mistakes. If at all possible, try to take a second to look back over your answer selection and make sure you've selected the correct answer choice and haven't made a costly careless mistake (such as marking an answer choice that you didn't mean to mark). This quick double check should more than pay for itself in caught mistakes for the time it costs.

⊘ Pace Yourself

It's easy to be overwhelmed when you're looking at a page full of questions; your mind is confused and full of random thoughts, and the clock is ticking down faster than you would like. Calm down and maintain the pace that you have set for yourself. Especially as you get down to the last few minutes of the test, don't let the small numbers on the clock make you panic. As long as you are on track by monitoring your pace, you are guaranteed to have time for each question.

⊘ Don't Rush

It is very easy to make errors when you are in a hurry. Maintaining a fast pace in answering questions is pointless if it makes you miss questions that you would have gotten right otherwise. Test writers like to include distracting information and wrong answers that seem right. Taking a little extra time to avoid careless mistakes can make all the difference in your test score. Find a pace that allows you to be confident in the answers that you select.

⊘ Keep Moving

Panicking will not help you pass the test, so do your best to stay calm and keep moving. Taking deep breaths and going through the answer elimination steps you practiced can help to break through a stress barrier and keep your pace.

Final Notes

The combination of a solid foundation of content knowledge and the confidence that comes from practicing your plan for applying that knowledge is the key to maximizing your performance on test day. As your foundation of content knowledge is built up and strengthened, you'll find that the strategies included in this chapter become more and more effective in helping you quickly sift through the distractions and traps of the test to isolate the correct answer.

Now that you're preparing to move forward into the test content chapters of this book, be sure to keep your goal in mind. As you read, think about how you will be able to apply this information on the test. If you've already seen sample questions for the test and you have an idea of the question format and style, try to come up with questions of your own that you can answer based on what you're reading. This will give you valuable practice applying your knowledge in the same ways you can expect to on test day.

Good luck and good studying!

Nature of Science

Safety

Safety Procedures

Everyone working in a lab setting should be careful to follow these rules to protect themselves and others from injury or accidents.

- Students should wear a **lab apron** and **safety goggles**.
- **Loose** or **dangling** clothing and jewelry, necklaces, and earrings should not be worn.
- Those with **long hair** should tie it back.
- Care should always be taken not to **splash chemicals**.
- **Open-toed shoes** such as sandals and flip-flops should not be worn, nor should wrist watches.
- **Glasses** are preferable to contact lenses since the latter carries a risk of chemicals getting caught between the lens and the eye.
- Students should always be **supervised** during an experiment.
- The area where the experiment is taking place and the surrounding floor should be **free of clutter**.
- **Food** and **drink** should also not be allowed in a lab setting.
- **Cords** should not be allowed to **dangle** from work stations.
- There should be no **rough-housing** in the lab.
- **Wash hands** before and after the lab is complete.

Safety Gloves

There are many types of **gloves** available to help protect the skin from cuts, burns, and chemical splashes. There are many considerations to take into account when choosing a glove. For example, gloves that are highly protective may limit grip or accuracy. Some gloves may not offer appropriate protection against a specific chemical. Disposable latex, vinyl, or nitrile gloves are usually appropriate for most circumstances, and offer protection from incidental splashes and contact.

Laboratory Accidents

Accidents happen in labs, so it is important to know how to clean up, stay safe, and report the accident to the teacher. Any spills or accidents should be **reported** to the teacher so that the teacher can determine the safest clean-up method. The student should start to wash off a **chemical** spilled on the skin while reporting the incident. Some spills may require removal of contaminated clothing and use of the **safety shower**. Broken glass should be disposed of in a designated container. If someone's clothing catches fire they should walk to the safety shower and use it to extinguish the flames. A fire blanket may be used to smother a **lab fire**. A fire extinguisher, phone, spill neutralizers, and a first aid box are other types of **safety equipment** found in the lab. Students should be familiar with **routes** out of the room and the building in case of fire.

Reusing and Disposing of Materials

When conducting an investigation, scientists try to **conserve** materials by making sure they are not overused or wasted. To prevent overuse, it is important for scientists to consider potential ways to **limit** the use of certain materials. For example, consider glass and plastic. In a lab, plastic is not the most durable material, so it is not often reusable. Because of this, a scientist would try to limit its use by using something more durable, like glass. By using a more durable material that can be reused, the scientist would reduce the amount of waste produced by the experiment. Next, scientists consider whether it is possible to **reuse** the material in another investigation.

Disposal

Materials made of glass or plastic may be reusable, depending on how they have been used. However, in some cases, the dangers of reusing equipment outweigh the benefits of conservation. For example, plastic containers can be degraded by harsh chemicals, and glass microscope slides used to look at harmful microbes can be difficult to sterilize. In these cases, scientists follow a set of procedures for the proper **disposal** of materials. **Plastics** should be rinsed thoroughly and recycled or disposed of according to local regulations. Contaminated or broken **glass** should be placed in a container separate from regular waste, such as a cardboard box or dedicated glass bin. Guidelines for **chemical** disposal vary widely based on the properties of the chemical, and some chemicals are unsafe to dispose of down the drain or in the trash. Therefore, it is important that scientists research and consider the proper disposal method of any chemicals prior to using them in an investigation.

Science Knowledge and Scientific Process

Scientific knowledge is knowledge about the world that we understand by observing and testing. The **scientific process** is how we try to gain scientific knowledge. The steps are to make an initial observation, make a hypothesis, test the hypothesis with an experiment, draw conclusions from the experiment, then start over with new observations.

Scientific Knowledge

Scientific knowledge refers to any topic that is studied **empirically**, meaning that it is based on observation of a **phenomenon** in an objective way. The body of **scientific knowledge** is often broken down into several domains including biology, ecology, Earth science, space science, physics, and chemistry. These each have further subdomains and are overlapping in many ways. For instance, ecology is the study of ecosystems, which are made up of biological factors and geological factors, so it contains elements of both biology and Earth science. Each of these domains is subject to the concepts of scientific inquiry, such as the scientific method, scientific facts, hypotheses, and scientific laws.

Important Terminology

- A **phenomenon** is an event or effect that is observed.
- A **scientific fact** is considered an objective and verifiable observation. Usually, a fact can be repeated or demonstrated to others.
- A **scientific theory** is a proposition explaining why or how something happens and is built on scientific facts and laws. Scientific theories can be tested, but are not fully proven. If new evidence is found that disproves the theory, it is no longer considered true.
- A **hypothesis** is an educated guess that is not yet proven. It is used to predict the outcome of an experiment in an attempt to solve a problem or answer a question.

- A **law** is an explanation of events that always leads to the same outcome. It is a fact that an object falls. The law of gravity explains why an object falls. The theory of relativity, although generally accepted, has been neither proven nor disproved.
- A **model** is used to explain something on a smaller scale or in simpler terms to provide an example. It is a representation of an idea that can be used to explain events or applied to new situations to predict outcomes or determine results.

HISTORY OF SCIENTIFIC KNOWLEDGE

When one examines the history of **scientific knowledge**, it is clear that it is constantly **evolving**. The body of facts, models, theories, and laws grows and changes over time. In other words, one scientific discovery leads to the next. Some advances in science and technology have important and long-lasting effects on science and society. Some discoveries were so alien to the accepted beliefs of the time that not only were they rejected as wrong, but were also considered outright blasphemy. Today, however, many beliefs once considered incorrect have become an ingrained part of scientific knowledge, and have also been the basis of new advances. Examples of advances include: Copernicus's heliocentric view of the universe, Newton's laws of motion and planetary orbits, relativity, geologic time scale, plate tectonics, atomic theory, nuclear physics, biological evolution, germ theory, industrial revolution, molecular biology, information and communication, quantum theory, galactic universe, and medical and health technology.

SCIENTIFIC INQUIRY AND SCIENTIFIC METHOD

Scientists use a number of generally accepted techniques collectively known as the **scientific method**. The scientific method generally involves carrying out the following steps:

- Identifying a problem or posing a question
- Formulating a hypothesis or an educated guess
- Conducting experiments or tests that will provide a basis to solve the problem or answer the question
- Observing the results of the test
- Drawing conclusions

An important part of the scientific method is using acceptable experimental techniques. Objectivity is also important if valid results are to be obtained. Another important part of the scientific method is peer review. It is essential that experiments be performed and data be recorded in such a way that experiments can be reproduced to verify results. Historically, the scientific method has been taught with a more linear approach, but it is important to recognize that the scientific method should be a cyclical or **recursive process**. This means that as hypotheses are tested and more is learned, the questions should continue to change to reflect the changing body of knowledge. One cycle of experimentation is not enough.

Review Video: The Scientific Method
Visit mometrix.com/academy and enter code: 191386

OBSERVATIONS

An **observation** is something specific you notice about the world or an event. For instance, a very obvious event that takes place is if we leave milk out on the counter overnight, the milk will go bad. We observe this event by using our five senses: sight, taste, smell, touch, and sound. When milk goes bad, there are several ways it changes.

ASKING QUESTIONS

Observations may inspire new questions. These questions can be used to form a hypothesis, which can be used to design an experiment. When trying to gain scientific knowledge, it is best to ask questions that are clear and specific, or well defined. This can make answering the question easier. When a question is not clear or is not specific, it may have several possible answers. It also may have an answer that only leads to more questions. For example, the question "what will happen if you drop an egg" is not a well-defined question. The result of dropping an egg depends on many factors, and there are many possible answers to the question. However, the question "what will happen if you drop an uncooked egg on concrete" is a well-defined question. The question is specific and clear, and it can be tested using a simple experiment.

HYPOTHESIS

The next step of the scientific process is to make a hypothesis. A **hypothesis** is a proposed explanation for the expected results of an experiment. A testable hypothesis is one that is written prior to an investigation and can be easily supported or opposed using evidence from an experiment. A hypothesis about milk might be that if I keep milk above a certain temperature for a long time, it will go bad. Hypotheses need to be specific and testable so we can decide if it is true or false.

EXPERIMENT

The step after making a hypothesis is to check if it is true by testing it with an **experiment**. An experiment should be a controlled, specific situation that shows whether or not a hypothesis is correct. Experiments need to ask questions about **facts**, rather than **opinions**. Usually, the more specific the experiment, the clearer the answer will be. For instance, if I test my hypothesis by putting milk outside overnight, but do not set a timer, then I can get an answer, but I will not be able to record how time affected the experiment. Similarly, if the milk is outside and the temperature changes overnight, I will not be able to learn much about what effect the temperature had on the milk.

VARIABLES

These two aspects of the experiment are examples of variables. **Variables** are parts of the experiment that can change. An **independent variable** is a variable that the experimenter will change during the experiment, so it is **controlled**. A **dependent variable** is a variable that changes in response to changes to an independent variable, and it is **observed**. For instance, we cannot control time, but we can observe the milk over time by checking it every half hour. Temperature, on the other hand, can be controlled with technology. We can keep the milk inside the house, where the temperature will always be around 70 degrees, or we can keep it in the refrigerator, where the milk will stay close to 40 degrees. These variables need to be controlled as best as possible to get the most specific results.

EXPERIMENTS TESTING ONE VARIABLE

Experiments should be designed to only test the effects of one variable. This helps experimenters make sure that the cause of the experiment's results is clear and certain. To make sure that the experiment only tests one variable, the experiment should only have one independent variable. For example, the height that sunflowers would grow in different circumstances depends on many factors that could be changed by the experimenter. Sunflowers are affected by the amount of water and sunlight they receive, the soil in which they are planted, the amount of space they have to grow, and the temperature of the air around them. If more than one of these factors are independent variables, then the experimenter may not be able to tell which factor affected growth of the sunflower. If only one of these factors is an independent variable, then the experimenter will know which factor affected the sunflower, since it will be the only thing that was changed by the experimenter.

Constants and Controls

To ensure that there is only one independent variable, other factors cannot be changed by the experimenter. These factors are called **constants**. Another aspect of an experiment is the control. A **control** is an example where the independent variable is not manipulated. The group in which the independent variable was manipulated can then be compared to the control group.

Collecting Information During an Experiment

An experimenter makes observations during an experiment, writes them down, and then uses those observations to **draw conclusions**. Observations made during an experiment become **data**. Accurately **measuring** and **recording** data is necessary for an effective scientific investigation. **Accuracy** describes how close a measurement is to the true value. Not accurately measuring during an experiment may cause an experimenter to misunderstand the results of the experiment. For example, investigating how much plants grow when given different amounts of water would require the experimenter to accurately measure and record how much water each plant received and how much each plant grew daily. When an experimenter is writing and sharing the conclusion of a scientific investigation, accurate information and specific observations are needed so the experiment can be repeated and considered to be reliable.

Observed and Measured Data

Data can be either measurable or observable. **Observable data** is often referred to as **qualitative data**, because it describes specific **qualities** of something being observed. An example of this is color or smell. It is very difficult to find numbers to describe a color or smell, but it is not hard to describe that a liquid changed from red to blue. **Measurable data** is also known as **quantitative data** because it refers to the quantity or amount of something. A good example of quantitative data is weight. Any time someone steps on a scale to know how much they weigh, they are looking at quantitative data. Both types of data are important to keep track of and record.

Validating Explanations Through Evidence

Whenever scientists try to explain an observation, they must test their ideas to see if those ideas are correct. During an experiment, scientists will observe any changes that happen and take measurements to either support or disprove their interpretation of the first observation. Without these observations and measurements, scientists would not have enough evidence to support their ideas and, therefore, no reason for other people to believe their ideas. For example, if a scientist notices that it rains a lot in the summer, the scientist may form an opinion that summer has the rainiest months. To find out if this idea is correct, the scientist would need to measure the amount of rainfall each season by collecting rain throughout the year. The measurements of how much rain fell each season are data that will support or disprove the scientist's idea that summer has the rainiest months.

Repeating Experiments

Experiments should be **repeated** to see if the same result happens every time. For example, if you can get the same result in only three out of ten attempts, then the result is not reliable, and the experiment should be changed and tried again.

The results of an investigation that is only run once are not completely reliable. When an investigation is run the exact same way again and again and the result is the same every time, then the result is more likely to be considered reliable. If the investigation has only been completed once, or even just a few times, the results may be a result of chance or an error. When an investigation can be repeated, there is an opportunity for other discoveries to occur. An investigation may be repeated and produce different results. While those results may not be reliable, they can still lead to a new discovery or idea that can be investigated. The results of a repeated investigation may become a scientific theory, which is an explanation of an event that has become widely accepted by the science community.

Reflect

After an experiment is complete, the scientist needs to **reflect** on what happened by asking questions:

- Did the experiment answer the question?
- Was the hypothesis true or false?
- Did repeated attempts produce the same results?
- Is there anything I should change for future attempts?
- What did I learn?
- What questions can I ask now that I have learned something?

Making Observations After an Experiment

Once an investigation is complete, scientists will make more observations and try to interpret the data, which can be done in multiple ways. One way is by looking for **patterns**. For example, a scientist might notice a pattern in the data that shows when one variable is increased, another variable increases as well. Alternatively, increasing one variable could result in a decrease in another. These patterns help scientists to develop explanations for phenomena by determining how two variables are related.

Repeat the Process

After the experiment and reflection is over, the scientist hopefully learned something and can ask new questions. These questions should be more specific, or the experiment should be improved to get better answers.

Replicability by Others

When scientists investigate their observations, they must write down or draw everything they observe, measure, and interpret from their experiments. One of the main reasons to record this information is to allow other scientists to perform the same experiment. Without detailed notes about how the experiment is set up and performed, another scientist would not have adequate instructions to re-create the experiment. It is important that other scientists perform the same experiment to find out if others can get the same results as the first scientist. If the scientists who re-creates the experiment get the same results, that further supports the first scientist's ideas. If the first scientist's results cannot be replicated, that scientist's ideas will be rejected. For example, a sick patient would not want to take a new medicine that was only tested and found safe for one person in one experiment. The patient would want the medicine to be proven to work in many tests on many people to make sure it is safe.

Replication Versus Repetition

Replication is a necessary part of the scientific process of discovery. It involves different scientists performing the same experiment to see if they can replicate the initial results. Replication is necessary for scientists to either validate or invalidate others' discoveries or results. Repetition, on the other hand, happens when the original scientist runs multiples trials of the initial experiment. This is essential to scientific discovery because verifying an experiment lets a scientist know if the results are repeatable and testable instead of something that happened by chance.

Other Types of Scientific Investigations

While many scientists use the scientific method to guide their research and experiments, scientists also use other methods for studying and learning. Some scientists work by observing something, asking a question about it, investigating, collecting information, trying to understand the information, and then sharing their interpretation of what the information means with others. Other kinds of scientists might ask themselves how to solve a problem, imagine the solution, make plans for a machine or system to solve the problem, build it, and then test and improve on what they made. Scientific research can also happen without using a method, but science always involves observations. Observations occur when someone notices something about the world using their senses. Scientists test their observations to understand them. Testing helps scientists develop reasons why the thing they observed happened.

Experiment Versus Other Scientific Investigations

An experiment is an important form of scientific investigation that involves the identification and control of variables. Variables are quantities that can change and be measured during an experiment, which helps scientists support, refute, or validate their hypothesis. Experiments are not the only form of scientific investigation, however, since variables cannot always be identified or controlled. For example, weather patterns cannot be controlled, as humans do not have power over the water cycle or the many other elements that influence weather. Any scientific discoveries without variables should be called investigations, which lack a hypothesis. Investigations can be represented through modeling, research, data collection, or other methods.

Methods Used Throughout Different Fields of Study

Scientists use many methods when searching to understand scientific phenomena in different fields of study. Models like diagrams, pictures, computer programs, and physical representations can be helpful for visualizing information or concepts that do not exist physically or that are too small, too big, too fast, or too dangerous; however, models often over-simplify information. Scientists also use research and investigation to learn more about their fields of study. Research and investigation helps scientists understand the history of their research topic and form ideas around observations; however, research and investigation require a lot of time and access to information. Many scientists also use experiments to answer questions. Experimenting allows scientists to test their hypotheses and find out if the results do or do not support them; however, experiments are not suitable for questions that lack controllable and definable variables.

Sharing Results

The result of a scientific investigation is valuable information that others may want to know. These results may help other scientists learn new information that is related to their own research and investigations. They may also help others if the information changes the way people may look at an everyday product or activity. However, results can be communicated in different ways, depending on whether the data is qualitative or quantitative. **Qualitative data** is valuable for understanding changes that cannot be represented by numbers, such as color changes in a chemical reaction. Meanwhile, **quantitative data** provides measurements that helps scientists to understand how two variables are connected. Qualitative data is best suited to a drawing, diagram, or a list of written descriptions, while quantitative data is typically represented in the form of a table or graph.

Referring to Results

Whenever scientists perform an experiment or an investigation, they do not refer to their results as "proof" of their hypothesis because the word "proof" implies that there is no other explanation. Since every explanation or factor cannot be investigated in a natural environment, scientists instead state that their "results support" their hypothesis or that their results "fail to support" their hypothesis.

Lab Reports

A **lab report** should begin with a statement describing the problem or question being investigated. It should also include the hypothesis and list the variables in the experiment. Both a list of all materials used and the detailed procedure that was followed during the investigation are important to include. These will allow other scientists to replicate the investigation. A lab report should also list the results of an investigation. Any data tables or observations that are part of the results need to be labeled correctly and include accurate measurements and calculations. Finally, a lab report should conclude with an explanation that uses the evidence that was found during the investigation to state whether the hypothesis was supported or not supported. Also, the conclusion should include a detailed summary of the data collected during the investigation, and it should describe any errors that might have occurred during the investigation.

VENN DIAGRAMS

One helpful way of sorting out information when comparing two things is a **venn diagram.** This tool is essentially just two circles that overlap, and it is used to display what aspects of one thing are similar or different from another thing. In the following diagram, notice how fish and frogs are similar in some ways, but different in others.

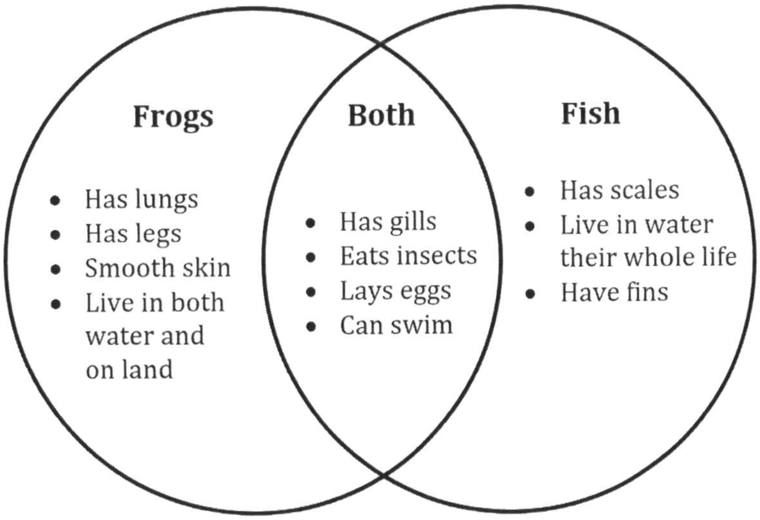

FREQUENCY TABLES

Frequency tables show how frequently each unique value appears in a set. A **relative frequency table** is one that shows the proportions of each unique value compared to the entire set. Relative frequencies are given as percentages; however, the total percent for a relative frequency table will not necessarily equal 100 percent due to rounding. An example of a frequency table with relative frequencies is below.

Favorite Color	Frequency	Relative Frequency
Blue	4	13%
Red	7	22%
Green	3	9%
Purple	6	19%
Cyan	12	38%

CIRCLE GRAPHS

Circle graphs, also known as *pie charts*, provide a visual depiction of the relationship of each type of data compared to the whole set of data. The circle graph is divided into sections by drawing radii to create central angles whose percentage of the circle is equal to the individual data's percentage of the whole set. Each 1% of data is equal to 3.6° in the circle graph. Therefore, data represented by a 90° section of the circle graph makes up 25% of the whole. When complete, a circle graph often looks like a pie cut into uneven wedges. The pie chart below shows the data from the frequency table referenced earlier where people were asked their favorite color.

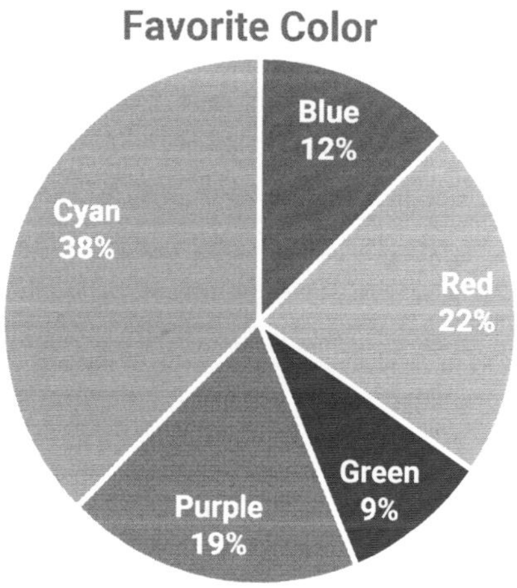

Pictographs

A **pictograph** is a graph, generally in the horizontal orientation, that uses pictures or symbols to represent the data. Each pictograph must have a key that defines the picture or symbol and gives the quantity each picture or symbol represents. Pictures or symbols on a pictograph are not always shown as whole elements. In this case, the fraction of the picture or symbol shown represents the same fraction of the quantity a whole picture or symbol stands for. For example, a row with $3\frac{1}{2}$ ears of corn, where each ear of corn represents 100 stalks of corn in a field, would equal $3\frac{1}{2} \times 100 = 350$ stalks of corn in the field.

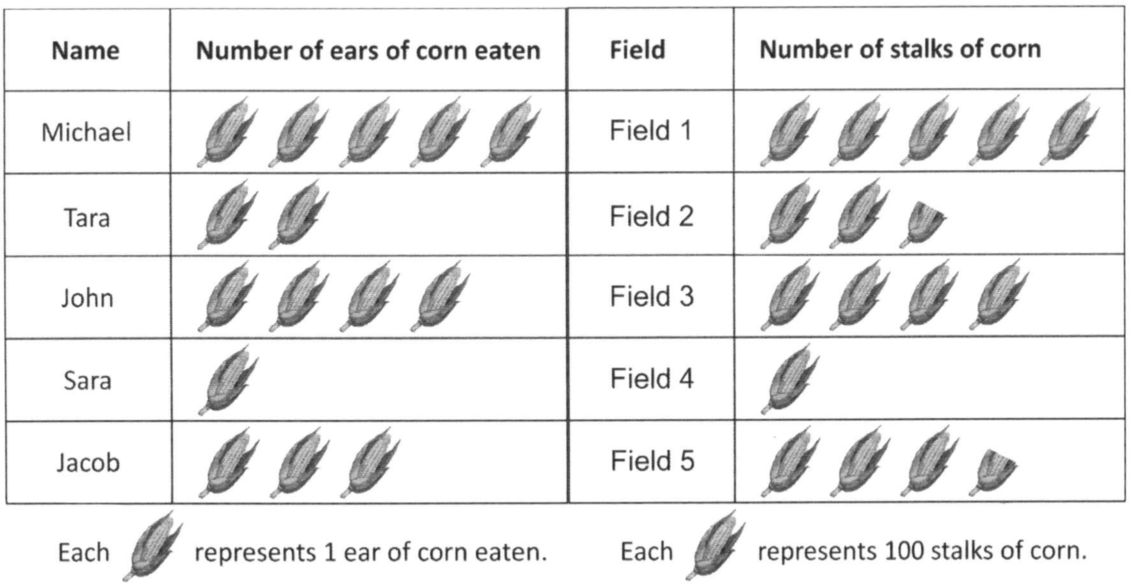

Review Video: Pictographs
Visit mometrix.com/academy and enter code: 147860

Line Graphs

Line graphs have one or more lines of varying styles (solid or broken) to show the different values for a set of data. The individual data are represented as ordered pairs, much like on a Cartesian plane. In this case, the x- and y-axes are defined in terms of their units, such as dollars or time. The individual plotted points are joined by line segments to show whether the value of the data is increasing (line sloping upward), decreasing (line sloping downward), or staying the same (horizontal line). Multiple sets of data can be graphed on the same line graph to give an easy visual comparison. An example of this would be graphing achievement test scores for different groups of students over the same time period to see which group had the greatest increase or decrease in performance from year to year (as shown below).

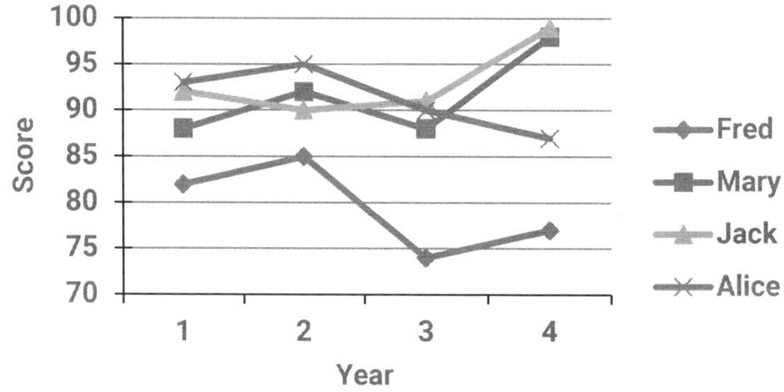

Review Video: How to Create a Line Graph
Visit mometrix.com/academy and enter code: 480147

LINE PLOTS

A **line plot**, also known as a *dot plot*, has plotted points that are not connected by line segments. In this graph, the horizontal axis lists the different possible values for the data, and the vertical axis lists the number of times the individual value occurs. A single dot is graphed for each value to show the number of times it occurs. This graph is more closely related to a bar graph than a line graph. Do not connect the dots in a line plot or it will misrepresent the data.

Review Video: Line Plot
Visit mometrix.com/academy and enter code: 754610

STEM AND LEAF PLOTS

A **stem and leaf plot** is useful for depicting groups of data that fall into a range of values. Each piece of data is separated into two parts: the first, or left, part is called the stem; the second, or right, part is called the leaf. Each stem is listed in a column from smallest to largest. Each leaf that has the common stem is listed in that stem's row from smallest to largest. For example, in a set of two-digit numbers, the digit in the tens place is the stem, and the digit in the ones place is the leaf. With a stem and leaf plot, you can easily see which subset of numbers (10s, 20s, 30s, etc.) is the largest. This information is also readily available by looking at a histogram, but a stem and leaf plot also allows you to look closer and see exactly which values fall in that range. Using a sample set of test scores (82, 88, 92, 93, 85, 90, 92, 95, 74, 88, 90, 91, 78, 87, 98, 99), we can assemble a stem and leaf plot like the one below.

Test Scores

7	4	8							
8	2	5	7	8	8				
9	0	0	1	2	2	3	5	8	9

Review Video: Stem-and-Leaf Plots
Visit mometrix.com/academy and enter code: 302339

BAR GRAPHS

A **bar graph** is one of the few graphs that can be drawn correctly in two different configurations – both horizontally and vertically. A bar graph is similar to a line plot in the way the data is organized on the graph. Both axes must have their categories defined for the graph to be useful. Rather than placing a single dot to mark the point of the data's value, a bar, or thick line, is drawn from zero to the exact value of the data, whether it is a number, percentage, or other numerical value. Longer bar lengths correspond to greater data values. To read a bar graph, read the labels for the axes to find the units being reported. Then, look where the bars end in relation to the scale given on the corresponding axis and determine the associated value.

The bar chart below represents the responses from our favorite-color survey.

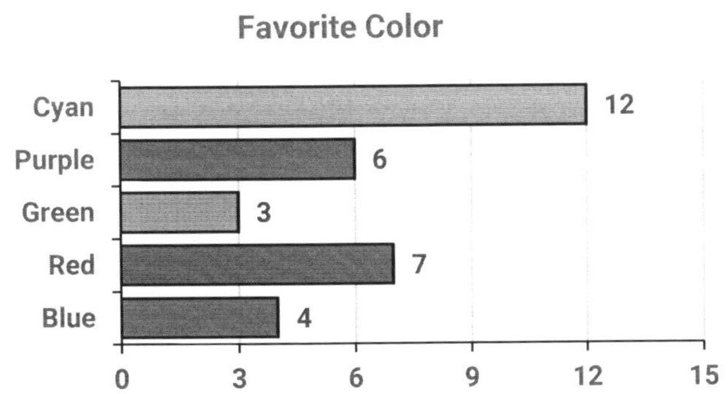

Constructing Explanations

In science, an explanation is only considered credible if it is based upon and supported by **empirical** evidence, which includes data from an experiment and unbiased observations. Scientists construct credible explanations by analyzing data. The first step of constructing an explanation is deciding whether the data **supports** or **opposes** the hypothesis. When the data supports a scientist's hypothesis, the scientist can make a **conclusion** about the relationship he or she studied. This conclusion is combined with scientific reasoning and existing information to form a well-rounded explanation. When the data does not support a scientist's initial hypothesis, the scientist can make a conclusion about what is not true and suggest potential explanations that could be tested in future experiments. When a scientific idea is consistently supported by evidence and data from many experiments, it may be referred to as a **theory**, which is a well-tested and widely accepted explanation for a phenomenon.

SCIENTIFIC THEORIES

A scientific theory is a well-supported and widely accepted explanation of nature or happenings in the universe. While scientific theories have not been proven, they have been tested and re-tested to the point that they are generally accepted to be true. Because of this rigorous testing, scientific theories are not simply claims that a person makes. The word "theory" in daily conversation refers to what someone thinks about something, but an everyday theory like this does not require testing like scientific theories do. Therefore, scientific theories are only made by scientists and must be supported by many other scientists as well.

Theories cannot be proven, so they are modified over time as more scientific discoveries are made. Instead of starting anew every time a scientific theory is shown to be inaccurate, scientists usually modify the existing theories. Given that theories are based on observations made at the time, greater scientific advancement can allow scientists to refine an older theory. The older theory still explains what scientists of the past observed, which is important for understanding the development of scientific thought. Thus, theories are modified instead of thrown out.

Scientific Theories Versus Laws

A theory explains why natural things happen or how they happen. For example, the theory of plate tectonics explains that volcanoes, mountains, and valleys are formed by the movement of tectonic plates below the Earth's surface. A law, however, describes an observation of natural events or the results of an experiment. For example, the law of conservation of mass states that mass cannot be created or destroyed, only changed. This law does not state why mass cannot be created or destroyed; it only states the observed phenomenon. Laws are, therefore, used to predict the behavior of the natural world, while theories attempt to explain why phenomena occur.

Predicting Trends and Patterns

When analyzing scientific data, scientists look for **patterns** or associations, which can be used to make predictions or generalizations about the natural world. One method for making predictions is to identify the relationship between two factors. For example, a data set may show that cities with more buildings have higher amounts of light pollution. This connection is called a **correlation**. When two variables are correlated, it is usually possible to predict an effect. For example, when given the number of buildings in a certain city, a scientist could make a reasonable prediction about the amount of light pollution in that city. In addition, scientists can use previous research and scientific explanations to predict **trends**. Trends show the relationship of two factors over a certain period of time.

Evaluating Scientific Explanations

The results of an investigation and the conclusions that scientists make after studying data are used to create scientific explanations. **Explanations** seek to describe why natural events happen and provide new details about scientific discoveries. However, some explanations are not reliable. When new scientific explanations are made, it is important to evaluate them to see if they are reliable and possible. Important factors to think about and questions to ask when evaluating a scientific explanation are:

- **Logic:** Does the explanation make sense? Is the explanation reasonable? Does it seem possible?
- **Question or Problem:** Was the question or problem that the investigation studied well-defined? Did the investigation results answer that question?
- **Experimental methods:** Is the method used in the experiment reliable? Did the experimenter record their process? Was the experiment performed properly and carefully?
- **Tools:** Did the tools used take accurate measurements? Were the correct tools used?
- **Evidence:** Is the explanation based on direct or indirect evidence? Does the evidence support the explanation well?
- **Research:** Did the investigator use reliable, scientific resources when doing research related to the investigation or experiment?

EVALUATING CONFLICTING EXPLANATIONS

When a scientist is presented with two opposing explanations of a scientific phenomenon, it is important that he or she first look at the **evidence** used to support each explanation. All strong scientific explanations are supported by experimental evidence, typically in the form of data from an investigation. In addition, scientists must carefully analyze the **methods** of an experiment to make sure the experiment was well-designed. Checking that the experiment was well designed helps to determine whether the evidence itself is valid. Lastly, scientists might question the conclusion and explanation itself by asking whether the data could be explained by an **alternative explanation.** In this case, scientists can conduct **follow-up experiments** to help rule out opposing explanations.

Scientific Models

Scientists often create **models** to help express and understand scientific ideas. A model is a representation of an idea that is used to experience something that cannot be experienced directly. For instance, we cannot see and experience evaporation directly, but we can easily draw out the process of evaporation, condensation, and precipitation. Having a drawing helps us to understand the concept since we cannot experience it directly. Models can be three-dimensional, such as something you can hold, or they can be simple diagrams demonstrating a process. For instance, a planetarium is a large model that helps someone see the size of planets and stars and how they interact. More typical models in the classroom include baking soda and vinegar volcanoes, solar system mobiles, or atoms and molecules made from foam and straws. Other models can include a diagram showing the water cycle.

LIMITATIONS OF MODELS

Models can be helpful for experiencing a scientific process that normally could not be observed directly, but they are limited. Models are usually used to display a very large thing in a small way, such as a volcano or the Earth in a way that a human can look at it and touch it. Models are also often used to express very small things or invisible things in a more observable way. Changing the size or the materials used to express something limits how similar a model can be to the real thing. For instance, if a model of the water cycle used cotton balls to show clouds, it limits our understanding of clouds. Clouds are not made of dry, solid cotton, but are made up of vapor filled with water. Volcanos made from clay that use baking soda and vinegar do not demonstrate the extreme heat or mass of volcanic materials. Similarly, a mobile of the solar system cannot express how extremely large the sun and planets are. When using a model to understand a concept, the observer needs to be aware that they are probably only getting a clear picture of a small part of the concept, not gaining full understanding from the model.

Measurement

Tools for Measuring and Observation

Purpose	Tool
Measuring Length	Rulers, meter sticks
Measuring Weight or Mass	Spring scales, pan balances
Measuring Volume	Beakers, graduated cylinders
Measuring Time	Timers, clocks
Measuring Temperature	Thermometer
Measuring Light	Spectroscope (or spectrometer)
Recording Information	Journals, notebooks
Observing Animals and Plants	Terrariums, aquariums, collecting nets
Observing Weather	Rain Gauges, wind vanes, anemometers, psychrometers
Observing effects of heat	Hot plates
Models for Understanding Concepts	Sun-Earth-Moon System Models, volcano models, water cycle models
Visual Observation	cameras, hand lenses, microscopes
Making calculations	Calculators, computers
Holding substances	Test Tubes

Metric and International System of Units

The **metric system** is the accepted standard of measurement in the scientific community. The **International System of Units (SI)** is a set of measurements (including the metric system) that is almost globally accepted. The United States, Liberia, and Myanmar have not accepted this system. **Standardization** is important because it allows the results of experiments to be compared and reproduced without the need to laboriously convert measurements. The SI is based partially on the **meter-kilogram-second (MKS) system** rather than the **centimeter-gram-second (CGS) system**. The MKS system considers meters, kilograms, and seconds to be the basic units of measurement, while the CGS system considers centimeters, grams, and seconds to be the basic units of measurement. Under the MKS system, the length of an object would be expressed as 1 meter instead of 100 centimeters, which is how it would be described under the CGS system.

Review Video: Metric System Conversions
Visit mometrix.com/academy and enter code: 163709

Metric System

The **metric system** is the accepted standard of measurement in the scientific community. **Standardization** is important because it allows the results of experiments to be compared and reproduced without the need to convert measurements. The metric system uses similar conversions between all types of measurement, including length, mass, volume, time, and temperature.

Customary and Metric (Scientific) Units of Measurement

The customary system commonly used in the United States is not based on consistent smaller units. Thus, 12 inches equal 1 foot, 3 feet equal 1 yard, and 5,280 feet equal 1 mile. The metric system used in science and in most countries is based on units of 10. Therefore, 1000 millimeters and 100 centimeters equal 1 meter, and 1,000 meters equal 1 kilometer. The same pattern is true for the other units of measurement in the two systems. The following table shows the different units.

Unit	Customary System	Metric System
length	inch, foot, mile	centimeter, meter, kilometer
mass, weight	net weight ounce, pound	gram, kilogram, newton
volume	fluid ounce, pint, quart	milliliter, liter
temperature	Fahrenheit degree	Celsius degree

Fahrenheit and Celsius Temperature Scales

In the Fahrenheit scale the point where water freezes and ice melts is set at 32°, and the point where water boils and water vapor condenses is 212°. That means a difference of 180° between the freezing and boiling points of water. In the Celsius scale, the freezing/melting point is set at 0°and the boiling/condensation point at 100°, making this scale much easier to use.

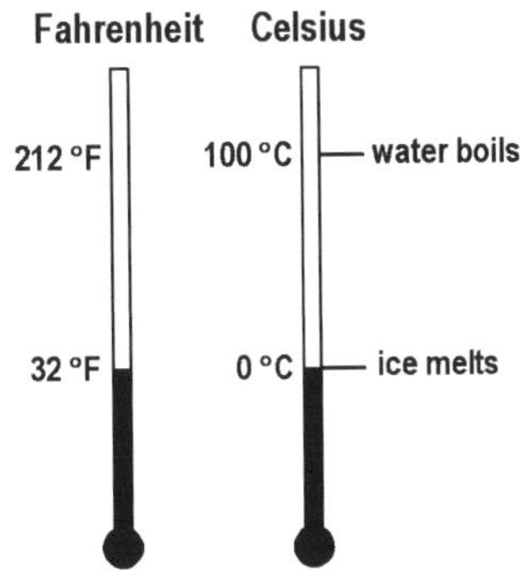

Basic Units of Measurement

The **metric system** is generally accepted as the preferred measurement system. Having a **universal standard** allows individuals to interpret measurements more easily, regardless of where they are located. The basic units of measurement are the **meter**, which measures length; the **liter**, which measures volume; and the **gram**, which measures mass. The metric system starts with a base unit and increases or decreases in units of 10. The prefix and the base unit combined are used to indicate an amount. For example, deka- is 10 times the base unit. A decameter, or dekameter, is 10 meters; a decaliter, or dekaliter, is 10 liters; and a decagram, or dekagram, is 10 grams. The prefix hecto- refers to 100 times the base amount and kilo- is 1,000 times the base amount. The prefixes that indicate a fraction of the base unit are deci-, which is 1/10 of the base unit; centi-, which is 1/100 of the base unit; and milli-, which is 1/1000 of the base unit.

COMMON PREFIXES

The prefixes for **multiples** are as follows:

Deca or Deka	(da)	10
Hecto	(h)	100
Kilo	(k)	1,000
Mega	(M)	100,000

The prefixes for **subdivisions** are as follows:

Deci	(d)	1/10
Centi	(c)	1/100
Milli	(m)	1/1,000
Micro	(μ)	1/100,000

Contributions of Scientists

- **Sir Francis Bacon** – contributed many ideas that helped develop the modern scientific method.
- **Gallileo Galilei**– one of the first people to use a telescope and contributed ideas about how gravity works. He also contributed the idea that the Earth revolved around the Sun, and not the other way around.
- **Leonardo da Vinci** – known for his contributions to art and to science, he was an avid inventor, designing a submarine, an armored tank, and several aircraft far before any of which were actually built.
- **Sir Isaac Newton** – best known for his contributions to physics. He described the principals of inertia and friction.
- **Louis Pasteur** – discovered bacteria and invented the process of pasteurization and developed some of the first vaccines.
- **Thomas Edison** – invented many distinct devices, including the phonograph, improved upon the telephone, the lightbulb, and the kinetoscope, an early form of movie projector.
- **Albert Einstein** – studied theoretical physics with the use of mathematics and is particularly famous for his theory of relativity.

Earth and Space Science

Sun

The **Sun** is the vital force of life on Earth. It is also the central component of our solar system. It is basically a sphere of extremely hot gases (close to 15 million degrees at the core) held together by gravity. Some of these gaseous molecules are ionized due to the high temperatures. The balance between its gravitational force and the pressure produced by the hot gases is called **hydrostatic equilibrium**. The source of the solar energy that keeps the Sun alive and plays a key role in the perpetuation of life on Earth is located in the Sun's core, where nucleosynthesis produces heat energy and photons. The Sun's atmosphere consists of the photosphere, the surface visible from Earth, the chromosphere, a layer outside of and hotter than the photosphere, the transition zone (the region where temperatures rise between the chromosphere and the corona), and the corona, which is best viewed at x-ray wavelengths. A solar flare is an explosive emission of ionized particles from the Sun's surface.

Solar Properties

The Sun completes a rotation once every 27 days; however, because it is gaseous and not solid like Earth, the Sun's equator and poles typically complete a rotation every 24 days. The Sun is divided into six layers: the core (the hot center where nuclear reactions occur), the radiative zone (energy moves slowly out through this layer), the convection zone (energy moves to the Sun's surface with convection currents), the photosphere (what is seen when observing the Sun), the chromosphere (a layer of atmosphere where prominences form), and the corona (the outer layer where plasma escapes the Sun). Convection is the transference of the Sun's energy to the photosphere, and prominences refer to large plasma features on the corona with high temperatures. Solar flares occur in the chromosphere and corona; these flares are eruptions of energy near sunspots, which are pockets of magnetism on the photosphere known to have cooler temperatures.

Position of the Sun

The Sun, which is at the center of our solar system and is the closest star to Earth, is a medium-sized, main sequence star orbited by eight main planets along with several dwarf planets. The solar system is positioned within the spiral-shaped Milky Way galaxy and located on one of the outer arms of the galaxy's spiral shape. Earth is the third planet from the Sun and is approximately 93 million miles away from it. This is equivalent to one astronomical unit. In comparison, the second closest star to Earth is Proxima Centauri, at about 25 trillion miles or 40 trillion kilometers away from Earth. It is over 250,000 times farther away from Earth than the Sun is.

Review Video: The Sun
Visit mometrix.com/academy and enter code: 699233

Earth's Rotation

The **Earth rotates** west to east about its axis, an imaginary straight line that runs nearly vertically through the center of the planet. This rotation (which takes 23 hours, 56 minutes, and 5 seconds) places each section of the Earth's surface in a position facing the Sun for a period of time, thus creating the alternating periods of light and darkness we experience as **day and night**. This rotation constitutes a sidereal day; it is measured as the amount of time required for a reference star to cross the meridian (an imaginary north-south line above an observer). Each star crosses the meridian once every (sidereal) day. Since the speed at which Earth rotates is not exactly constant, we use the mean solar day (a 24-hour period) in timekeeping rather than the slightly variable sidereal day.

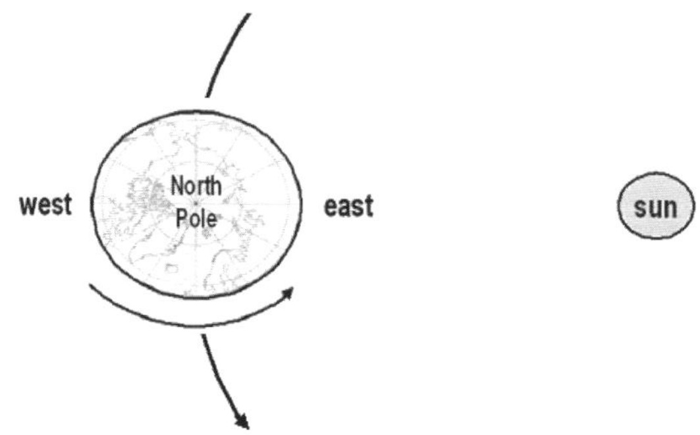

Earth's Revolution Around the Sun

Like all celestial objects in our solar system, planet **Earth** revolves around the **Sun**. This process takes approximately 365 1/4 days, the period of time that constitutes a calendar year. The path of the orbit of Earth around the Sun is not circular but **elliptical**. Therefore, the distances between the Earth and the Sun at points on either extreme of this counterclockwise orbit are not equal. In other words, the distance between the two objects varies over the course of a year. At **perihelion**, the minimum heliocentric distance, Earth is 147 million kilometers from the Sun. At **aphelion**, the maximum heliocentric distance, Earth is 152 million kilometers from the Sun. This movement of the Earth is responsible for the apparent annual motions of the Sun (in a path referred to as the ecliptic) and other celestial objects visible from Earth's surface.

Earth's Tilt and Seasons

The orbital path the Earth follows around the Sun helps create the **seasons**: winter, spring, summer, and fall. Earth is closest to the Sun in January and farthest in July. However, there is also a tilt to the Earth's axis. During July, the Northern Hemisphere is tilted towards the Sun. This causes the light and heat the Sun gives off to reach the Northern Hemisphere at a more direct angle. This is why July has hotter temperatures than January in the Northern Hemisphere, even though Earth is farthest away from the Sun during that time. These conditions are the opposite in the Southern Hemisphere, as the region's hottest temperatures occur in January. The Earth's tilt and orbit also affect the number of daylight hours a region experiences at different times, as people in the

Northern Hemisphere experience longer days and summertime in July, and people in the Southern Hemisphere experience shorter days and winter in July.

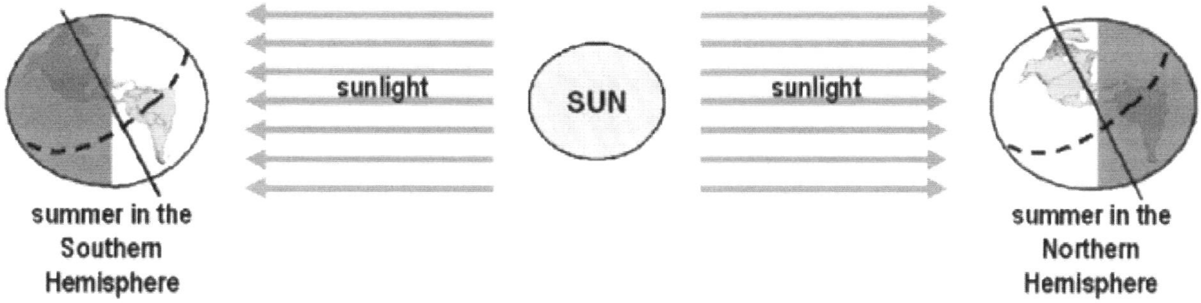

Review Video: Earth's Tilt and Seasons
Visit mometrix.com/academy and enter code: 602892

EXAMPLE

A disappointed traveler from the United States visits Australia in July, only to discover that it is wintertime. Which of the following correctly explains this phenomenon?

a. As Earth rotates, part of the Earth is facing away from the Sun.
b. Earth's orbit is not a perfect circle, causing it to be farther away from the Sun at certain times of the year.
c. Earth is tilted on its axis, resulting in part of the Earth getting more direct sunlight.
d. The Earth's magnetic field causes the Northern and Southern Hemispheres to have opposite seasons.

Choice A has to do with the rotation of the Earth. Earth rotates on its axis once every 24 hours, resulting in day and night, not seasons.

The part of the Earth facing away from the Sun is experiencing nighttime, not necessarily winter. Choice A is incorrect.

Choice B has to do with Earth's elliptical orbit, which resembles a squished circle in which the Sun is slightly offset. While it is true that the Earth is farther away from the Sun at certain times of the year, the effects on temperature are relatively minuscule and do not explain seasons. Choice B is not the answer.

Choice C has to do with Earth's tilt on its axis. Because Earth is tilted at 23.5°, one hemisphere is tilted more toward the Sun and receives more direct sunlight, resulting in summer. When the Earth reaches the other side of its orbit, the opposite hemisphere experiences summer and the hemisphere tilted away from the Sun experiences winter.

This explains seasons as well as the fact that the Southern Hemisphere, where Australia is located, experiences opposite seasons to the Northern Hemisphere. Choice C is the correct answer.

Choice D has to do with the Earth's magnetic field, which protects the Earth from cosmic rays and solar winds by deflecting them away from the planet. The Earth's magnetic poles have nothing to do with seasons. Choice D is incorrect.

Choice C is the correct answer because Earth's seasons are a result of the 23.5° axis tilt, which also explains the differences in seasons between the Northern and Southern Hemispheres that caused the traveler's disappointment.

Moon

Earth's Moon is historically one of the most studied celestial bodies. Its mass is approximately 1.2% of the Earth's mass, and its radius is just over one-fourth of the size of the Earth's radius. Measurements of the Moon's density suggest that its characteristics are similar to those of the rocks that make up Earth's crust. The **landscape** of the Moon consists mostly of mountains and craters formed by collisions of this surface with meteors and other interplanetary materials. The Moon's crust (estimated to be 50 to 100 kilometers in thickness) is made up of a layer of regolith (lunar soil) supported by a layer of loose rocks and gravel. Beneath the crust is a mantle made up of a solid lithosphere and a semiliquid asthenosphere. The Moon's **core** (the innermost 500 kilometers of the body) is not as dense as that of the Earth. The Moon is made up mostly of refractory elements with high melting and boiling points with low levels of heavy elements such as iron.

Formation Theories

The **fission model** of Moon origin suggests that the Moon is actually a piece of the Earth that split off early during the planet's formation. In this model, a portion of the Earth's mantle fissioned off during a liquid stage in its formation, creating the Moon. According to the **capture model**, the Moon formed elsewhere in the solar system and was subsequently captured by the Earth's gravitational field. The **double-impact model** states that the Earth and the Moon formed during the same period of time from the same accretion material. Each of these theories has its strengths, but none of them can explain all of the properties of the Moon and its relationship to the Earth. Recently, a fourth (widely accepted) hypothesis has been suggested, which involves the **collision** between the Earth and a large asteroid. This hypothetical collision is said to have released a large amount of Earth's crustal material into its orbit; the Moon accreted from that material and the material displaced from the asteroid due to the collision.

Earth-Moon System

While the Moon is commonly referred to as a satellite of the Earth, this is not entirely accurate. The ratio of the masses of the two bodies is much larger than that of any other planet-satellite system. Also, the Moon does not truly **revolve** around the Earth. Rather, the two bodies revolve around a common center of mass beneath the surface of the Earth (approximately 4,800 kilometers from Earth's core). The **orbital planes** of the Moon and the Earth are nearly aligned; therefore, the Moon moves close to the ecliptic, as seen from Earth. Due to the Moon's synchronous rotation (its rotation period and orbital period are equal); the same side of the Moon is always facing Earth. This occurs because of the **mutual gravitational pull** between the two bodies. These mutual gravitational pulls play a role in changing the ocean tides as well. The moon pulls the oceanic waters toward itself, causing high tide in the side closest to the moon and low tides in areas further from the moon.

Phases

The **sidereal period** of the Moon (the time it takes the Moon to orbit the Earth with the fixed stars as reference points) is about 27 days. The **lunar month** (or synodic period) is the period of time required for the Moon to return to a given alignment as observed from the Earth with the Sun as a reference point; this takes 29 days, 12 hours, 44 minutes, and 28 seconds. A discrepancy exists between the two periods of time because the Earth and the Moon move at the same time. Sunlight reflected off of the Moon's surface at different times during the lunar month causes its apparent shape to change. The sequence of the Moon's shapes is referred to as the **phases of the Moon**. The full Moon can be viewed when the body is directly opposite from the Sun. The opposite end of the cycle, the new Moon, occurs when the Moon is not visible from Earth because it is situated between the Earth and the Sun.

CONFIGURATIONS

The **configurations of the Moon** describe its position with respect to the Earth and the Sun. We can thus observe a correlation between the phases of the Moon and its configuration. The Moon is at **conjunction** at the time of the new Moon—it is situated in the same direction as the Sun. **Quadrature** (which signals the first quarter phase) is the position of the Moon at a right angle between the Earth-Sun line; we see exactly half of the Moon's sunlit hemisphere. This is the **waxing crescent phase**, in which we see more of the Moon each night. Then comes opposition (which occurs when the Moon lies in the direction opposite the Sun)—we see the full Moon. After this point, the Moon enters its **waning gibbons phase** as it travels back toward quadrature. When it reaches that point again, it has entered the third-quarter phase. Finally, as the Moon circles back toward conjunction, it is in its waning crescent phase.

Phases of the Moon

The light of the Moon is a reflection of sunlight that reaches the Moon. As the moon revolves around Earth approximately every 27.3 days, light from the Sun hits it from different angles. The Moon is always orbiting Earth, and as Earth and the Moon both move throughout their orbits, sunlight reaches different areas of the Moon. A **moon phase** describes the appearance of the Moon. Moon phases depend on the position of the Moon, Earth, and Sun.

A **new moon** occurs when the Moon is between the Sun and Earth. During this phase, the Moon is not visible because the Sun is illuminating the side of the Moon that is facing away from Earth. When any sunlight reaches the side of the Moon that is facing Earth, the appearance of the Moon will depend on its phase. For example, following a new moon, the right edge of the visible side of the Moon will look like a crescent. This phase is called a **waxing crescent**. During the next phase, the **first quarter**, the right half of the visible side of the moon will be lit up in a half-circle shape. Following that phase, the moon will then appear to be in an oval shape during its **waxing gibbous** phase. After that phase is the **full moon**, where the moon appears as a bright, white circle. Then, the

Moon returns to a new moon as it goes through these phases in the opposite order and direction. These phases are known as the **waning gibbous**, **third quarter**, and **waning crescent** phases.

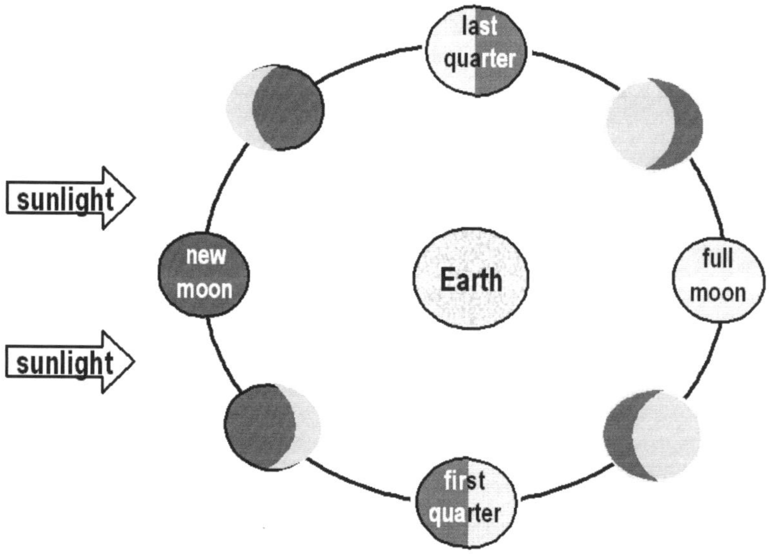

EXAMPLE

A group of students uses a calendar to keep track of the Moon's phase each night for a month. Their moon calendar so far shows the following sequence: new moon, waxing crescent, first quarter. Which moon phase can they expect to come next in the sequence?

a. Full moon
b. New moon
c. Waning gibbous
d. Waxing gibbous

Choice A: full moon. The most recent phase in the sequence is a first quarter moon, meaning the Moon appears half-illuminated in the sky. Therefore, the next phase should be more than half-illuminated but less than fully illuminated. Choice A can be eliminated.

Choice B: new moon. The first phase in the sequence is a new moon. Since the Moon has not completed a whole lunar cycle, there will not be another new moon until it does. Choice B is not the correct answer.

Choice C: waning gibbous. A gibbous is between half-illuminated and fully illuminated. A waning gibbous happens after a full moon as the illuminated portion of the moon gets smaller, so choice C is not the correct answer.

Choice D: waxing gibbous. A waxing gibbous means the illuminated moon is growing, which happens between a first quarter moon and a full moon. Choice D is the correct answer.

Choice D, waxing gibbous, is the correct answer because it follows a first quarter in the lunar sequence.

ECLIPSE

An **eclipse** occurs when either the Moon or Earth blocks the light from the Sun. Types of eclipses include solar eclipses and lunar eclipses. A **solar eclipse** is when the Moon is directly in between the Sun and Earth in a straight or nearly straight line. This is very similar to a new moon, but what makes it different is that the Moon is at a specific location between Earth and the Sun. In addition, instead of the Moon appearing to be gone, the moon is outlined with sunlight. A **lunar eclipse** is when Earth is directly in between the Sun and the Moon, in a straight or nearly straight line. Just as a solar eclipse is similar to a new moon, a lunar eclipse is similar to a full moon and occurs when the Moon is at a specific location on the opposite side of Earth as the Sun. During a lunar eclipse, the Moon will still appear as a full circle, but it will appear dim and red instead of bright and white.

Review Video: Moon
Visit mometrix.com/academy and enter code: 880415

Influence of the Sun and Moon on Tides

The relative positions of the Sun, Moon, and Earth influence the large-scale motions of Earth's oceans, and these motions make up **tides**. While the Sun has a much larger mass than the Moon, and therefore a larger gravitational pull, the Moon has a stronger impact on tides because it is closer to Earth than the Sun. As the Moon orbits around the Earth, it is always exerting a gravitational pull on the Earth's surface. This gravitational pull is strongest on the side of Earth that is closest to the Moon, and it pulls the oceans upward, creating a **high tide**. On the opposite side of Earth, this effect is also occurring, so there is a high tide there as well. The oceans on both sides are bulging upward. Between these areas, the ocean water levels are lower, and at their lowest, they create the **low tides**.

Earth rotates on its axis every 24 hours, so as it rotates, the areas experiencing high and low tides will change. The Sun's gravitational pull also influences the tides. When the Moon aligns with the Sun in its orbit, the gravitational forces of the Sun and the Moon have an additive effect, resulting in even higher high tides. Thus, full moon and new moon positions result in the highest high tides. Conversely, when the Moon is in first quarter and last quarter positions, the gravitational pulls of the Sun and Moon partially cancel out, causing lower high tides than other positions.

Solar System

The solar system consists of the Sun and eight **planets**. In order from the Sun, the planets are Mercury, Venus, Earth, Mars, Jupiter, Saturn, Uranus and Neptune. Six of the planets have one or more **moons**. The solar system also contains countless **meteoroids, asteroids,** and **comets.**

SOLAR SYSTEM PROPERTIES

In the solar system, the Sun is the largest celestial body and has the greatest gravitational pull. Some planets, like Earth, have enough gravitational pull to have moons. Mercury is unable to have a moon because of its proximity to the Sun. Venus also has no moon, but scientists do not know why. The Earth's moon, unlike the moons of other planets, lacks an atmosphere and an icy covering. The Earth has an orbital velocity (orbiting the Sun) slower than the planets closer to the Sun, like Mercury and Venus, and faster than those further away from the Sun, like Uranus and Neptune. This is because of the Sun's gravity. The strong effect of the Sun's gravity also means that the Earth's orbital path is also not as large as the paths of the planets further away, but it is longer than those of the planets closer to the Sun. Due to the Sun's heat emissions, Earth is also one of the warmer planets. Only the two closest planets to the Sun are warmer than Earth. The planets further from the Sun are much colder because they do not receive as much heat. While Mercury does not have atmospheres because of the Sun's heat, Earth and the other planets do. The atmosphere of Venus is so thick that temperatures on the planet's surface can melt lead, while Earth's atmosphere allows for life to occur.

HISTORICAL MODELS OF THE SOLAR SYSTEM

While today it is commonly accepted that the Sun is the center of the solar system, the geocentric model proposed that Earth was at the center. According to the geocentric model, the other planets and stars were believed to revolve around Earth. This model was accepted for nearly 2,000 years. The current model of the solar system is the heliocentric model, which states that the Sun is at the center of the solar system and all the planets revolve around it. The heliocentric model is the accepted theory today, but there have been many other propositions throughout the years.

PLANETS

All the planets revolve around the Sun, which is an average-sized star in the spiral Milky Way galaxy. They revolve in the same direction in nearly circular orbits. If the planets were viewed by looking down from the Sun, they would rotate in a counter-clockwise direction. All the planets are in, or near, the same plane, called the ecliptic, and their axis of rotation is nearly perpendicular to the ecliptic. The only exception is Uranus, which is tipped on its side.

TERRESTRIAL PLANETS, JOVIAN PLANETS, AND MASS OF PLANETS

The **Terrestrial Planets** are: Mercury, Venus, Earth, and Mars. These are the four planets closest to the Sun. They are called terrestrial because they all have a compact, rocky surface similar to the Earth's. Venus, Earth, and Mars have significant atmospheres, but Mercury has almost no atmosphere.

The **Jovian Planets** are: Jupiter (the largest planet), Saturn, Uranus, and Neptune. They are called Jovian (Jupiter-like) because of their huge sizes in relation to that of the Earth, and because they all have a gaseous nature like Jupiter. Although gas giants, some or all of the Jovian Planets may have small, solid cores.

The Sun represents 99.85% of all the matter in our solar system. Combined, the planets make up only 0.135% of the mass of the solar system, with Jupiter having twice the mass of all the other planets combined. The remaining 0.015% of the mass comes from comets, planetary satellites, asteroids, meteoroids, and interplanetary medium.

Review Video: Terrestrial Planets
Visit mometrix.com/academy and enter code: 100346

Definition of Planet

On August 24, 2006, the International Astronomical Union redefined the criteria a body must meet to be classified as a planet, stating that the following conditions must be met:

- "A planet orbits around a star and is neither a star nor a moon."
- "Its shape is spherical due to its gravity."
- "It has 'cleared' the space of its orbit."

A **dwarf planet** such as Pluto does not meet the third condition. Small solar system bodies such as asteroids and comets meet only the first condition.

Terrestrial Planets

The term **terrestrial planets** refers to the four planets closest to the Sun (Mercury, Venus, Earth, and Mars). They are classified together because they share many similarities that distinguish them from the giant planets. The terrestrial planets have **high densities and atmospheres** that constitute a small percentage of their total masses. These atmospheres consist mostly of heavy elements, such as carbon dioxide, nitrogen, and water, and are maintained by the gravitational field of the planets (which could not prevent hydrogen from escaping). These planets exhibit magnetic fields of varying intensity. An important characteristic that distinguishes the terrestrial planets from the giant planets is the evidence of various levels of internally generated activity, which caused these planets to evolve from their original states. These processes are thought to have been caused by constant meteoritic impacts during the first few hundred million years of the planets' existence. Radioactive decay of certain isotopes increased the internal temperatures of these planets, leading to volcanic activity on all of the terrestrial planets except Venus.

Mercury

Mercury, the smallest interior planet, is the least well known of the four. This is due to its close proximity to the Sun and high temperatures. Mercury's atmosphere is not very dense; this means that the planet's surface experiences wide temperature differentials from day to night. Mercury's density is close to that of Earth. As the smallest planet known to have experienced planetary evolution, Mercury's internal activity ceased (it became extinct) thousands of millions of years ago. The size of the planet is relevant because less massive bodies cool more quickly than larger ones after cessation of radioactivity. Mercury's surface is characterized by craters produced by meteoritic impact.

Venus

Venus is comparable to Earth in both mass and density. Venus is the brightest planet in the sky (partially due to the fact that it is proximate to the Sun), which makes exploration of its surface difficult. This planet's atmosphere consists mainly of carbon dioxide, with trace amounts of water and carbon oxide molecules, as well as high levels of sulfuric, nitric, and hydrofluoric acids in the clouds that characterize this atmosphere. The concentration of clouds, coupled with the chemical makeup of Venus's atmosphere, result in a strong greenhouse effect at the planet's surface. This surface consists of large plains (thought to be created by either volcanic activity, which remains unproven, or by meteoritic impacts) and large impact craters. The materials that compose Venus's surface are highly radioactive. Some astronomers have suggested past single-plate tectonic activity; again, however, the planet's dense atmosphere makes valid surface observation quite difficult.

Mars

Mars and Earth exhibit many similarities. For example, Mars has an internal structure that includes a central metallic core, a mantle rich in olivine and iron oxide, and a crust of hydrated silicates. Martian soil consists largely of basalts and clay silicate, with elements of sulfur, silicon oxide, and iron oxide. The planet's surface belies high levels of past volcanic activity (though, due to its relatively small mass, it is probably extinct). In fact, Mars is home to the largest known volcano in the solar system. The Martian landscape also includes two major basins, ridges and plateaus, and, most notably, apparent evidence of fluvial (water-based) erosion landforms, such as canyons and canals. It is possible that the past pressures and temperatures on Mars allowed water to exist on the red planet. Some have gone so far as to suggest that this planet was a site of biochemical evolution. So far, however, no evidence of life has been found.

Mars's Satellites

Two Martian satellites have been observed: **Phobos** and **Deimos**. Each of these bodies is ellipsoidal; the circular orbits of the two satellites lie in Mars's equatorial plane. The gravitational forces between this planet and Phobos and Deimos have caused both satellites to settle into synchronous rotation (the same parts of their surfaces are always facing Mars). This feature exerts a braking force on Phobos's orbit. In other words, its orbit is decreasing in size. The relationship between Deimos and Mars is similar to the Earth-Moon system, in which the radius of the satellite's orbit is gradually growing. The differential compositions and densities of Mars and its satellites indicate that Phobos and Deimos probably did not break off from Mars.

Giant Planets

The **large diameters** of Jupiter, Saturn, Uranus, and Neptune gave rise to the name of the category into which they fall. The **hypothetical icy cores** of these planets cause them to exhibit primary atmospheres, because the large levels of mass they accreted prevented even the lightest elements from escaping their gravitational pulls. The atmospheres of the giant planets thus consist mostly of hydrogen and helium. The giant planets do not have solid surfaces like those of the terrestrial planets. Jupiter probably consists of a core (made of ice and rock) surrounded by a layer of metallic hydrogen, which is covered by a convective atmosphere of hydrogen and helium. Saturn is believed to have the same type of core and hydrogen mantle, enriched by the helium missing from the atmosphere, surrounded by a differentiation zone and a hydrogenic atmosphere. Uranus and Neptune probably have the same type of core, surrounded by ionic materials, bounded by methane-rich molecular envelopes. Uranus is the only giant planet that exhibits no evidence of internal activity.

Rings

Each of the four giant planets exhibits **rings**. These are flat disks of fragmented material that orbit just next to their respective planets. Many of the giant planets' smaller satellites are embedded in these rings. There are two main hypotheses regarding the formation of such rings. One theory suggests that the tidal force exerted on a satellite by its planet may surpass the **Roche limit** (the point at which particle cohesion is no longer possible) and break the satellite into fragments, which then collide and become smaller. This material then spreads out and forms a ring. An alternate theory of the formation of the rings of the giant planets suggests that there was unaccreted material left over after the formation of these planets. Below the Roche limit (within a certain vicinity to the planet), these particles could not join together to form satellites and would consequently settle into orbital rings.

GIANT PLANET SATELLITES

Each of the giant planets possesses a number of **satellites**. **Jupiter** has over 50 known satellites—they are grouped according to size. Each of the four largest satellites of Jupiter exhibits evidence of internal activity at some point in their evolutions. In fact, Io, the densest satellite and the one closest to Jupiter, is the only celestial body besides Earth known to be currently volcanically active. **Saturn** has 21 satellites. Titan, the second-largest known satellite, has its own atmosphere. The other six largest of Saturn's satellites all have icy surfaces; some of these show evidence of past internal activity. The smaller 14 are relatively unknown. **Uranus** has five satellites. Each of them displays evidence of geological activity, in the form of valleys, smoothed surfaces, cliffs, mountains, and depressions. **Neptune** has eight known satellites. The larger, Triton, is similar to Titan in that it has an atmosphere. The other seven satellites of Neptune are relatively unknown.

Review Video: Giant Planets
Visit mometrix.com/academy and enter code: 563115

PLUTO AND CHARON

Though Charon was originally considered a satellite of Pluto, it now appears that the two are more accurately described as a double dwarf planet system (largely because of the similarity in the sizes of the two and the recurring debate over how Pluto should be classified). It is believed that these bodies formed from the solar nebula like most other objects in the solar system. Pluto has a highly irregular orbit, which places it closer to the Sun than Neptune for periods of time. In sharp contrast to its giant neighbors, this planet's density is higher than that of water ice. The surface of Pluto consists of high levels of methane absorbed into ice, with trace amounts of carbon oxide and nitrogen. Charon resembles the major Uranian satellites more so than it does Pluto. It consists of water ice with a siliceous or hydrocarbonate contaminant.

Review Video: Pluto and Charon
Visit mometrix.com/academy and enter code: 426296

COMETS, ASTEROIDS, AND METEOROIDS

Comets are celestial bodies composed of dust, rock, frozen gases, and ice. They range from tens of yards to tens of miles in diameter. They orbit the Sun with periods of a few years to hundreds of thousands of years. Invisible until they near the Sun, comets emit volatile components in jets of gas and dust when exposed to the Sun's heat. The **coma** is the comet's fog-like envelope that glows as it reflects sunlight and releases radiation. **Solar winds** blow a comet away from the Sun and give it a tail of dust or electrically charged molecules. Each orbit of a comet causes it to lose matter until it breaks up or vaporizes into the Sun. Halley's comet, shown below, orbits the Sun every 75 to 76 years.

Asteroids are irregularly-shaped boulders, usually less than 60 miles in diameter, that orbit the Sun. Most are made of graphite; about 25% are silicates, or iron and nickel. Collisions or gravitational forces can cause them to fly off and possibly hit a planet.

Meteoroids are fragments of asteroids of various sizes. They hurl through the solar system at speeds of between 15 and 45 miles per second. If they come through Earth's atmosphere, they are called meteors or shooting stars. In the atmosphere, they burn up and leave a visible fiery trail of gas and debris called a *meteor*. If they are large enough and do not completely burn up, they land on Earth, and they are called *meteorites*, and create craters on impact (the Barringer Crater in Arizona).

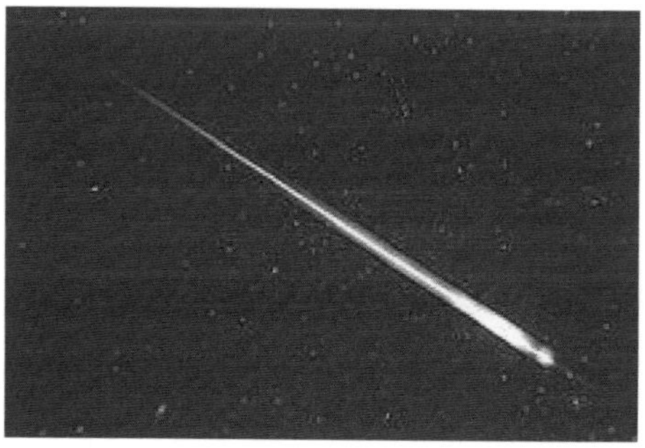

Milky Way

On a clear dark moonless night far from city lights a broad white band of stars that stretches across the sky can be seen. This is the Milky Way galaxy, and our Sun and the solar system are part of it. The Milky Way is a huge flat disk containing between 200 billion and 400 billion stars. Because Earth is in that disk, we see it edge on, which is why it appears to us as a broad band of light.

The Milky Way is a flat, disk-shaped spiral galaxy with a central bar-like bulge of stars. It is huge—between 100,000 and 120,000 light-years in diameter. A light-year is a unit of distance, not time. It is the distance light travels in one year, about 6 trillion miles. The Milky Way is between 600

thousand trillion and 700 thousand trillion miles across. Our solar system lies about two thirds of the way out on one of the spiral arms.

The Effect of Gravity in Our Solar System

Gravity is an attractive force that impacts the motion of the bodies in our solar system. The Sun at the center of our solar system has a mass that is more than 300,000 times the mass of Earth. Due to the Sun's large mass, it exerts a strong gravitational field on nearby planets, causing them to orbit around the Sun. In order to stay in orbit, a planet must have enough **speed** to keep moving. As it moves, the Sun's gravity pulls the planet inward like an invisible leash, resulting in a circular or elliptical orbit. Gravity is also responsible for the orbit of a planet's moons, including Earth's Moon. Although Earth's mass is much smaller than the Sun, the gravitational force from the Earth holds the Moon in orbit. This happens because gravity depends on both distance and mass, and the Moon is close enough to Earth to be affected more strongly by Earth's gravity than that of the Sun.

Review Video: Astronomy
Visit mometrix.com/academy and enter code: 640556

Review Video: The Solar System
Visit mometrix.com/academy and enter code: 273231

Components of the Universe

The universe is made up of many types of celestial objects, including stars, planets, nebulae, and galaxies, among others.

- **Stars** are giant balls of plasma that are mostly composed of helium and hydrogen. Stars have very large masses and extremely high temperatures, ranging from approximately 2,000 to 50,000 °C. There are different types of stars, and a star's type is based upon its mass, age, size, color, luminosity, and temperature. There are billions of stars in each galaxy.
- **Planets** are self-contained, spherical bodies that are shaped by their own gravitational force. Most planets rotate on their own axis and orbit a star. Planets can be made up of rocky material, gases, or different types of ice. They have much smaller masses and lower temperatures than stars.
- **Nebulae** are gigantic clouds of gas and dust where new stars are often born. They come in a range of shapes and sizes and are bigger than stars but smaller than galaxies. They are more diffuse and much less dense than stars and planets.
- **Galaxies** are vast systems of stars, planets, and nebulae held together by gravity. There are billions of galaxies in the universe. Planetary systems, consisting of planets orbiting stars, are positioned within larger galaxies such as the Milky Way, which is where our planetary system, the solar system, resides. Many galaxies have a spiral shape, but there are other shapes, such as elliptical and irregular.

Structures of Galaxies

Elliptical galaxies are roughly spherical. Within this category, subgroups based on the degree of flattening exhibited in the galaxy's shape range from E0 (spherical) to E7 (flat). A dwarf elliptical galaxy has a spheroidal shape, with low mass and low luminosity. An S0 galaxy is similar in shape to a spiral galaxy, but lacks spiral arms. **Spiral galaxies** such as the Milky Way are characterized by disk-like nuclei with spiral arms. Subtypes of this category are determined by the tightness of the spiral arms and the size of the nucleus; a spiral galaxy of Sa type has a large nucleus and tightly wound arms, and an Sc-type galaxy consists of a small nucleus with open spiral arms. A barred spiral galaxy exhibits an elongated nucleus. The subtypes of barred spiral galaxies are determined like those of spiral galaxies. Some **irregular galaxies** (type I) display a loose spiral structure with high levels of disorganization. Other irregular galaxies (type II) can be of any shape.

Review Video: Galaxies
Visit mometrix.com/academy and enter code: 226539

Distance in Space

An astronomical unit (AU) is equal to 93 million miles, and is far smaller than a light year or a parsec. A light year is defined as the distance light can travel in a vacuum in one year, and is equal to roughly 64,341 AU. A parsec is the parallax of one arcsecond, and is equal to $206.26 \times 10^{\Delta 3}$ AU.

Using Electromagnetic Waves to Learn About the Universe

While the naked eye can only detect electromagnetic waves in the visible light spectrum, scientists can use equipment such as various types of **telescopes** to detect other frequencies of radiation and gain new information about the universe. For example, **radio telescopes** detect radio waves emitted from objects in space. They are especially useful because they can be used during the day and cloudy weather, unlike telescopes that rely on visible light. **Infrared telescopes** detect infrared radiation and are useful in detecting objects that cannot be seen by the human eye, such as those with low luminosity. **Ultraviolet telescopes** observe the universe from outside Earth's atmosphere and are useful for determining what planets and other celestial bodies are made of. **X-ray telescopes** have a unique structure and have been used to estimate the mass of some stars and detect other bodies in space. **Gamma ray telescopes** are similar to x-ray telescopes and detect unique objects like black holes.

Example

Which of the following best explains the relationship between stars and nebulae?

a. Nebulae are clouds of dust and gas where new stars are formed.
b. Nebulae are the remnants of dying stars that eventually become galaxies.
c. Nebulae are the outer cloud of young stars where planets are formed.
d. Nebulae are the remnants of stars that have collided with one another.

Choice A states that nebulae are giant clouds of dust and gas in space where new stars can be formed. Nebulae are sometimes referred to as stellar nurseries because the density of dust and gas can lead to the formation of the new stars. Choice A could be the answer.

Choice B states that nebulae form from dying stars and eventually become galaxies. While the dust and gas that make up nebulae sometimes come from dying stars, they do not turn into galaxies, which are ginormous and complex structures. Choice B is incorrect.

Choice C states that a nebula is the outer cloud of a young star where planets are formed. While it is true that planets are formed in the outer part of young stars, this outer disk is part of the forming star and not a nebula. Choice C is incorrect.

Choice D states that nebulae are the remnants of stars that have collided with one another. While stars do occasionally collide with one another, this does not result in a nebula. Choice D is not the answer.

Choice B is the correct answer because it accurately describes the relationship between nebulae and stars: nebulae are clouds of dust and gas where new stars are formed.

Theories Relating to the Origin of the Universe

Model of the Inflationary Universe

Hubble's law states that the speed at which a galaxy appears to be moving away from the Earth is proportional to its distance from Earth. This relatively simple formula ($v = Hr$, where v is the **velocity of a receding galaxy**, r is its distance from Earth, and H is the Hubble constant) had an important implication at the time that it was developed—the universe is expanding. This fact, in turn, implies that the universe began at a **specific point** in the past. This model suggests that a random conglomeration of quarks and leptons, along with the strong force (all the forces in the universe unified as one), existed in the very dense, very hot, early universe. When the universe was a certain age (about 10–35 seconds old), the strong force separated out from the mass. This enabled the rapid expansion of the particles that formed the universe.

Big Bang Theory

The **theory of the big bang** expands upon the model of the **inflationary universe**. This theory hypothesizes that the early universe consisted of elementary particles, high energy density and high levels of pressure and heat. This single mass experienced a **phase change** (similar to that of freezing water) when it cooled and expanded. This transition caused the early universe to expand exponentially; this period of growth is called **cosmic inflation**. As it continued to grow, the temperature continued to fall. At some point, **baryogenesis** (an unknown process in which quarks and gluons become baryons, such as protons and neutrons) occurred, somehow creating the distinction between matter and antimatter. As the universe continued to cool, the **elementary forces** reached their present form, and **elementary particles** engaged in big bang **nucleosynthesis** (a process that produced helium and deuterium nuclei). **Gravity** became the predominant force governing interactions between particles; this enabled increasing accretion of particles of matter, which eventually formed the universal constituents as we recognize them today.

Stars

Stellar Observation

The observation of stars relates to one of three stellar properties: position, brightness, and spectra. **Positional stellar observation** is principally performed through study of the positions of stars on multiple photographic plates. Historically, this type of analysis was done through measurement of the angular positions of the stars in the sky. **Parallax** of a star is its apparent shift in position due to the revolution of the Earth about the Sun; this property can be used to establish the distance to a star. Observation of the **brightness** of a star involves the categorization of stars according to their magnitudes. There is a fixed intensity ratio between each of the six magnitudes. Since stars emit light over a range of wavelengths, viewing a star at different wavelengths can give an indication of its temperature. The analysis of stars' **spectra** provides information about the temperatures of stars—the higher a star's temperature, the more ionized the gas in its outer layer. A star's spectrum also relates to its chemical composition.

Binary Star

Binary star systems, of which about fifty percent of the stars in the sky are members, consist of two stars that orbit each other. The orbits of and distances between members of a binary system vary. A **visual binary** is a pair of stars that can be visually observed. Positional measurements of a visual binary reveal the orbital paths of the two stars. Astronomers can identify astrometric binaries through long-term observation of a visible star—if the star appears to wobble, it may be inferred that it is orbiting a companion star that is not visible. An **eclipsing binary** can be identified through observation of the brightness of a star. Variations in the visual brightness of a star can occur when one star in a binary system passes in front of the other. Sometimes, variations in the spectral lines of a star occur because it is in a binary system. This type of binary is a spectroscopic binary.

Review Video: Types of Stars
Visit mometrix.com/academy and enter code: 831934

Sizes of Stars

Stars come in a large variety of sizes. They can be the size of a large town or larger than the Sun. The largest stars are called **supergiant** stars, and can be 1,500 times larger than the Sun. The smallest stars are called **red dwarf** stars. The Sun is considered a medium-sized star. The size of a star can be affected by the gravitational pull acting on the star and the star's radiation. As energy is released from the center of the star, the star will grow. However, gravity from the center of the star pulls against that growth and can shrink or limit the star's size. The mass and density of the star will also generally influence its size. From Earth, scientists can determine the size of a star by the star's **luminosity**, which is the total energy a star can radiate in one second, and its **temperature**. The **Hertzsprung-Russell Diagram** was created to compare stars based on these characteristics. Stars with higher temperature and luminosity are larger in size, while stars with lower temperature and lower luminosity are smaller in size.

Brightness of Stars

The brightness of a star when viewed from Earth is its **apparent brightness**. The difference in apparent brightness among stars can be affected by two factors: the distance from the star to Earth and the amount of light put out by the star. Two stars can put out the same amount of light, but from Earth, one may appear to be dimmer than the other. That is because the one that looks dimmer is further away from Earth. The closest star to the Earth is the Sun, which is why it appears to be the brightest of all the stars from Earth. Some stars are so far away that they cannot be seen from Earth, and they may only be discovered and identified by studying the motion of other stars or planets around them. The brightness of a star will vary throughout its life cycle. The more energy a star produces, the more light it will give off. Sometimes the energy produced by a star becomes greater than the gravitational pull on the star. This causes the star to explode and create a supernova, which will shine very brightly for many days.

Hertzsprung-Russell Diagram

The **Hertzsprung-Russell (H-R) diagram** was developed to explore the relationships between the luminosities and spectral qualities of stars. This diagram involves plotting these qualities on a graph, with absolute magnitude (luminosity) on the vertical and spectral class on the horizontal. Plotting a number of stars on the H-R diagram demonstrates that stars fall into narrowly defined regions, which correspond to stages in stellar evolution. Most stars are situated in a diagonal strip that runs from the top-left (high temperature, high luminosity) to the lower-right (low temperature, low luminosity). This diagonal line shows stars in the **main sequence** of star evolution. Stars that fall above this line on the diagram (low temperature, high luminosity) are believed to be much larger than the stars on the main sequence (because their high luminosities are not due to higher temperatures than main sequence stars). They are termed **giants** and **supergiants**. Stars below the main sequence (high temperature, low luminosity) are called **white dwarfs**. The H-R diagram is useful in calculating distances to stars.

Types of Stars

Stars are categorized by several characteristics, including temperature, mass, age, size, and **luminosity**, or brightness. Different types of stars form due to processes that depend on the mass and age of a star.

- **Main sequence stars** are the most abundant type in the galaxy and are characterized by the fusion of hydrogen atoms into helium atoms that occurs in their cores. They range in size, temperature, and luminosity. The Sun at the center of our solar system sits in the middle of the range, possessing average characteristics for a main sequence star.
- **Giant stars** form when main sequence stars run out of fusible hydrogen in their core. They are characterized by their larger size and higher luminosity. On average, giant stars have lower temperatures than main sequence stars.
- **White dwarf** stars are later life-cycle stars that form after giant stars run out of energy. Giant stars shed their outer layers, which become planetary nebulae, and the small, dense core that remains is the white dwarf, with high temperatures and low luminosity.
- **Supergiant stars** have similar characteristics to giant stars, but even larger masses and higher luminosity. They are formed when larger-than-average main sequence stars run out of hydrogen in their core. They tend to become supernovas, followed by neutron stars or black holes.

Stellar Evolution

The life cycle of a star is closely related to its **mass**—low-mass stars become white dwarfs, while high-mass stars become **supernovae**. A star is born when a **protostar** is formed from a **collapsing interstellar cloud**. The temperature at the center of the protostar rises, allowing nucleosynthesis to begin. **Nucleosynthesis**, or hydrogen-burning through fusion, entails a release of energy. Eventually, the star runs out of fuel (hydrogen). If the star is relatively low mass, the disruption of hydrostatic equilibrium allows the star to contract due to gravity. This raises the temperature just outside the core to a point at which nucleosynthesis and a different kind of fusion (with helium as fuel) that produces a carbon nucleus can occur. The star swells with greater energy, becoming a red giant. Once this phase is over, gravity becomes active again, shrinking the star until the degeneracy pressure of electrons begins to operate, creating a white dwarf that will eventually burn out. If the star has a high mass, the depletion of hydrogen creates a supernova.

Supernova

When a star on the main sequence runs out of hydrogen fuel, it begins to burn helium (the by-product of nucleosynthesis). Once helium-burning is complete in a massive star, the mass causes the core temperature to rise, enabling the fusion of carbon, then silicon, and a succession of other atomic nuclei, each of which takes place in a new shell further out of the core. When the fusion cycle reaches iron (which cannot serve as fuel for a nuclear reaction), an iron core begins to form, which accumulates over time. Eventually, the temperature and pressure in the core become high enough for electrons to interact with protons in the iron nuclei to produce neutrons. In a matter of moments, this reaction is complete. The core falls and collides with the star's outer envelope, causing a massive explosion (a supernova). This continues until the neutrons exert degeneracy pressure; this creates a pulsar. In more massive stars, nothing can stop the collapse, which ends in the creation of a black hole.

Technology in Space Exploration and Discovery

Technology plays an important role in the development and maintenance of scientific explorations. It allows scientists to access remote locations like outer space with tools like telescopes which allow observation, rovers which allow the collection of physical and photographic data, satellites which measure and store data from the Earth's surface, and spaceships which allow humans to physically access distant places in space. Even technology as simple as a program designed to help scientists maintain and compare data is essential for the communication of ideas and the understanding of collected information.

Rock Cycle

The **rock cycle** is the process whereby the materials that make up the Earth transition through the three types of rock: igneous, sedimentary, and metamorphic. Rocks, like all matter, cannot be created or destroyed; rather, they undergo a series of changes and adopt different forms through the functions of the rock cycle. Plate tectonics and the water cycle are the driving forces behind the rock cycle; they force rocks and minerals out of equilibrium and force them to adjust to different external conditions. Viewed in a generalized, cyclical fashion, the rock cycle operates as follows: rocks beneath Earth's surface melt into magma. This **magma** either erupts through volcanoes or remains inside the Earth. Regardless, the magma cools, forming igneous rocks. On the surface, these rocks experience **weathering** and **erosion**, which break them down and distribute the fragments across the surface. These fragments form layers and eventually become **sedimentary rocks**. Sedimentary rocks are then either transformed to **metamorphic rocks** (which will become magma inside the Earth) or melted down into magma.

Rock Formation

Igneous Rocks: Igneous rocks can be formed from sedimentary rocks, metamorphic rocks, or other igneous rocks. Rocks that are pushed under the Earth's surface (usually due to plate subduction) are exposed to high mantle temperatures, which cause the rocks to melt into magma. The magma then rises to the surface through volcanic processes. The lower atmospheric temperature causes the magma to cool, forming grainy, extrusive igneous rocks. The creation of extrusive, or volcanic, rocks is quite rapid. The cooling process can occur so rapidly that crystals do not form; in this case, the result is a glass, such as obsidian. It is also possible for magma to cool down inside the Earth's interior; this type of igneous rock is called intrusive. Intrusive, or plutonic, rocks cool more slowly, resulting in a coarse-grained texture.

Sedimentary Rocks: Sedimentary rocks are formed when rocks at the Earth's surface experience weathering and erosion, which break them down and distribute the fragments across the surface. Fragmented material (small pieces of rock, organic debris, and the chemical products of mineral sublimation) is deposited and accumulates in layers, with top layers burying the materials beneath. The pressure exerted by the topmost layers causes the lower layers to compact, creating solid sedimentary rock in a process called lithification.

Fossil Fuels

Sedimentary rock can contain the remains of living organisms. This happens when clasts are deposited on top of remains or pieces of remains are deposited among the clasts. Over time and with pressure, these remains become substances called **fossil fuels** that can fuel machines. Some examples of fossil fuels are oil and coal.

EXAMPLE

Which of the following best explains how fossil fuels are formed?

a. Fossils created from the mass extinction of dinosaurs gradually broke down into fuel such as oil.
b. Decaying plants and animals at the bottom of the ocean were compressed into fuel such as oil.
c. The remains of animals encased in ice from the last ice age melted, releasing fuel such as oil.
d. Fossils and bones are processed by humans to create fuels such as oil.

Choice A states that fossil fuels were formed from dinosaur fossils. The production of fossil fuels is unrelated to fossils, despite their name. Fossil fuels are formed from the remains of ancient plants and animals, not dinosaur fossils. Choice A is incorrect.

Choice B proposes that fossil fuels were formed from the remains of plants and animals in the ocean. Over very long periods of time, pressure and heat can turn these remains into fossil fuels. Choice B could be the correct answer.

Choice C states that fossil fuels are the result of animal remains that have become encased in ice during an ice age melting. When this happens, it typically preserves the remains of the animals, and they do not decay or transform into materials such as fossil fuels. Choice C is not the answer.

Choice D has to do with fossils being processed by humans to create fossil fuels. Fossil fuels do not actually come from fossils, and they are created through natural processes over hundreds of millions of years, not by humans. Choice D is incorrect.

Choice B is the correct answer. Fossil fuels are created not from fossils, but from decaying remains of plants and animals in the ocean due to extreme amounts of time, pressure, and heat.

Metamorphic Rocks: Metamorphic rocks are igneous or sedimentary rocks that have "morphed" into another kind of rock. In metamorphism, high temperatures and levels of pressure change preexisting rocks physically and/or chemically, which produces different species of rocks. In the rock cycle, this process generally occurs in materials that have been thrust back into the Earth's mantle by plate subduction. Regional metamorphism refers to a large band of metamorphic activity; this often occurs near areas of high orogenic (mountain-building) activity. Contact metamorphism refers to metamorphism that occurs when "country rock" (that is, rock native to an area) comes into contact with high-heat igneous intrusions (magma).

ROLE OF WATER

Water plays an important role in the rock cycle through its roles in **erosion** and **weathering**: it wears down rocks; it contributes to the dissolution of rocks and minerals as acidic soil water; and it carries ions and rock fragments (sediments) to basins where they will be compressed into **sedimentary rock**. Water also plays a role in the **metamorphic processes** that occur underwater in newly-formed igneous rock at mid-ocean ridges. The presence of water (and other volatiles) is a vital component in the melting of rocky crust into magma above subduction zones.

Review Video: Igneous, Sedimentary, and Metamorphic Rocks
Visit mometrix.com/academy and enter code: 689294

Soils

Soils are formed when rock is broken down into smaller and smaller fragments by physical, chemical, and biological processes. This is called **weathering**. *Physical processes* include **erosion** and **transportation** by water and wind, freezing and thawing, and slumping due to gravity. *Chemical changes* alter the original substances present in rocks and early-stage soils. *Biological processes* include burrowing by animals like earthworms and rodents and penetration by plant roots. As plants and animals die and **decay**, soils become rich in dark organic matter called *humus*.

Properties of Soil

Since soil is a mixture of rock fragments and biological materials, it varies significantly. The composition of soil determines whether it will be good for plant life or not. Several properties of soil can be used to identify its composition, which can be helpful for adjusting it for suitability for plant growth.

- **Texture** refers to the size of the particles, which are classified as sand, silt, or clay, depending on the size and mixture of the particles.
- **Structure** refers to the density and arrangement of the soil particles. Soil can be compacted, making it dense and rock-like or it can be loose and easy to work with when planting.
- **Porosity** refers to how well water flows through the soil. A higher sand content usually allows water to flow through the soil more easily, whereas clay tends to hold onto water.
- **Chemistry** cannot be seen, but can be tested for the actual elements present in a sample of soil.
- **Color** of soil changes based on the types of minerals and organic matter in the soil. Redder soil may indicate that there is oxidized (rusted) iron in the soil, for instance.

Weathering

The rocks at Earth's surface experience physical, biological, and chemical processes that are much different from the processes ambient during their formations. The operation of these processes on Earth materials is called weathering.

Mechanical Weathering

Mechanical weathering causes disintegration of rocks and minerals. In this process, the affected rocks break apart into small fragments but retain their chemical compositions. This type of weathering occurs due to the presence of joints, or cracks, in rocks that allow the penetration of water and vegetative roots. Mechanical weathering occurs most often in cooler climates. The subtypes of mechanical weathering are pressure release, exfoliation, freeze-thaw, and salt-crystal growth:

- **Pressure release**, or surface unloading, occurs when erosion removes materials overlying rock. Decreased pressure causes the underlying rocks to expand and fracture.
- **Exfoliation** often occurs in regions with some moisture that experience substantial diurnal temperature changes. Rocks are subjected to heat during the day, which causes them to expand. At night, the much cooler temperatures cause the rocks to compact. The repeated expansion and contraction creates stress in the outer layers of the rocks, which eventually begin to "peel" off in thin layers. Exfoliation can also be caused by pressure release.
- **Freeze-thaw** operates when water, which has penetrated the joints of a rock, freezes and expands. The resultant pressure widens the joints and can even shatter the rock. If the rock does not fracture, the thawing of ice in the joints admits water further into the rock. Continuous, long-term freeze-thaw activity weakens rocks.
- In **salt-crystal growth**, the evaporation of saline solutions within rocks leaves salt crystals behind. Pressures accompanying this crystallization can be very high.

Chemical Weathering

Chemical weathering refers to the processes by which rocks experience chemical changes (such as decomposition and decay) due to the influence of organic acids. Chemical weathering occurs most often in high temperature, high humidity climates. The two types of weathering are not mutually exclusive; they often occur side by side. The subtypes of chemical weathering are hydration, hydrolysis, oxidation, and solution:

- **Hydration** occurs when salt minerals, which are part of a rock, expand and change due to the absorption of water. For example, anhydrite changes to gypsum with the addition of water. Hydration can cause rocks to fragment mechanically.
- **Hydrolysis** involves a chemical reaction between acidic water and a rock-forming mineral. The interaction breaks the rock down into new materials. For instance, the chemical reaction between feldspar and acidic water produces quartz and clay.
- **Oxidation**, or rusting, which results in yellow, brown, or red discoloration, occurs in iron-bearing minerals when they are exposed to the atmosphere.
- **Solution** is the weathering process whereby an organic acid interacts with certain minerals in a rock, producing ions that are then washed away by erosion. Solution, therefore, is a gradual dissolving process. It produces underground channels and caverns.

Erosion

Erosion is a natural process whereby Earth's landforms are broken down through weathering. Rain and wind wear away solid matter. Over time, rain reduces mountains to hills. Rocks break off from mountains and, in turn, disintegrate into sand. Weathering and the resulting erosion always occur in downhill directions. Rain washes rocks off mountains and down streams. Rains, rivers, and streams wash soils away, and ocean waves break down adjacent cliffs. Rocks, dirt, and sand change their form and location through erosion. They do not simply vanish. These transformations and movements are called mass wasting, which occurs chemically (as when rock is dissolved by chemicals in water) or mechanically (as when rock is broken into pieces). Because materials travel as a result of mass wasting, erosion can both break down some areas and build up others. For example, a river runs through and erodes a mountain, carrying the resulting sediment downstream. This sediment gradually builds up, creating wetlands at the river's mouth. A good example of this process is Louisiana's swamps, which were created by sediment transported by the Mississippi River.

Layers of the Earth

The Earth has several distinct layers, each with its own properties:

- **Crust** – This is the outermost layer of the Earth that is comprised of the continents and the ocean basins. It has a variable thickness (35-70 km in the continents and 5-10 km in the ocean basins) and is composed mostly of alumino-silicates.
- **Mantle** – This is about 2900 km thick, and is made up mostly of ferro-magnesium silicates. It is divided into an upper and lower mantle. Most of the internal heat of the Earth is located in the mantle. Large convective cells circulate heat, and may cause plate tectonic movement.
- **Core** – This is separated into the liquid outer core and the solid inner core. The outer core is 2300 km thick (composed mostly of nickel-iron alloy), and the inner core (almost entirely iron) is 12 km thick. The Earth's magnetic field is thought to be controlled by the liquid outer core.

Layers of the Earth

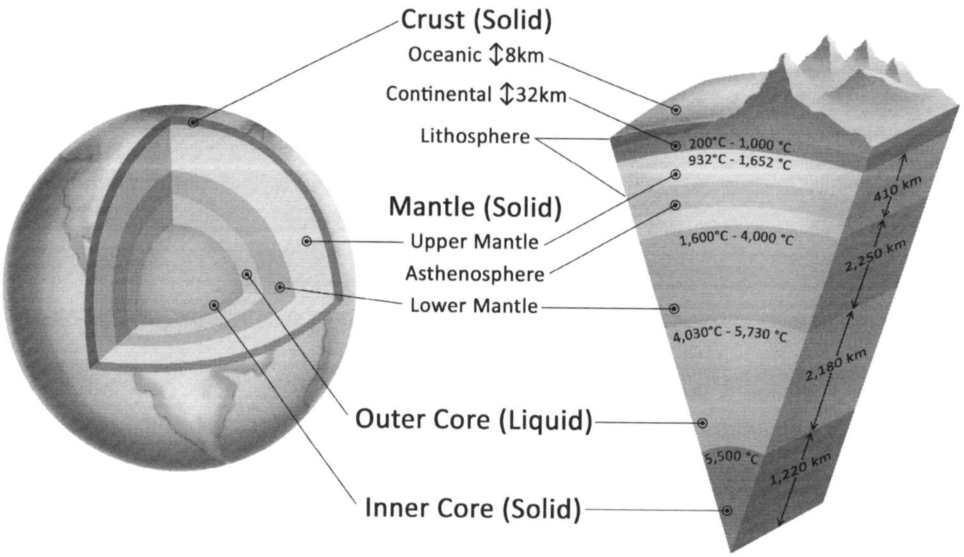

Plate Tectonics

Main Concepts

Plate tectonics is a geological theory that was developed to explain the process of continental drift. The theoretical separation of the Earth's lithosphere and asthenosphere is based upon the mechanical properties of the materials in the two respective layers and is distinct from the chemical separation of Earth's crust, mantle, and core. According to the theory of plate tectonics, the Earth's lithosphere is divided into **ten major plates**: African, Antarctic, Australian, Eurasian, North American, South American, Pacific, Cocos, Nazca, and Indian; it floats atop the asthenosphere. The plates of the lithosphere abut one another at plate boundaries (divergent, convergent, or transform fault), where the formation of topological features of Earth's surface begins.

Seafloor Spreading

Seafloor spreading was originally put forth as an explanation for the existence of midocean ridges such as the Mid-Atlantic Ridge. These ridges were identified as features of a vast undersea mountain system that spans the globe. Seafloor spreading postulates that the ocean floor expands outward from these ridges. The process occurs when the upper mantle layer of the Earth (the asthenosphere), just beneath the planet's crust, is heated through convection. The heat causes the asthenosphere to become more elastic and less dense. This heated material causes the crust to bow outward and eventually separate. The lighter material then flows out through the resultant rift and hardens, forming new oceanic crust. If a rift opens completely into an ocean, the basin will be flooded with seawater and create a new sea. Often, the process results in failed rifts, rifts that stopped opening before complete separation is achieved.

Continental Drift

Continental drift is a theory that explains the separation and movement of the continents based on shifts in a plastic layer of Earth's interior caused by the planet's rotation (seafloor spreading). Continental drift is part of the larger theory of plate tectonics. In the early twentieth century, many scientists and scholars noted that the edges of certain continents seemed to look like connecting pieces of a puzzle. Due to this observation, as well as the fact that similar geologic features, fossils, fauna, and flora existed on the Atlantic coasts of continents like South America and Africa, these observers theorized the previous existence of a supercontinent (referred to as Pangaea), in which all of the discrete continents identifiable today were joined together.

Theory

This theory of plate tectonics arose from the fusion of **continental drift** (first proposed in 1915 by Alfred Wegener) and **seafloor spreading** (first observed by Icelandic fishermen in the 1800s and later refined by Harry Hess and Robert Dietz in the early 1960s) in the late 1960s and early 1970s. Prior to this time, the generally accepted explanation for continental drift was that the continents were floating on the Earth's oceans. The discovery that mountains have "roots" (proved by George Airy in the early 1950s) did not categorically disprove the concept of floating continents; scientists were still uncertain as to where those mountainous roots were attached. It was not until the identification and study of the Mid-Atlantic Ridge and magnetic striping in the 1960s that plate tectonics became accepted as a scientific theory. Its conception was a landmark event in the field of Earth sciences—it provided an explanation for the empirical observations of continental drift and seafloor spreading.

Tectonic Plate Motion

The two main sources of **tectonic plate motion** are **gravity** and **friction**. The energy driving tectonic plate motion comes from the dissipation of heat from the mantle in the relatively weak asthenosphere. This energy is converted into gravity or friction to incite the motion of plates. Gravity is subdivided by geologists into ridge-push and slab-pull. In the phenomenon of **ridge-push**, the motion of plates is instigated by the energy that causes low-density material from the mantle to rise at an oceanic ridge. This leads to the situation of certain plates at higher elevations; gravity causes material to slide downhill. In **slab-pull**, plate motion is thought to be caused by cold, heavy plates at oceanic trenches sinking back into the mantle, providing fuel for future convection. Friction is subdivided into mantle drag and trench suction. Mantle drag suggests that plates move due to the friction between the lithosphere and the asthenosphere. Trench suction involves a downward frictional pull on oceanic plates in subduction zones due to convection currents.

Review Video: Plate Tectonic Theory
Visit mometrix.com/academy and enter code: 535013

Results of Tectonic Plate Motion

Earthquakes result from the movement of a dozen or so major lithospheric (crustal) plates that float upon Earth's mantle (asthenosphere). These **plates** move about each other, at **transform boundaries**, in response to complex convection cells set in motion by Earth's interior heat. Two plates move apart from each other at **divergent boundaries**, or spreading centers, and come together at **convergent boundaries**. When thin, denser, iron- and magnesium- rich oceanic crust collides with thicker, lighter, silica-rich continental crust, the former is **subducted** beneath the latter. The subducted material carries scraped-off continental crust and seawater down with it. As this material melts, it rises as a mixture of magma and steam to produce explosive **volcanic mountain ranges** such as those surrounding the Pacific Ocean Basin. A **hot spot** is an area of the Earth's surface that experiences high levels of volcanic activity, created by hypothetical phenomena called mantle plumes. Mantle plumes are exceptionally hot portions of the Earth's mantle that rise (through convection) to the crust. Hot spots are responsible for the formation of volcanic chains such as the Hawaiian Islands. When two continental plates collide at convergent boundaries, the crust buckles and thrusts up massive mountain ranges such as the Alps and Himalayas.

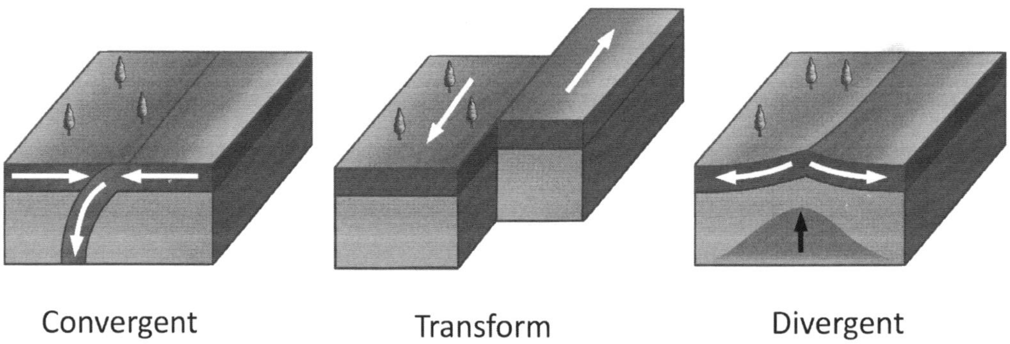

Example

The Andes volcanic mountain range on the western coast of South America is the longest mountain range in the world, consisting of hundreds of volcanoes. Which of the following processes is most likely responsible for the formation of these volcanoes?

a. Convergence of a continental plate and oceanic plate
b. Two tectonic plates moving side-by-side
c. Divergence of two tectonic plates
d. Existence of a hotspot

Choice A describes a continental plate, also referred to as a land plate, colliding with an oceanic plate. When this happens, the oceanic plate slides underneath the continental plate, which is called subduction. This results in long chains of volcanoes, such as the Cascades in the United States, along with earthquakes and sometimes tsunamis. The Andes are a long chain of volcanoes, so Choice A could be correct.

Choice B describes two tectonic plates moving side-by-side. When this happens, it causes earthquakes and rolling hills, not volcanoes. Choice B is not the answer.

Choice C describes the divergence, or separation, of two continental plates. This results in large troughs in the land called rift valleys, not volcanoes. Choice C is not the answer.

Choice D describes the existence of a hotspot, which is a high-temperature spot below Earth's crust that causes magma to rise up through the crust. Hotspots form individual volcanoes or small volcanic groups, such as those in Hawaii and Yellowstone. However, the Andes are a long chain of volcanic mountains, which are not associated with hotspots. Choice D is incorrect.

Choice A is the correct answer. Chains of volcanic mountains like the Andes are formed through subduction when an oceanic plate slides underneath a continental plate.

Determining the Order in Which Geologic Events Occurred Using the Rock Record

The **Law of Superposition** logically assumes that the bottom layer of a series of sedimentary layers is the oldest, unless it has been overturned or older rock has been pushed over it. In addition, igneous intrusions can cut through or flow above already present rocks (e.g., lava flows). This is a further indication that the lower rock layers are older. Another guideline for the rock record is that **rock layers** are older than the folds and faults in them because the rocks must exist before they can be folded or faulted. If a rock contains **atomic nuclei**, reference tables of the half-lives of commonly used radio isotopes can be used to match the decay rate of known substances to the nuclei in a rock, and thereby determine its age. Ages of rocks can also be determined from **contact metamorphism**, the re-crystallization of pre-existing rocks due to changes in physical and chemical conditions, such as heat, pressure, and chemically active fluids that might be present in lava or polluted waters.

Matching Rocks and Geologic Events in One Place with Those of Another

Geologists physically follow rock layers from one location to another by a process called "walking the outcrop." Geologists walk along the outcropping to see where it goes and what the differences and similarities of the neighboring locations they cross are. Similar rock **types** or **patterns** of rock layers that are similar in terms of thickness, color, composition, and fossil remains tell geologists that two locations have a similar geologic history. Fossils are found all over the Earth, but are from a relatively **small time period** in Earth's history. Therefore, fossil evidence helps date a rock layer, regardless of where it occurs. **Volcanic ash** is a good time indicator since ash is deposited quickly over a widespread area. Matching the date of an eruption to the ash allows for a precise identification of time. Similarly, the **meteor impact** at the intersection of the Cretaceous and Tertiary Periods left a time marker. Wherever the meteor's iridium content is found, geologists are able to date rock layers.

Sequencing the Earth's Geologic History from the Fossil and Rock Record

Reference tables are used to match specimens and time periods. For example, the fossil record has been divided into time units of the Earth's history. Rocks can therefore be dated by the fossils found with them. There are also reference tables for dating plate motions and mountain building events in geologic history. Since humans have been around for a relatively short period of time, **fossilized human remains** help to affix a date to a location. Some areas have missing **geologic layers** because of erosion or other factors, but reference tables specific to a region will list what is complete or missing. The theory of **uniformitarianism** assumes that geologic processes have been the same throughout history. Therefore, the way erosion or volcanic eruptions happen today is the same as the way these events happened millions of years ago because there is no reason for them to have changed. Therefore, knowledge about current events can be applied to the past to make judgments about events in the rock record.

Revealing Changes in Earth's History by the Fossil and Rock Records

Fossils can show how animal and plant life have changed or remained the same over time. For example, fossils have provided evidence of the existence of dinosaurs even though they no longer roam the Earth, and have also been used to prove that certain insects have been around for hundreds of millions of years. Fossils have been used to identify four basic eras: **Proterozoic**, the age of primitive life; **Paleozoic**, the age of fishes; **Mesozoic**, the age of dinosaurs; and **Cenozoic**, the age of mammals. Most ancient forms of life have disappeared, and there are reference tables that list when this occurred. Fossil records also show the evolution of certain life forms, such as the horse from the eohippus. However, the majority of changes do not involve evolution from simple to complex forms, but rather an increase in the variety of forms.

Paleontology

Paleontology is the study of prehistoric plant and animal life through the analysis of **fossil remains**. These fossils reveal the ecologies of the past and the path of evolution for both extinct and living organisms. A historical science, paleontology seeks information about the identity, origin, environment, and evolution of past organisms and what they can reveal about the past of the Earth as a whole. Paleontologists seek to explain causes rather than conduct experiments to observe effects. It is related to the fields of biology, geology, and archaeology, and is divided into several sub-disciplines concerned with the types of fossils studied, the process of fossilization, and the ecology and climate of the past. Paleontologists also help identify the composition of the Earth's rock layers by the fossils that are found, thus identifying potential sites for oil, mineral, and water extraction.

Landforms

Deltas, Canyons, and Dunes

A **delta** is landform that is created where a river flows into a larger body of water. The river carries sediment. When it reaches the larger body of water, the water from the river spreads out and the sediment is deposited. Sediment is **deposited** by a river when the movement of the river causes it to move to a different area and it is able to fall through the water and settle. An example is the Mississippi Delta, where the Mississippi River meets the Gulf of Mexico. A **canyon** is a deep ravine between two cliffs. Canyons are usually formed by erosion caused by flowing water over extended periods of time. An example of this is the Grand Canyon in Arizona. A **sand dune** is a mound of sand built by a natural force, such as wind, over time. Forces like wind can create sand dunes by moving grains of sand until they form a mound. Great Sand Dunes National Park, located in Colorado, is home to the tallest sand dunes in the United States.

Example

The Grand Canyon, located in Northern Arizona, is the largest canyon in the United States. It reaches a maximum of 6,000 feet deep. Which of the following factors is most likely to be responsible for the formation of the Grand Canyon?

a. Erosion by water and wind
b. Cracking of the soil resulting from hot and dry weather
c. Accumulation of sediment on the sides of the river
d. Tectonic plate movement

Choice A proposes that the Grand Canyon was formed through erosion and weathering. Over very long periods of time, water and wind can have drastic effects on a landscape and even wear away at rock. Choice A could be correct.

Choice B proposes that the Grand Canyon was formed from soil cracking due to hot weather. While this does happen in certain types of soil, it would not be forceful enough to create such a large canyon. Choice B is not the answer.

Choice C proposes that the sediment carried by the river accumulated on both sides, creating the high walls of the canyon. While this is true for the creation of most riverbanks, this process would not be able to create the enormous heights of the Grand Canyon's walls. Choice C can be eliminated.

Choice D proposes that the Grand Canyon is the result of tectonic plate movement. While tectonic plate movement is likely responsible for the formation of the high ground or plateau that the canyon cuts through, it would not have created the canyon itself. This choice is incorrect.

Choice A proposes the best explanation for the formation of the Grand Canyon, which was formed through the effects of moving water over the course of a very long period of time.

Glaciers

Glaciers start high in the mountains, where snow and ice accumulate inside a cirque (a small semicircular depression). The snow becomes firmly packed into masses of coarse-grained ice that are slowly pulled down a slope by gravity. Glaciers grow with large amounts of snowfall and retreat (diminish) if warm weather melts more ice than can be replaced. Glaciers once covered large areas of both the northern and southern hemispheres with mile-thick ice that carved out valleys, fjords, and other land formations. They also moved plants, animals, and rocks from one area to another. There were two types of glaciers: **valley**, which produced U-shaped erosion and sharp-peaked mountains; and **continental**, which moved over and rounded mountain tops and ridges. These glaciers existed during the ice ages, the last of which occurred from 2.5 million years ago to 12,000 years ago.

Mountains

A **mountain** is a portion of the Earth that has been raised above its surroundings by volcanic action or tectonic plate movement. Mountains can be made of any type of rock and most lie along active plate boundaries. There are two major mountain systems. The **Circum-Pacific** encircles the entire Pacific Ocean, from New Guinea up across Japan and the Aleutians and down to southern South America. The **Alpine-Himalaya** stretches from northern Africa across the Alps and to the Himalayas and Indonesia. **Orogeny** is the term for the process of natural mountain formation. Therefore, physical mountains are orogens. **Folded mountains** are created through the folding of rock layers when two crustal plates come together. The Alps and Himalayas are folded mountains. The latter was formed by the collision of India with Asia. **Fault-block mountains** are created from the tension forces of plate movements. These produce faults that vertically displace one section to form a mountain. **Dome mountains** are created from magma pushing up through the Earth's crust.

Oceans, Seas, Lakes, Rivers, and Canals

- **Oceans** are the largest bodies of water on earth and cover nearly 71% of the earth's surface. There are five major oceans: Atlantic, Pacific (largest and deepest), Indian, Arctic, and Southern (surrounds Antarctica).
- **Seas** are smaller than oceans and are somewhat surrounded by land like a lake, but lakes are fresh water and seas are salt water. Seas include the Mediterranean, Baltic, Caspian, Caribbean, and Coral.

- **Lakes** are bodies of water in a depression on the earth's surface. Examples of lakes are the Great Lakes and Lake Victoria.
- **Rivers** are a channeled flow of water that start out as a spring or stream formed by runoff from rain or snow. Rivers flow from higher to lower ground, and usually empty into a sea or ocean. Great rivers of the world include the Amazon, Nile, Rhine, Mississippi, Ganges, Mekong, and Yangtze.
- **Canals** are artificial waterways constructed by humans to connect two larger water bodies. Examples of canals are the Panama and the Suez.

Hydrosphere and Hydrologic Cycle

The **hydrosphere** is anything on Earth that is related to water, whether it is in the air, on land, or in a plant or animal system. A water molecule consists of only two atoms of hydrogen and one of oxygen, yet it is what makes life possible. Unlike any other planets that have been discovered, Earth is able to sustain water in a liquid state most of the time. Water vapor and ice are of no use to living organisms. The **hydrologic cycle** is the journey water takes as it proceeds through different forms. Liquid surface water evaporates to form the gaseous state of a cloud, and then becomes liquid again in the form of rain. This process takes about 10 days. This cycle is for surface water only: rivers, lakes, groundwater, ocean surface, etc. Water in the deep ocean and in the heart of glaciers is typically sequestered from the cycle for many thousands of years.

Water Cycle

- **Evaporation** refers to liquid water heating up and changing to into a gas, known as water vapor.
- **Transpiration** is where water inside of plants evaporates directly out of plant leaves.
- **Condensation** refers to the water vapor cooling down and beginning to turn back into a liquid form, causing clouds to form.
- **Precipitation** refers to the rain, snow, hail, or sleet that falls from clouds once the water vapor has condensed enough.

- The **storage** stage of the water cycle refers to the water being stored in the ground, trees, or bodies of water on the earth. Water is either trapped in vegetation (interception) or absorbed into the surface (infiltration). Runoff, caused by gravity, physically moves water downward into oceans or other water bodies.

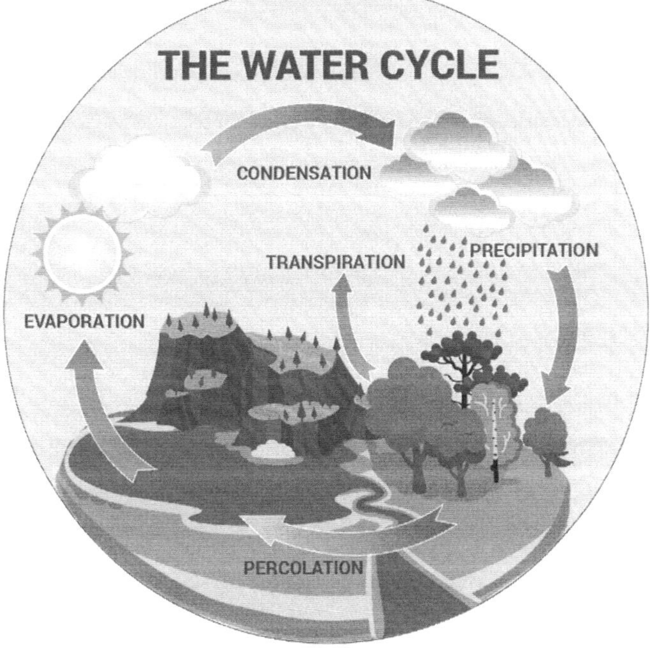

Review Video: Hydrologic Cycle
Visit mometrix.com/academy and enter code: 426578

Biosphere

Biosphere is the term used by physical geographers to describe the living world of trees, bugs, and animals. It refers to any place where life exists on Earth, and is the intersection of the hydrosphere, the atmosphere, the land, and the energy that comes from space. The biosphere includes the upper areas of the atmosphere where birds and insects can travel, areas deep inside caves, and hydrothermal vents at the bottom of the ocean.

Factors that affect the biosphere include:

- The **distance and tilt** between the Earth and the Sun – This produces temperatures that are conducive to life and causes the seasons.
- **Climate, daily weather, and erosion** – These change the land and the organisms on and in it.
- Earthquakes, tornadoes, volcanoes, tsunamis, and other **natural phenomena** – These all change the land.
- **Chemical erosion** – This changes the composition of rocks and organic materials.
- **Biological erosion** – This is bacteria and single-celled organisms breaking down organic and inorganic materials.

Earth's Atmosphere

Earth's gravity is strong enough to attract the molecules of the gases in the atmosphere and keep them in a layer surrounding the planet. The gravity of smaller celestial bodies like Mercury and Earth's moon is not strong enough to do this, and their atmospheres long ago diffused out into space.

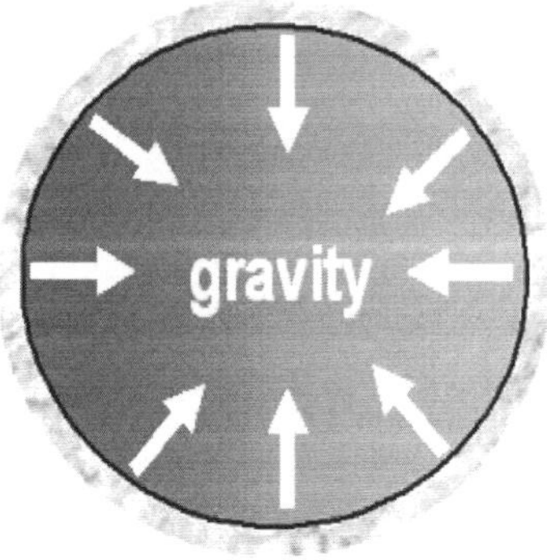

Composition of Earth's Atmosphere

The Earth's atmosphere is 79% nitrogen, 20% oxygen, and 1% other gases. The oxygen was originally produced almost entirely by algae-type plants. The atmosphere has four layers:

- **Troposphere** – This is the layer closest to the Earth where all weather takes place. It is the region that contains rising and falling packets of air. Air pressure at sea level is 0.1 atmospheres, but the top of the troposphere is about 10% of that amount.
- **Stratosphere** – In this layer, air flow is mainly horizontal. The upper portion has a thin layer of concentrated ozone (a reactive form of oxygen) that is largely responsible for absorbing the Sun's ultraviolet rays.
- **Mesosphere** – This is the coldest layer. Temperatures drop to -100°C at the top.
- **Thermosphere** – This is divided into the lower ionosphere and the higher exosphere. This layer is very thin and has many ionized atoms with a net electrical charge. The aurora and Van Allen Belts are here. This layer also absorbs the most energetic photons from the Sun and reflects radio waves, enabling long distance radio communication.

Review Video: Earth's Atmosphere
Visit mometrix.com/academy and enter code: 417614

Geosphere and Cryosphere

The geosphere refers to the land, rocks, sand, mountains, volcanoes, and soil that make up the planet. By contrast, the cryosphere is the frozen water on the planet, which includes glaciers, icebergs, ice caps, and snow. The geosphere and cryosphere interact when glaciers and ice erode rocks or when large glaciers pass over the land and carve out large structures, such as Michigan's Lake Erie. Furthermore, the ground can become permanently frozen; it is then known as permafrost and included in the cryosphere instead of the geosphere. Ice also breaks down pieces of rocks in a process called weathering, which is an essential step in the rock cycle.

Weather and Climate

Weather describes conditions or changes in sunshine, temperature, cloud coverage, precipitation, warm and cold fronts, and more during a specific time in a specific area. These components can change throughout a day, week, or month. Meteorologists track and report what is happening in the atmosphere to help predict how the weather will change in the near future. Weather data is collected and studied over long periods of time, often multiple decades, to evaluate the climate of a particular area. **Climate** refers to patterns in weather conditions, such as temperature, precipitation, and any extremes related to them, in a specific area over a very long period of time. A large factor that influences climate is latitude, which is the distance of an area from the equator.

Weather

Heat energy from the Sun warms different parts of the planet in different ways at different times. As warm air rises it expands and cools. This causes moisture to condense as liquid drops or freeze as ice crystals to form clouds. When the water drops or ice crystals become too large to stay aloft, they fall as precipitation. As warm air rises it also leaves a low-pressure zone behind. This causes air from high surrounding high-pressure zones to rush in as wind.

Climate

Climate is usually defined as the "**average weather**" in a particular area on Earth. The timespan over which climate is measured is variable, but it is generally accepted that the climate of an area does not vary during a human life span (though climate is extremely various in geologic time). This may change, however, due to the increasing greenhouse effect. Meteorologists measure climate by averaging certain quantifiable elements such as rainfall or temperature. Climate may be studied on several different scales:

- **Local climate** refers to the climate of small geographic areas (generally up to tens of miles wide). The local climate of an area is affected by things such as its location relative to an ocean and the presence of mountains near the location.
- A **regional climate** is the climate of a larger geographic area, such as a country. A regional climate may also be delineated due to climate features that are distinctive from the surrounding climate.
- **Global climate** refers to the average weather experienced across the Earth.

Climate Zones

Climate zones are areas of regional climate. These zones are created by the general circulation of the air in Earth's atmosphere. Generally, the warmest air moves from the equator (where the greatest amount of solar energy is received) toward the higher latitudes at the poles. The latitudinal temperature gradient produces atmospheric pressure. At the equator, solar energy heats air near the surface, causing it to rise and decreasing air pressure. The risen air is transported by winds to cooler areas at higher latitudes, where the air then descends (because cool air is heavier than warmer air), creating an area of high pressure. The descended air is then moved by surface winds, either back to the equator or up to higher latitudes, where it encounters colder air. The air then rises again in an area of low pressure. The air in polar regions is very cold, which causes it to sink, creating high pressure. Winds are thus generated to move air from warmer regions to colder ones.

Review Video: Rotation of Low Pressure Systems
Visit mometrix.com/academy and enter code: 258356

Clouds

Clouds form when water vapor in the atmosphere cools to the point where it **condenses** and becomes water droplets or small particles of frozen ice crystals. Clouds form when moisture is added to the air through evaporation until the air becomes **saturated** and cannot hold any more water. Then, the water vapor can condense into visible droplets.

Precipitation

Precipitation is water that falls back to the surface of the Earth from the atmosphere. This water may be in the form of **rain**, which is water in liquid form. Raindrops are formed in clouds due to **condensation**. When the drops become too large to remain in the clouds, gravity causes them to fall toward the surface of the Earth. Extremely small raindrops are called **drizzle**. If the temperature of a layer of air through which rain passes is below the freezing point of water, the rain may take the form of **sleet**, which is partially frozen water. Precipitation may also fall in the form of **snow**, which is made of ice crystals. When clumps of snowflakes melt and refreeze, **hail** is formed. Hail may also be formed when liquid water gathers on the surface of a snowflake and then freezes.

Temperature

Temperature describes the amount of **heat** in an area. The Earth's tilt and shape impact the average temperatures in each region. The Sun shines on the areas closest to the equator most directly, causing those areas to have warmer average temperatures. All other areas receive energy from the Sun at different angles, causing lower average temperatures. The farther North or South an area is from the equator, the less directly the Sun will shine on them. Since temperature is an important part of the water cycle, it also has an effect on the humidity, precipitation, and air pressure in an area. Since weather processes are like cycles, these factors can also impact the temperature in an area. Temperature can be predicted based on an area's location, the time of year, the moisture in an area, and the air pressure in an area.

Wind

When the Sun shines, it heats the surface of Earth, including Earth's atmosphere. This heating does not occur evenly because some places on Earth, such as the equator, receive more direct sunlight than others. When air is heated and becomes warmer, it rises due to decreased density, causing more dense air from colder parts of the planet to rush in under it. As the warm air moves in the atmosphere, it cools and begins to sink again. This creates a cycle of heat movement within Earth's atmosphere called **convection**. This circular motion of air in the atmosphere is responsible for winds.

Air Pressure

Pressure describes the amount of force applied to an object over a certain area. For example, a person standing on a bed sinks deeper into the bed than a person laying on it. This occurs because the same amount of force is applied to a smaller area, which means the pressure is higher. Pressure applies to all forces that are applied to other objects, including air. The pressure applied by air in a given place is called **air pressure**, or **barometric pressure**. Because air has mass, and gravity is pulling it toward the Earth, air applies force on everything beneath it. Air pressure changes with **altitude**, which is the height of an object above sea level. The lower the altitude, the higher the air pressure. This is because the air at higher altitudes is weighing on the air underneath it. Similarly, air pressure is lower at higher altitudes.

Pressure Systems

The atoms in warm air are less densely packed, causing them to exert less pressure. In contrast, cold air is characterized by closely packed atoms, which means it has high density and exerts much pressure. A **low-pressure system** attracts air from surrounding areas, causing it to rise and condense higher in the atmosphere, leading to clouds and precipitation such as rain. A **high-pressure system** blows air away from itself and is associated with fewer clouds and calmer weather. The boundary where two systems interact is called a **front** and is associated with turbulent, stormy weather. Scientists like **meteorologists** use **pressure maps** to predict the weather, usually for a specific area that is local to them. By mapping out the location of high- and low-pressure systems and examining the boundaries between them, meteorologists can predict future weather based on the weather patterns associated with each system and type of boundary.

Impact of Temperature and Humidity on Air Pressure

Humidity and temperature also affect air pressure. **Humidity** refers to how much moisture is in the air. Air that contains more water molecules contains more mass than drier air. Therefore, gravity pulls more on air that has higher humidity, which causes increased air pressure. Similarly, **temperature** can affect the density of air. Gases do not have a constant volume, but the space between the molecules in a gas grows and shrinks with changes in temperature, causing changes in air pressure.

Impact of Air Pressure on Climate and Weather

Weather systems are often described based on air pressure. A **high-pressure system** means that an area has higher air pressure, while a **low-pressure system** has a lower pressure. Pressure will move toward **equilibrium**, or a state of **balance**. Therefore, high- and low-pressure systems naturally interact with each other. Low pressure systems try to **pull air** toward them to reach equilibrium. This causes condensation to form and can eventually produce storms. High pressure systems **push air** away from them and are usually associated with sunny or clear weather.

Lightning Bolt

Lightning is a huge electric spark that can occur inside a cloud, go from one cloud to another, or go from a cloud to the ground. The turbulent rising air and rising and falling raindrops or ice crystals in a thunderstorm cause differences in electric charge in different parts of the cloud and between the bottom of the cloud and the ground. When the difference in charge is large enough, a lightning bolt will discharge which neutralizes the difference.

Thunder

As a lightning bolt travels through the air, it pushes the air aside faster than the speed of sound. This produces a shock wave of very hot air that creates a loud sonic boom, which we hear as thunder. If a person can hear thunder, he needs to get indoors quickly as possible since he could be struck by lightning.

We hear thunder later because sound travels much slower than light. Light travels so fast that it is almost instantaneous from one point to another anywhere on Earth. Sound travels much more slowly—about one mile every five seconds or so. Light would travel one mile in only about 5 millionths of a second. Therefore, the distance from a lightning flash can be determined by counting the number of seconds until the thunder it made is heard.

Tornado

A tornado is a violent rotating column of air that is in contact with both the ground and a cloud. The column is visible because the very low pressure causes water vapor to condense out as visible water droplets. Where the tornado touches the ground it usually stirs up a cloud of dirt and debris like the one in this photo. Tornadoes are the most violent storms on Earth, and the strongest spin at 300 miles per hour.

Review Video: Tornadoes
Visit mometrix.com/academy and enter code: 540439

Tropical Cyclones

A tropical cyclone is potentially the most destructive and dangerous type of cyclone. Such a formation is referred to as a **hurricane** when it occurs over the Atlantic Ocean or as a **typhoon** when it occurs over the Pacific or Indian Oceans. **Tropical cyclones** develop at low latitudes (specifically, between 8 and 15 degrees North or South latitude) when the surface waters below reach temperatures of 81 degrees Fahrenheit or above. From their zone of origination, tropical cyclones often travel westward through the trade-wind belt; westerly winds may push the storm northward as well. This type of cyclone is associated with high wind speeds and high levels of rainfall. A tropical cyclone also displays extremely low pressure in its center, or eye, where weather conditions are fair (in contrast to the rest of the storm). These weather systems occur seasonally: in the Northern Hemisphere, cyclonic activity is highest from May to November; in the Southern Hemisphere, the cyclone season is roughly the opposite.

HURRICANE

A **hurricane** is a very large tropical storm that forms over the open ocean and produces very strong winds and heavy rains. A **tropical storm** forms when warm water evaporates and the saturated air rises and forms a column of condensed water vapor. As the wind speed increases the pressure falls even more and a hurricane can be born. Sinking air in the center of the storm produces an **eye** (arrow) where the weather is quite calm and free of clouds.

MEASURING WEATHER

Weather can be measured by a variety of methods. The simplest include measurement of rainfall, sunshine, pressure, humidity, temperature, and cloudiness with basic instruments such as thermometers, barometers, and rain gauges. However, the use of **radar** (which involves analysis of microwaves reflecting off of raindrops) and satellite imagery grants meteorologists a look at the big picture of weather across, for example, an entire continent. This helps them understand and make predictions about current and developing weather systems. Infrared (heat-sensing) imaging allows meteorologists to measure the temperature of clouds above ground. Using weather reports gathered from different weather stations spread over an area, meteorologists create synoptic charts. The locations and weather reports of several stations are plotted on a chart; analysis of the pressures reported from each location, as well as rainfall, cloud cover, and so on, can reveal basic weather patterns.

Heat Transfer

Heat is a type of energy. Heat transfers from the hot object to the cold object through the three forms of heat transfer: conduction, convection, and radiation.

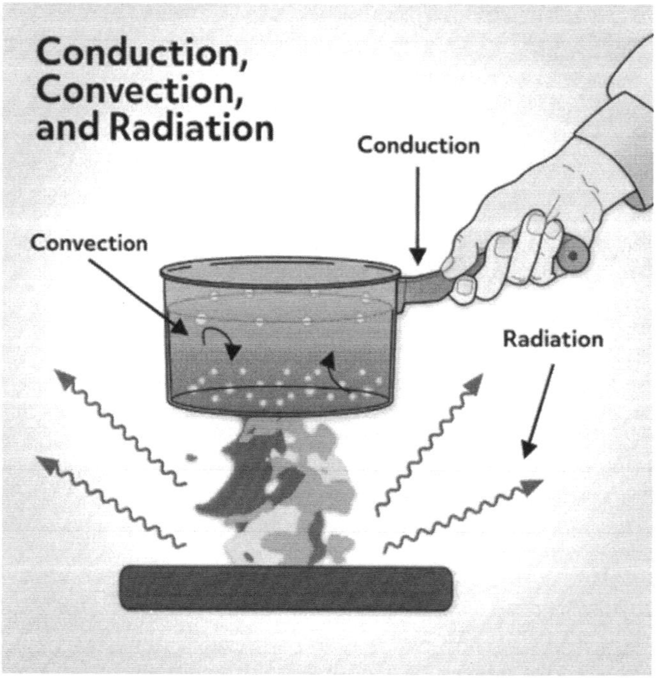

Conduction is the transfer of heat by physical contact. When you touch a hot pot, the pot transfers heat to your hand by conduction.

Convection is the transfer of heat by the movement of fluids. When you put your hand in steam, the steam transfers heat to your hand by convection.

Radiation is the transfer of heat by electromagnetic waves. When you put your hand near a campfire, the fire heats your hand by radiation.

Review Video: Heat Transfer
Visit mometrix.com/academy and enter code: 451646

Effects of Natural Processes on Climate Change

Natural Processes That Impact the Climate

Many natural processes have extreme effects on Earth systems. **Volcanic eruptions** have largely short-term effects on global temperature due to the emissions of ash and CO_2, which affect how sunlight is absorbed and reflected in the atmosphere. **Asteroids** usually burn up in the atmosphere, but impacts of significant sizes can cause similar effects to that of volcanos, such as introducing chemicals into the atmosphere or severely damaging ecosystems. **Meteoroids** are fragments of asteroids of various sizes. If they come through Earth's atmosphere, they are called meteors or shooting stars. If they land on Earth, they are called meteorites, and create craters on impact (the Barringer Crater in Arizona). **Ocean currents** and **subsurface processes** within the earth also can change how temperature variation is distributed across the Earth. **Magmatic cycles** of temperature change cause surface level heating and cooling, referred to as **El Nino** (heating) and **La Nina** (cooling). **Solar variations** usually come in cycles which also have powerful effects on the temperature of the planet. These temperature changes affect temperature of the climate directly, but also influence systems such as weather, oceanic currents, and ecological systems.

Global Warming

The **natural greenhouse effect** of the atmosphere is beneficial to life on Earth; it keeps temperatures on the planet 33 degrees higher than they would be without this phenomenon. Originally, this helped sustain life. However, it has been discovered in the last 20 years that this effect is being intensified by the actions of humans. In the twentieth century, certain activities of mankind, including the burning of fossils fuels like coal and oil, have resulted in an **increase in the levels of greenhouse gases** (such as methane and carbon dioxide) being released into the atmosphere. Also, increasing deforestation has affected the number of photosynthesis-practicing plants. The combined effect of these trends is a higher-than-normal concentration of greenhouse gases in the atmosphere. This, in turn, produces the effect of global warming. The average temperature at the Earth's surface has gone up 0.6 degrees Celsius in the last 100 years. Continuation of this trend is likely to have a detrimental effect on many of the planet's ecosystems, including that of human beings.

Environmental Impacts

Greenhouse Effect

The **greenhouse effect** refers to a naturally occurring and necessary process. **Greenhouse gases**, which are ozone, carbon dioxide, water vapor, and methane, trap infrared radiation that is reflected toward the atmosphere. Without the greenhouse effect, it is estimated that the temperature on Earth would be 30 degrees less on average. The problem occurs because human activity generates more greenhouse gases than necessary. Practices that increase the amount of greenhouse gases include the burning of natural gas and oil, farming practices that result in the release of methane and nitrous oxide, factory operations that produce gases, and deforestation practices that decrease the amount of oxygen available to offset greenhouse gases. Population growth also increases the volume of gases released. Excess greenhouse gases cause more infrared radiation to become trapped, which increases the temperature at the Earth's surface. Venus experiences a greenhouse effect similar to that observed on Earth as its dense atmosphere traps the solar radiation and creates a greenhouse effect. The greenhouse gases, including ozone, carbon dioxide, water vapor, and methane, trap infrared radiation that is reflected back toward the atmosphere. While both Venus and Earth experience the greenhouse effect, Venus's greenhouse effect is much more severe.

Ozone Depletion

Ultraviolet light breaks O_2 into two very reactive oxygen atoms with unpaired electrons, which are known as **free radicals**. A free radical of oxygen pairs with another oxygen molecule to form **ozone** (O_3). Ultraviolet light also breaks ozone (O_3) into O_2 and a free radical of oxygen. This process usually acts as an ultraviolet light filter for the planet. Other free radical catalysts are produced by natural phenomena such as volcanic eruptions and by human activities. When these enter the atmosphere, they disrupt the normal cycle by breaking down ozone so it cannot absorb more ultraviolet radiation. One such catalyst is the chlorine in chlorofluorocarbons (CFCs). CFCs were used as aerosols and refrigerants. When a CFC like CF_2Cl_2 is broken down in the atmosphere, chlorine free radicals are produced. These act as catalysts to break down ozone. Whether a chlorine free radical reacts with an ozone or oxygen molecule, it is able to react again.

Human Impacts on Ecosystems

Human impacts on **ecosystems** take many forms and have many causes. They include widespread disruptions and specific niche disturbances. Humans practice many forms of **environmental manipulation** that affect plants and animals in many biomes and ecosystems. Many human practices involve the consumption of natural resources for food and energy production, the changing of the environment to produce food and energy, and the intrusion on ecosystems to provide shelter. These general behaviors include a multitude of specific behaviors, including the use and overuse of pesticides, the encroachment upon habitat, over hunting and over fishing, the introduction of plant and animal species into non-native ecosystems, deforestation and clearing land for agriculture, logging, mining, and urbanization, and the introduction of hazardous wastes and chemical byproducts into the environment. These behaviors have led to a number of consequences, such as acid rain, ozone depletion, deforestation, urbanization, accelerated species loss, genetic abnormalities, endocrine disruption in populations, and harm to individual animals.

Global Warming

Global warming may cause the permanent loss of glaciers and permafrost. There might also be increases in air pollution and acid rain. Rising temperatures may lead to an increase in sea levels as polar ice melts, lower amounts of available fresh water as coastal areas flood, species extinction because of changes in habitat, increases in certain diseases, and a decreased standard of living for humans. Less fresh water and losses of habitat for humans and other species can also lead to decreased agricultural production and food supply shortages. Increased desertification leads to habitat loss for humans and other species. There may be more moisture in the atmosphere due to evaporation.

Acid Rain and Eutrophication

Acid rain is made up water droplets for which the pH has been lowered due atmospheric pollution. The common sources of this pollution are **sulfur** and **nitrogen** that have been released through the burning of fossil fuels. This can lead to a lowering of the pH of lakes and ponds, thereby destroying aquatic life, or damaging the leaves and bark of trees. It can also destroy buildings, monuments, and statues made of rock.

Eutrophication is the depletion of oxygen in a body of water. It may be caused by an increase in the amount of nutrients, particularly **phosphates**, which leads to an increase in plant and algae life that use up the oxygen. The result is a decrease in water quality and death of aquatic life. Sources of excess phosphates may be detergents, industrial run-off, or fertilizers that are washed into lakes or streams.

Waste Disposal Methods

- Landfills – **Methane** (CH_4) is a greenhouse gas emitted from landfills. Some is used to generate electricity and some gets into the atmosphere. CO_2 is also emitted, and landfill gas can contain nitrogen, oxygen, water vapor, sulfur, mercury, and radioactive contaminants such as tritium. **Landfill leachate** contains acids from car batteries, solvents, heavy metals, pesticides, motor oil, paint, household cleaning supplies, plastics, and many other potentially harmful substances. Some of these are dangerous when they get into the ecosystem.
- Incinerators – These contribute to air pollution in that they can release nitric and sulfuric oxides, which cause **acid rain**.
- Sewage – When dumped in raw form into oceans, sewage can introduce **fecal contaminants** and **pathogenic organisms**, which can harm ocean life and cause disease in humans.

Effects of Consumerism

Economic growth and quality of living are associated with a wasteful cycle of production. Goods are produced as cheaply as possible with little or no regard for the **ecological effects**. The ultimate goal is profitability. The production process is wasteful, and often introduces **hazardous byproducts** into the environment. Furthermore, byproducts may be dumped into a landfill instead of recycled. When consumer products get dumped in landfills, they can leach **contamination** into groundwater. Landfills can also leach gases. These are or have been dumping grounds for illegal substances, business and government waste, construction industry waste, and medical waste. These items also get dumped at illegal dump sites in urban and remote areas.

Energy Production

- **Coal-fired power plants**: These generate electricity fairly cheaply, but are the largest source of **greenhouse gases**.
- **Gasoline**: Gasoline is cheap, generates less CO_2 than coal, and requires less water than coal. But it nevertheless releases a substantial amount of CO_2 in the aggregate and is a limited resource. The burning of gas and other fossil fuels releases carbon dioxide (a greenhouse gas) into the atmosphere.
- **Nuclear power plants**: A small nuclear power plant can cheaply produce a large amount of electricity. But the waste is potentially harmful and a substantial amount of **water** is required to generate electricity. The cost of storing and transporting the **radioactive waste** is also very large.
- **Hydropower**: Hydropower is sustainable and environmentally benign once established. A disadvantage is that the building of a dam and the re-routing of a river can be very **environmentally disruptive**.
- **Wind power**: Wind power is sustainable, non-polluting, and requires little to no cooling water. But it will not produce power in the absence of **wind** and requires a large area over which the turbines can be laid out.
- **Solar power**: Solar power is sustainable, can be used for a single house or building, and generates peak energy during times of peak usage. But production is limited to when the sun is shining, the panels themselves are expensive to make, and making the panels generates harmful **toxins**.
- **Geothermal power:** Geothermal power is sustainable, relatively cheap, and non-polluting. Disadvantages are that it can only be utilized in areas with specific **volcanic activity**.

American Land Use for Transportation

In the United States, up to 70 percent of urban land is used for transportation—for parking lots, roads, and highways, as well as for light rail trains and subways and for airports. The national highway system includes about 160,000 miles. The areas devoted to automobile use have high concentrations of pollutants from gasoline and from wear and tear on tires, brake pads, and lubricating oil. Air pollutants from automobiles include hydrocarbons, carbon dioxide, carbon monoxide, nitrogen oxides, ozone, and volatile organic compounds (VOCs). Water is polluted by many of the same chemicals when it runs off the roads.

In some places, large areas are used for canals and channels that provide routes for transportation by water and/or reroute water to allow transportation by land. In Florida, canals cover thousands of miles; New Orleans is famous for its canals. In addition to navigation, canals are important for flood control and agricultural irrigation.

Overfishing

Efficient modern fishing methods (including GPS systems, spotter planes, and factory ships) and government subsidies allow more fish to be taken than in the past. The **larger fish species** (tuna, cod) have been harvested to the point where they are not as profitable. This has shifted the fishing to smaller individuals of the large species and then to smaller species of fish (mackerel). This is called **fishing down the food chain** (or web). Catching these smaller fish for human consumption makes them unavailable for the remaining larger fish, which fail to reestablish their populations. The result of this **overfishing** is that we are left with fewer and fewer food fish. Integrated coastal management programs and marine reserves can improve the numbers (and biodiversity) of fish in the ocean. The United Nations Convention on the Law of the Sea (UNCLOS) sets guidelines for sustainable use of ocean fishes. However, these guidelines are not followed by many fishing nations or by pirate fishers.

Effects of Burning Fossil Fuels on the Environmental

Burning fossil fuels (naturally-occurring hydrocarbon compounds that may be used by humans for fuel), especially coal, releases harmful elements into the atmosphere. The chemical reaction of coal combustion produces, for example, large amounts of carbon dioxide. When these gases reach the atmosphere, they inhibit the release of infrared photons into space—carbon dioxide molecules absorb the photons and may reflect them inward, back toward the Earth. This phenomenon is called the **greenhouse effect**. While the greenhouse effect is desirable, to a certain degree, to maintain a comfortable climate on the planet, increased levels of carbon dioxide can change the balance of energy in the atmosphere. This is termed **global warming**. Coal burning can also cause acid rain. Sulfur dioxide, a byproduct of burning coal, rises to the atmosphere and combines with water molecules to form sulfuric acid. This acid rain falls back to Earth, where it can cause harm to plants, animals, water bodies, and exposed structures. Burning gasoline can also contribute to the formation of acid rain.

Outdoor and Indoor Air Pollutants

The major outdoor air pollutants are carbon dioxide and carbon monoxide; sulfur dioxide and sulfuric acid; nitrogen oxides, nitric acid, and nitrates (or nitrate salts); particulates, or suspended particulate matter (SPM); ozone (at ground level); and VOCs (volatile organic compounds) such as hydrocarbons (including methane) and various solvents.

Indoor air pollutants include outdoor pollutants plus radioactive radon-222, cigarette smoke, cooking- and heating-fire smoke, formaldehyde, and very small particles.

Concentrations of most pollutants are measured in parts per million by volume (ppm or ppmv), milligrams per cubic meter of air (mg/m^3), or micrograms per cubic meter of air ($\mu g/m^3$). Radon is usually measured in picocuries per liter of air (pCi/L).

Water Pollution

Water pollution is a change in water that reduces the ability of water organisms to live in it or makes it unusable by humans. **Point source pollution**, as from the outflow pipe from a factory into a river, is traceable to a specific point, or polluter. **Nonpoint source pollution**, such as runoff from city streets, is spread out and cannot be traced to someone or somewhere specific. The top three sources of water pollution are agriculture, industry, and mining:

- Agriculture pollutes with water and sediments contaminated with such things as nitrates, phosphates, pesticides, oxygen-demanding wastes from plants and animals, and microbial pathogens such as viruses, bacteria, and protozoa.
- Industry pollutes with inorganic chemicals such as arsenic and mercury, organic chemicals such as petroleum products, and heat.
- Mining pollutes with sediments, sulfuric acid, and toxic chemicals, such as mercury and arsenic.

Eutrophication, death of aquatic organisms, buildup of toxins in fish, and early death for 3.2 million people per year are some effects of **water pollution**. Because many water sources are not suitable for human use, many countries purify their piped water as a government service. The first step is often holding the water in reservoirs to increase dissolved oxygen and decrease sediment. Commonly, the second step is disinfection with chlorine, ozone, or sunlight. Improving and maintaining water quality is a more sustainable way to provide potable water:

- In agriculture, organic farming would reduce nitrates, phosphates, and pesticides; oxygen-demanding plant and animal wastes would be composted for later application to the soil; this would keep many pathogens out of streams, and streamside areas could be kept planted to reduce erosion.
- In industry, arsenic, mercury, and other chemicals could be removed from industrial processes or reduced or at least removed from effluent (outgoing wastewater).

Watersheds

A **watershed** is a defined area where all the water from one place or multiple nearby places drains into a common location such as a river or ocean. A watershed is made up of two main types of water: surface water and ground water. **Surface water** is any water visible above ground, such as lakes and rivers, and **groundwater** is freshwater contained underneath the soil and fills the space between rocks and soil particles. Human activities can impact surface water through contamination, pollution, and the construction of dams. Human activities can also contaminate groundwater through the dumping of waste and the use of chemicals near the soil. Groundwater can also be depleted when people use wells to acquire drinking water. One of the most significant impacts on watersheds is **agricultural runoff**, which the result of fertilizers and pesticides from farms leaking into surface water and groundwater sources. Because all the water in a watershed drains into the same location, pollution present in any of the water sources can impact the entire watershed. This can potentially reduce the amount of freshwater available to humans and wildlife in an area.

Physical Science

Atomic Models and Theories

There have been many theories regarding the **structure** of atoms and their particles. Part of the challenge in developing an understanding of matter is that atoms and their particles are too small to be seen. It is believed that the first conceptualization of the atom was developed by **Democritus** in 400 B.C. Some of the more notable models are the solid sphere or billiard ball model postulated by **John Dalton**, the plum pudding or raisin bun model by **J.J. Thomson**, the planetary or nuclear model by **Ernest Rutherford**, the Bohr or orbit model by **Niels Bohr**, and the electron cloud or quantum mechanical model by **Louis de Broglie** and **Erwin Schrodinger**. Rutherford directed the alpha scattering experiment that discounted the plum pudding model. The shortcoming of the Bohr model was the belief that electrons orbited in fixed rather than changing ecliptic orbits.

Review Video: Atomic Models
Visit mometrix.com/academy and enter code: 434851

Review Video: John Dalton
Visit mometrix.com/academy and enter code: 565627

Thomson "Plum Pudding" Model

J.J. Thomson, the discoverer of the electron, suggested that the arrangement of protons and electrons within an atom could be approximated by dried fruit in a **plum pudding**. Thomson, whose discovery of the electron preceded that of the proton or neutron, hypothesized that an atom's electrons, the dried plums, were positioned uniformly inside the atom within a cloud of positive charge, the pudding. This model was later disproved.

Rutherford Scattering

Ernest Rutherford concluded from the work of Geiger and Marsden that the majority of the mass was concentrated in a minute, positively charged region, the **nucleus**, which was surrounded by **electrons**. When a positive alpha particle approached close enough to the nucleus, it was strongly repelled, enough so that it had the ability to rebound at high angles. The small nucleus size explained the small number of alpha particles that were repelled in this fashion. The scattering led to development of the **planetary model of the atom**, which was further developed by Niels Bohr into what is now known as the Bohr model.

Bohr Model

Niels Bohr postulated that the electrons orbiting the nucleus must occupy discrete orbits. These discrete orbits also corresponded to discrete levels of energy and angular momentum. Consequently, the only way that electrons could move between orbits was by making nearly instantaneous jumps between them. These jumps, known as **quantum leaps**, are associated with the absorption or emission of a quantum of energy, known as a photon. If the electron is jumping to a higher energy state, a photon must be absorbed. Similarly, if the electron is dropping to a lower energy state, a photon must be emitted.

Review Video: Structure of Atoms
Visit mometrix.com/academy and enter code: 905932

Basic Organization of Matter

An **element** is the most basic type of matter. It has unique properties and cannot be broken down into other elements. The smallest unit of an element is the **atom**. A chemical combination of two or more types of elements is called a compound. **Compounds** often have properties that are very different from those of their constituent elements. The smallest independent unit of an element or compound is known as a **molecule**. Most elements are found somewhere in nature in single-atom form, but a few elements only exist naturally in pairs. These are called diatomic elements, of which some of the most common are hydrogen, nitrogen, and oxygen. Elements and compounds are represented by chemical symbols, one or two letters, most often the first in the element name. More than one atom of the same element in a compound is represented with a subscript number designating how many atoms of that element are present. Water, for instance, contains two hydrogens and one oxygen. Thus, the chemical formula is H_2O. Methane contains one carbon and four hydrogens, so its formula is CH_4.

Review Video: Molecules
Visit mometrix.com/academy and enter code: 349910

Atom

A **neutral atom** consists of an extremely dense **nucleus** composed of one or more positively-charged **protons** and a varying number of uncharged **neutrons**, except for hydrogen-1 which contains no neutrons, surrounded by a cloud of one or more negatively-charged **electrons**. In a neutral atom, the number of electrons equals the number of protons in the nucleus. The protons and neutrons are bound together by the strong nuclear force, which overcomes the repulsive force the positive charges of the protons have for each other. The negatively-charged electrons are bound to the positively-charged protons by the attractive electromagnetic force. The number of protons, or the atomic number, determines the chemical element the atom represents. The number of electrons in the outermost shell determines how the atom interacts with other atoms or molecules.

Protons, Neutrons, and Electrons

The three major subatomic particles are the proton, neutron, and electron. The **proton**, which is located in the nucleus, has a relative charge of +1. The **neutron**, which is located in the nucleus, has a relative charge of 0. The **electron**, which is located outside the nucleus, has a relative charge of –1. The proton and neutron, which are essentially the same mass, are much more massive than the electron and make up the mass of the atom. The electron's mass is insignificant compared to the mass of the proton and neutron.

Atomic Number and Mass Number

The **atomic number** of an element is the number of protons in the nucleus of an atom of that element. This is the number that identifies the type of an atom. For example, all oxygen atoms have eight protons, and all carbon atoms have six protons. Each element is identified by its specific atomic number.

The **mass number** is the number of protons and neutrons in the nucleus of an atom. Although the atomic number is the same for all atoms of a specific element, the mass number can vary due to the varying numbers of neutrons in various isotopes of the atom.

Periodic Table

The **periodic table** groups elements with similar chemical properties together. The grouping of elements is based on atomic structure. It shows periodic trends of physical and chemical properties and identifies families of elements with similar properties. It is a common model for organizing and understanding elements. In the periodic table, each element has its own cell that includes varying amounts of information presented in symbol form about the properties of the element. Cells in the table are arranged in rows (periods) and columns (groups or families). At minimum, a cell includes the symbol for the element and its atomic number. The cell for hydrogen, for example, which appears first in the upper left corner, includes an "H" and a "1" above the letter. Elements are ordered by atomic number, left to right, top to bottom.

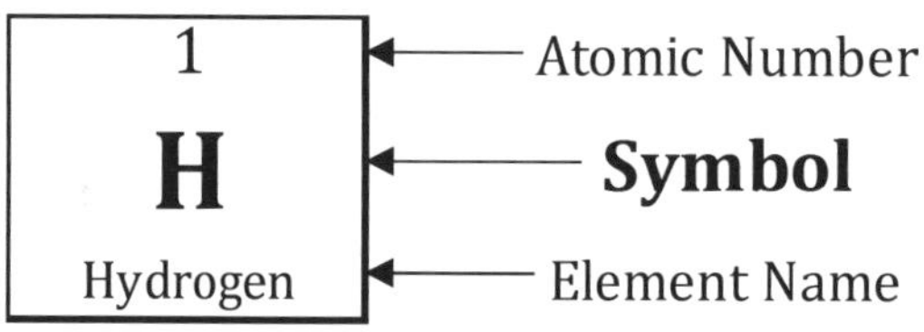

Review Video: The Periodic Table
Visit mometrix.com/academy and enter code: 154828

In the periodic table, the groups are the columns numbered 1 through 18 that group elements with similar outer electron shell configurations. Since the configuration of the outer electron shell is one of the primary factors affecting an element's chemical properties, elements within the same group have similar chemical properties. Previous naming conventions for groups have included the use of Roman numerals and upper-case letters. Currently, the periodic table groups are: Group 1, alkali metals; Group 2, alkaline earth metals; Groups 3-12, transition metals; Group 13, boron family; Group 14; carbon family; Group 15, pnictogens; Group 16, chalcogens; Group 17, halogens; Group 18, noble gases.

In the periodic table, there are seven periods (rows), and within each period there are blocks that group elements with the same outer electron subshell (more on this in the next section). The number of electrons in that outer shell determines which group an element belongs to within a given block. Each row's number (1, 2, 3, etc.) corresponds to the highest number electron shell that is in use. For example, row 2 uses only electron shells 1 and 2, while row 7 uses all shells from 1-7.

Groups and Periods in the Periodic Table

A **group** is a vertical column of the periodic table. Elements in the same group have the same number of **valence electrons**. For the representative elements, the number of valence electrons is equal to the group number. Because of their equal valence electrons, elements in the same groups have similar physical and chemical properties. A period is a horizontal row of the periodic table. Atomic number increases from left to right across a row. The **period** of an element corresponds to the **highest energy level** of the electrons in the atoms of that element. The energy level increases from top to bottom down a group.

Period ↓ / Group →	1	2	3	4	5	6	7	8	9	10	11	12	13	14	15	16	17	18
1	1 H																	2 He
2	3 Li	4 Be											5 B	6 C	7 N	8 O	9 F	10 Ne
3	11 Na	12 Mg											13 Al	14 Si	15 P	16 S	17 Cl	18 Ar
4	19 K	20 Ca	21 Sc	22 Ti	23 V	24 Cr	25 Mn	26 Fe	27 Co	28 Ni	29 Cu	30 Zn	31 Ga	32 Ge	33 As	34 Se	35 Br	36 Kr
5	37 Rb	38 Sr	39 Y	40 Zr	41 Nb	42 Mo	43 Tc	44 Ru	45 Rh	46 Pd	47 Ag	48 Cd	49 In	50 Sn	51 Sb	52 Te	53 I	54 Xe
6	55 Cs	56 Ba	*	72 Hf	73 Ta	74 W	75 Re	76 Os	77 Ir	78 Pt	79 Au	80 Hg	81 Tl	82 Pb	83 Bi	84 Po	85 At	86 Rn
7	87 Fr	88 Ra	**	104 Rf	105 Db	106 Sg	107 Bh	108 Hs	109 Mt	110 Ds	111 Rg	112 Cn	113 Uut	114 Fl	115 Uup	116 Lv	117 Uus	118 Uuo

*	57 La	58 Ce	59 Pr	60 Nd	61 Pm	62 Sm	63 Eu	64 Gd	65 Tb	66 Dy	67 Ho	68 Er	69 Tm	70 Yb	71 Lu
**	89 Ac	90 Th	91 Pa	92 U	93 Np	94 Pu	95 Am	96 Cm	97 Bk	98 Cf	99 Es	100 Fm	101 Md	102 No	103 Lr

Atomic Number and Atomic Mass in the Periodic Table

The elements in the periodic table are arranged in order of **increasing atomic number** first left to right and then top to bottom across the periodic table. The **atomic number** represents the number of protons in the atoms of that element. Because of the increasing numbers of protons, the atomic mass typically also increases from left to right across a period and from top to bottom down a row. The **atomic mass** is a weighted average of all the naturally occurring isotopes of an element.

Atomic Symbols

The **atomic symbol** for many elements is simply the first letter of the element name. For example, the atomic symbol for hydrogen is H, and the atomic symbol for carbon is C. The atomic symbol of other elements is the first two letters of the element name. For example, the atomic symbol for helium is He, and the atomic symbol for cobalt is Co. The atomic symbols of several elements are derived from Latin. For example, the atomic symbol for copper (Cu) is derived from *cuprum,* and the atomic symbol for iron (Fe) is derived from *ferrum.* The atomic symbol for tungsten (W) is derived from the German word *wolfram.*

ARRANGEMENTS IN THE PERIODIC TABLE

The three main sections of the periodic table are metals, nonmetals, and metalloids. There are also further subcategories for each section such as alkaline earth metals, transition metals, noble gases, etc.. The **metals** are located on the left side and center of the periodic table, and the **nonmetals** are located on the right side of the periodic table. The **metalloids** or **semimetals** form a zigzag line between the metals and nonmetals as shown below. Metals include the alkali metals such as lithium, sodium, and potassium and the alkaline earth metals such as beryllium, magnesium, and calcium. Metals also include the transition metals such as iron, copper, and nickel and the inner transition metals such as thorium, uranium, and plutonium. Nonmetals include the chalcogens such as oxygen and sulfur, the halogens such as fluorine and chlorine, and the noble gases such as helium and argon. Carbon, nitrogen, and phosphorus are also nonmetals. Metalloids or semimetals include boron, silicon, germanium, antimony, and polonium.

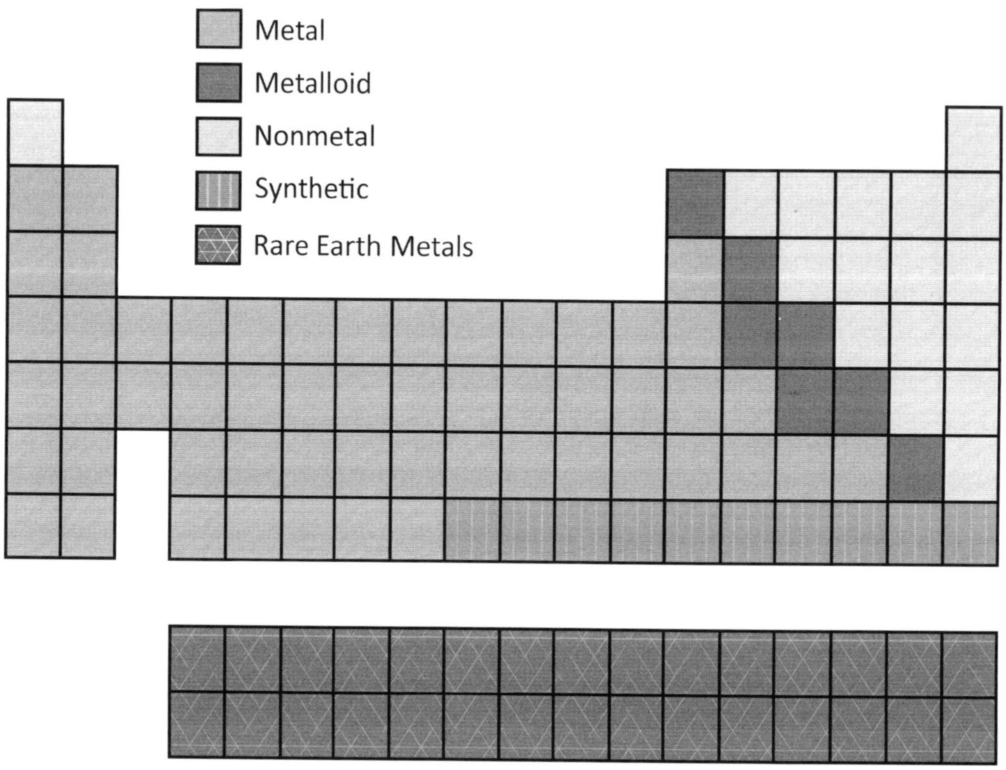

TRANSITION ELEMENTS

The **transition elements** belong to one of two categories—transition metals or inner transition metals. The **transition metals** are located in the middle of the periodic table, and the inner transition metals are typically set off as two rows by themselves at the bottom of the periodic table. The transition metals correspond to the "*d* block" for orbital filling, and the inner transition metals correspond to the "*f* block" for orbital filling. Examples of transition metals include iron, copper, nickel, and zinc. The inner transition metals consist of the *lanthanide* or *rare-earth series*, which corresponds to the first row, and the *actinide series*, which corresponds to the second row of the inner transition metals. The *lanthanide series* includes lanthanum, cerium, and praseodymium. The *actinide series* includes actinium, uranium, and plutonium.

Periodic Trends

Atomic Radius Size

Atomic radius size decreases across a period from left to right and increases down a group from top to bottom. The atomic radius decreases across a period due to the increasing number of protons and the attraction between those protons and the orbiting electrons. The atomic radius increases down a group due to the increasing energy levels. Atoms in the top-right corner of the periodic table (including hydrogen) have the smallest atomic radii, and atoms in the bottom-left corner of the periodic table have the largest atomic radii. Helium has the smallest atomic radius, and cesium has the largest confirmed atomic radius.

Ionic Radius Size

The **ionic radius size** increases down a group of the periodic table. This is due to the increasing energy levels and the fact that electrons are orbiting farther and farther from the nucleus. The trend seen across the periods of the periodic table is due to the formation of cations or anions. Metals form cations or positive ions. Cations are smaller than their neutral atoms due to the loss of one or more electrons. Nonmetals except the noble gases form anions or negative ions. Anions are larger than their neutral atoms due to the gain of one or more electrons.

Ionization Energy

Ionization energy is the amount of energy needed to remove an electron from an isolated atom. Ionization energy decreases down a group of the periodic table because the electrons get farther and farther from the nucleus making it easier for the electron to be removed. Ionization energy increases across a period of the periodic table due to the decreasing atomic size, which is due to the increasing number of protons attracting the electrons towards the nucleus. These trends of ionization energy are the opposite of the trends for atomic radius.

Electron Affinity

Electron affinity is the energy required to add an electron to a neutral atom in the gaseous phase of an element. If electrons are added to a halogen such as fluorine or chlorine, energy is released and the electron affinity is negative. If electrons are added to an alkaline earth metal, energy is absorbed and the electron affinity is positive. In general, electron affinity becomes more negative from left to right across a period in the periodic table. Electron affinity becomes less negative from the top to the bottom of a group of the periodic table.

Electronegativity

Electronegativity is a measure of the ability of an atom that is chemically combined to at least one other atom in a molecule to attract electrons to it. The Pauling scale is commonly used to assign values to the elements, with fluorine, which is the most electronegative element, being assigned a value of 4.0. Electronegativity increases from left to right across a period of the periodic table and decreases from top to bottom down a group of the periodic table.

Review Video: Electron Configuration
Visit mometrix.com/academy and enter code: 565113

Review Video: Electronegativity
Visit mometrix.com/academy and enter code: 823348

Physical Properties of the Elements in Relation to the Periodic Table

The **boiling point**, **melting point**, and **conductivity** of the elements depend partially on the number of valence electrons of the atoms of those elements. For the representative elements in groups 1A–8A, the number of valence electrons matches the group number. Because all of the elements in each individual group contain the same number of valence electrons, elements in the same groups tend to have similar boiling points, melting points, and conductivity. Boiling points and melting points tend to decrease moving down the column of groups 1A–4A and 8A but increase slightly moving down the column of groups 5A–7A.

Chemical Reactivity in Relation to the Periodic Table

Atoms of elements in the same **group** or **family** of the periodic table tend to have **similar chemical properties** and **similar chemical reactions**. For example, the alkali metals, which form cations with a charge of +1, tend to react with water to form hydrogen gas and metal hydroxides. The alkaline earth metals, which form cations with a charge of +2, react with oxygen gas to form metal oxides. The halogens, which form anions with a charge of −1, are highly reactive and toxic. The noble gases are unreactive and never form compounds naturally.

Chemical formulas

A chemical formula is a set of letters, numbers, and symbols that describe the elemental composition of a particular substance. Elements are listed by their periodic table symbol. A subscript number after the element symbol indicates the number of that type of element's atoms in the formula. If there is no subscript, there is only one atom of that type of element. There are three common types of chemical formulas to be familiar with:

1. The *molecular formula* describes the elemental composition of a single molecule of a substance. For instance, the molecular formula for glucose is $C_6H_{12}O_6$, because each molecule of glucose contains six atoms of carbon and oxygen, and twelve atoms of hydrogen.

2. The *empirical formula* is a reduced form of the molecular formula that gives only the ratios of the elements in a substance. For instance, the empirical formula for glucose is CH_2O, because the ratio of carbon to hydrogen to oxygen in glucose is 1 to 2 to 1. The empirical formula will be the same as the molecular formula for many simple substances.

3. The *structural formula* is an expanded formula that gives information about the way that the atoms in a molecule are bonded. Below is an example of the structural formula for ethane:

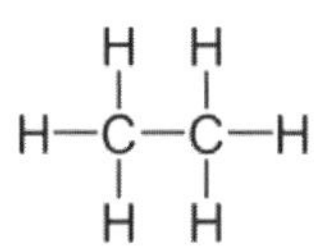

Chemical equation

Chemical equations describe chemical reactions. The reactants are on the left side before the arrow. The products are on the right side after the arrow. The arrow is the mark that points to the reaction or change. The coefficient is the number before the element. This gives the ratio of reactants to products in terms of moles.

The equation for making water from hydrogen and oxygen is $2H_{2(g)} + O_{2(g)} \rightarrow 2H_2O_{(l)}$. The number 2 before hydrogen and water is the coefficient. This means that there are 2 moles of hydrogen and 2 of water. There is 1 mole of oxygen. This does not need to have the number 1 before the symbol for the element. For additional information, the following subscripts are often included to indicate the state of the substance: (g) stands for gas, (l) stands for liquid, (s) stands for solid, and (aq) stands for aqueous. Aqueous means the substance is dissolved in water. Charges are shown by superscript for individual ions, not for ionic compounds. Polyatomic ions are separated by parentheses. This is done so the kind of ion will not be confused with the number of ions.

Review Video: The Process of a Reaction
Visit mometrix.com/academy and enter code: 808039

In a chemical equation, it is necessary to have the same number of atoms for each element on each side of the equation. Reactants appear on the left side of the equation and the products appear on the right. The elements are balanced by placing the necessary coefficients in front of each element or compound. In a simple example, diatomic hydrogen (H_2) combines with diatomic oxygen (O_2) to form water:

$$H_2 + O_2 \rightarrow H_2O$$

Adding up all the atoms for each element shows that there is one more oxygen on the reactant side than the product side of the equation. Since water contains twice as many hydrogen atoms as oxygen atoms, placing the coefficient 2 in front of both the hydrogen molecule on the reactant side and the water molecule on the product side balances the equation:

$$2\ H_2 + O_2 \rightarrow 2\ H_2O$$

Again, count the number of atoms of each element on both sides of the equation. There are 4 hydrogen atoms and 2 oxygen atoms on each side of the equation so it is balanced.

Review Video: Balancing Chemical Equations
Visit mometrix.com/academy and enter code: 341228

Law of Conservation of Mass

The **law of conservation of mass** is also known as the **law of conservation of matter**. This basically means that in a closed system, the total mass of the products must equal the total mass of the reactants. This could also be stated that in a closed system, mass never changes. A consequence of this law is that matter is never created or destroyed during a typical chemical reaction. The atoms of the reactants are simply rearranged to form the products. The number and type of each specific atom involved in the reactants is identical to the number and type of atoms in the products. This is the key principle used when balancing chemical equations. In a balanced chemical equation, the number of moles of each element on the reactant side equals the number of moles of each element on the product side.

Conversion of Energy Within Chemical Systems

Chemical energy is the energy stored in molecules in the bonds between the atoms of those molecules and the energy associated with the intermolecular forces. This stored **potential energy** may be converted into **kinetic energy** and then into heat. During a chemical reaction, atoms may be rearranged and chemical bonds may be formed or broken accompanied by a corresponding absorption or release of energy, usually in the form of heat. According to the first law of thermodynamics, during these energy conversions, the **total amount of energy must be conserved**.

Properties of Matter

Matter is anything that takes up space and has weight. Even air has weight and takes up space. All types of matter have different properties that can be observed or measured. There are many properties of matter, including temperature, mass, magnetism, and the ability to sink or float.

Intensive and Extensive Physical Properties of Matter

Intensive properties are those that do not depend upon the size of the sample. Examples are density, melting-freezing point, boiling point, color, chemical reactivity, luster, malleability, and electrical conductivity. **Extensive properties** do depend on the size of the sample. Examples include the amount of space occupied (volume), mass, and weight. Note that mass and weight are not the same thing. Mass is the amount of material present in a body, whereas weight is the gravitational force acting upon that mass in a specific gravitational field. A 100-kilogram object has the same mass on Earth as on the Moon, but its weight will change markedly. It will weigh 980.7 Newtons (220.5 pounds) here on Earth, but only 163.5 N (36.75 lbs) on the Moon. In outer space this object would weigh nothing at all, but would still have a mass of 100 kg.

Temperature

Temperature is a property that tells how hot or cold a thing is. **Temperature** also demonstrates how much **thermal energy** is in a thing. When an object is cold, it has very little thermal energy. For many substances, being hot makes the substance expand, while being cold makes it shrink. Temperature also tends to transfer from one object to another. For instance, when a cup is filled with ice and water, the ice and water exchange energy until they are the same temperature. The ice and water reach the same temperature eventually, usually resulting in the ice melting.

Mass and Weight

Mass is a measure of how much **matter** is in an object. **Mass** is usually measured by placing an object on a scale. The terms mass and weight are often used interchangeably, but they actually have different definitions. Mass is always the same for a specific object, but **weight** depends on other factors. For instance, 1,000 lb. car always has the same mass, but it would weigh different amounts depending on if the car were on Earth or on Mars, which has much lower gravity.

Volume and Density

Volume is a measure of the **size** of an object or how much space an object takes up. Volume affects several other factors like density. Density is the amount of **mass** (amount of matter) in a certain **volume**. The more matter there is, the more mass an object has. **Density** takes into account both the mass and volume of an object. For instance, an inflated balloon has very little mass in it, but it is fairly large. A watermelon is about the same size, but has much more mass in it, so the watermelon is denser than the balloon. Density is the reason things float or sink. One example is oil and water. Oil is usually thicker than water, but it is actually less dense. If you put oil and water in a cup, you can see that the oil always **floats** to the top. Another way of thinking about it is that the water is actually **sinking** in the oil.

Calculating Density

As stated before, density is the amount of mass in a certain volume. The formula used to find an object's density is Density $= \frac{\text{Mass}}{\text{Volume}}$. The formula is the same for liquid measurements of volume. Since volume is a measurement of the ratio of mass to volume, both units are required in the final answer.

For example, if a cube has a mass of 50 grams and the volume of 64 cm^3, the mass of 50 grams is divided by 64 to find that the density is 0.5 grams/cm^3.

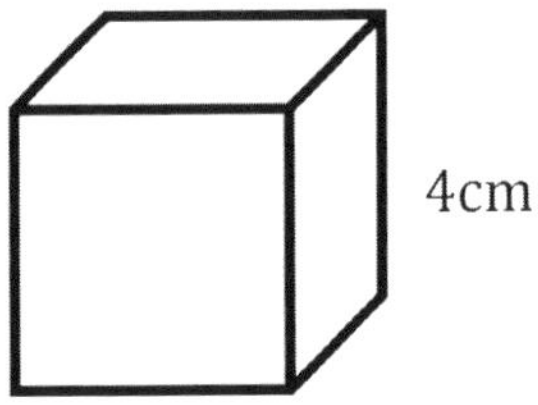

$$\text{Mass} = 50 \text{ grams}$$

$$\begin{aligned} \text{Volume} &= \text{side} \times \text{side} \times \text{side} \\ 64 &= 4 \times 4 \times 4 \\ \text{Density} &= \frac{\text{Mass}}{\text{Volume}} \\ D &= \frac{50\text{g}}{64\text{cm}^3} \\ \text{Density} &= 0.78 \text{ grams per cm}^3 \end{aligned}$$

Density of Water

Density is the **mass** (amount of matter) in a certain **volume**. The more **matter** there is, the more the object weighs. Most solids have more matter than the same volume of their liquids. This means that they are denser and sink in their own liquid. However, water is different. The molecules in ice are farther apart than they are in liquid water. That means that ice has less matter in it than the same volume of liquid water. Therefore, ice is less dense and floats in water.

Materials Denser Than Water

Ships and other floating objects made of materials that are denser than water float because of the empty space they contain inside their hulls. A ship weighing 5,000 tons overall will displace 5,000 tons of water, but this weight of water will occupy a smaller volume than the ship itself. Once this amount of water has been displaced the ship will not sink any deeper into the water and will float. Archimedes' principle states that the buoyant force is equal to the weight of the water (or any other fluid displaced). The reason a solid piece of iron or a rock sinks is that it weighs more than the volume of water it displaces. For the same reason, because a helium-filled balloon is lighter than air it will rise until the air's density is reduced such that the volume of air displaced is the same as the volume of the balloon.

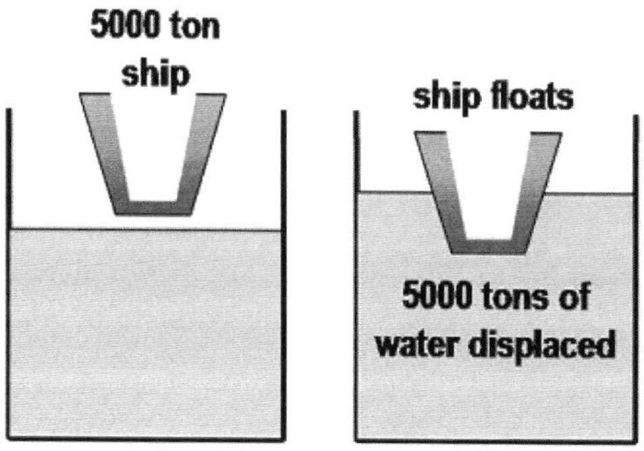

Density of Water and Ice

Most solids have more matter than the same volume of their liquids. This means that they are denser and sink in their own liquid. However, water is different. The molecules in ice are farther apart than they are in liquid water. That means that ice has less matter in it than the same volume of liquid water. Therefore, ice is less dense and floats in water.

Magnetism

Magnetism is a property that some rocks or metals can possess. **Magnetism** is a force that can push or pull on other magnetic materials. Magnets always have two poles, which attract the opposite pole and repel the same pole. Usually, the poles on a magnet are identified as being North or South, because the Earth's North and South Poles are actually magnetic as well. This is the reason that compasses work. The small needle in a compass is attracted to the Earth's poles and points in that direction. Many types of technology use magnetism, including electronics, motors, credit cards, and others.

Magnets

A magnet is a metal or object that produces a magnetic field. A magnetic field is mapped by invisible curved lines of force that attract magnets or certain metals like iron or nickel. A simple bar magnet has a south pole (S) at one end and a north pole (N) at the other. Each pole will attract the opposite pole of another magnet and repel the same pole. The north pole of a compass needle will point to the south pole of a magnet, while the south pole of the needle will be attracted to the north pole of the magnet.

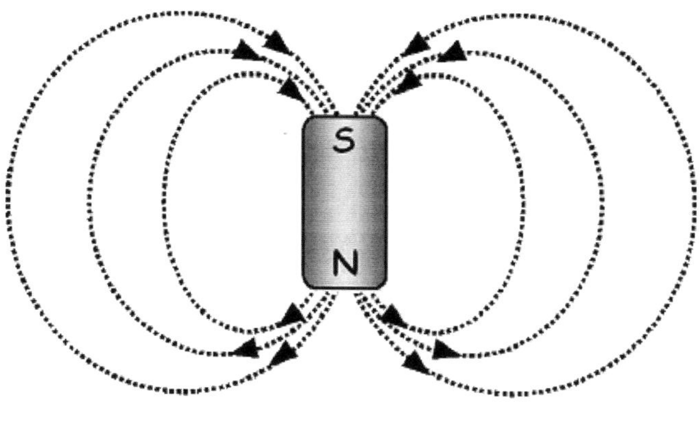

Opposite Poles of Two Magnets Attract Each Other

When two bar magnets are lined end to end with the north and south poles near each other, the lines of force run from the north pole of one magnet to the south pole of the other magnet indicating attraction.

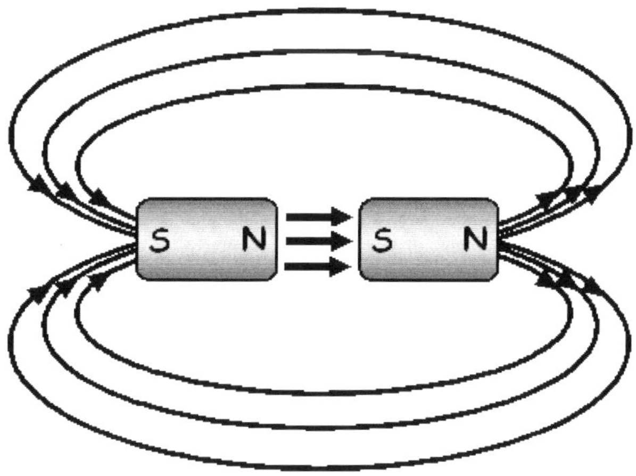

Cutting a Bar Magnet in Two

If a bar magnet is cut in two, two complete magnets will form, each with a north and south pole. If a bar magnet is cut it into three parts, three magnets will form.

Poles of Two Magnets Repel Each Other

When the like poles of two magnets are brought close to each other the lines of force run in opposite directions. This causes the two poles to push each other away.

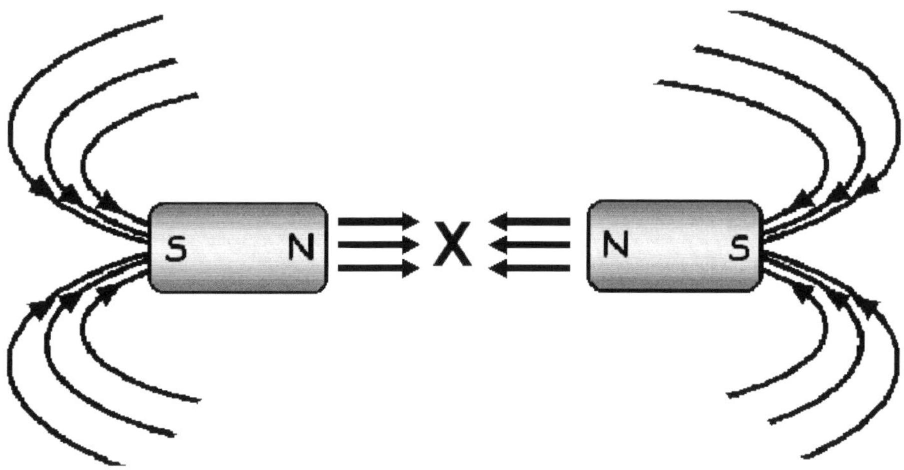

Needle of a Magnetic Compass

Planet Earth has a magnetic field just like a bar magnet. The north pole of a compass needle points to Earth's north pole because the magnetic pole near the North Pole is actually the south pole of Earth's magnetic field. Likewise, the south pole of the compass needle is attracted to the north pole of Earth's magnetic field near the south geographic pole. Just remember that each magnetic pole is attracted to its opposite pole on another magnet or magnetic object.

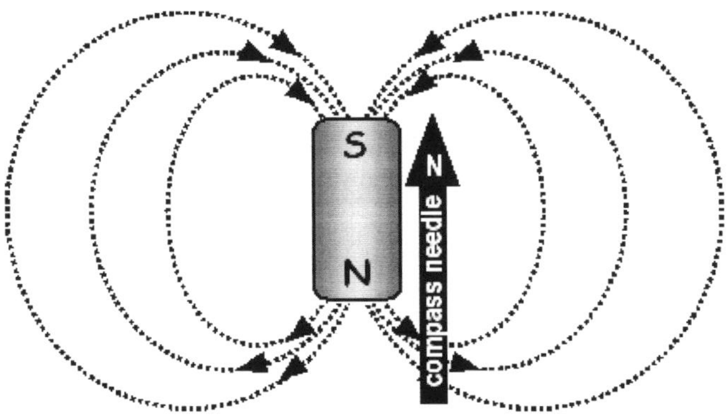

Conductivity

Conductivity is a property that describes how easily a material **transfers energy** to and from other materials. **Conductivity** usually refers to either heat energy or electrical energy. For instance, metals are usually good at conducting both heat and electricity, whereas plastic usually is not good at conducting these types of energy. Materials that are good at transferring energy are known as **conductors**, whereas materials that are not good at transferring energy are known as **resistors**.

Chemical and Physical Changes

Physical changes do not produce new substances. The atoms or molecules may be rearranged, but no new substances are formed. **Phase changes** or changes of state such as melting, freezing, and sublimation are physical changes. For example, physical changes include the melting of ice, the boiling of water, sugar dissolving into water, and the crushing of a piece of chalk into a fine powder.

Chemical changes involve a **chemical reaction** and do produce new substances. When iron rusts, iron oxide is formed, indicating a chemical change. Other examples of chemical changes include baking a cake, burning wood, digesting food, and mixing an acid and a base.

Physical Changes

Physical changes are those that do not affect the chemical properties of a substance. Changes in state are **physical changes**. For example, a liquid can freeze into a solid or boil into a gas without changing the chemical nature of the substance. It is all still the same substance. Ice, steam, and liquid water are all still water, H_2O. Physical properties include such features as shape, texture, size, volume, mass, and density. Cutting, melting, dissolving, mixing, breaking, and crushing are all types of physical changes.

Chemical Changes

Chemical changes occur when chemical bonds are broken and new ones are formed. The original substances are **transformed** into different substances. If vinegar and baking soda are mixed together, a lot of bubbles (carbon dioxide) and water will form. Burning wood in a fireplace is another type of chemical change. The carbon in the wood reacts with oxygen in the air to make ash, carbon dioxide, smoke and energy that we feel as heat and see as light.

Examples of chemical changes include the following:

- (a) The temperature of a system changes without any heating or cooling.
- (b) The formation of a gas (bubbles).
- (c) The formation of a precipitate (solid) when two liquids are mixed.
- (d) A liquid changes color.

A **chemical change** occurs when two or more substances come together and interact in such a way that they become completely new substances. For example, two hydrogen atoms and one oxygen atom combine to make a new compound—a water molecule, H_2O. Likewise, two oxygen atoms and one carbon atom combine to make one molecule of carbon dioxide—CO_2. The two substances that combine are called **reactants,** and the new compound that emerges is the **product**. Chemical reactions (changes) can be much more complicated than this.

States of Matter

The four states of matter are solid, liquid, gas, and plasma. **Solids** have a definite shape and a definite volume. Because solid particles are held in fairly rigid positions, solids are the least compressible of the four states of matter. **Liquids** have definite volumes but no definite shapes. Because their particles are free to slip and slide over each other, liquids take the shape of their containers, but they still remain fairly incompressible by natural means. **Gases** have no definite shape or volume. Because gas particles are free to move, they move away from each other to fill their containers. Gases are compressible. **Plasmas** are high-temperature, ionized gases that exist only under very high temperatures at which electrons are stripped away from their atoms.

Review Video: States of Matter
Visit mometrix.com/academy and enter code: 742449

Review Video: Properties of Liquids
Visit mometrix.com/academy and enter code: 802024

The following table shows similarities and differences between solids, liquids, and gases:

	Solid	**Liquid**	**Gas**
Shape	Fixed shape	No fixed shape (assumes shape of container)	No fixed shape (assumes shape of container)
Volume	Fixed	Fixed	Changes to assume shape of container
Fluidity	Does not flow easily	Flows easily	Flows easily
Compressibility	Hard to compress	Hard to compress	Compresses

Six Different Types of Phase Change

A substance that is undergoing a change from a solid to a liquid is said to be melting. If this change occurs in the opposite direction, from liquid to solid, this change is called freezing. A liquid which is being converted to a gas is undergoing vaporization. The reverse of this process is known as condensation. Direct transitions from gas to solid and solid to gas are much less common in everyday life, but they can occur given the proper conditions. Solid to gas conversion is known as sublimation, while the reverse is called deposition.

Review Video: Chemical and Physical Properties of Matter
Visit mometrix.com/academy and enter code: 717349

Phase States of Water

Water has three states of matter: ice, liquid water, and water vapor. Water freezes at 32 degrees Fahrenheit, where ice crystals form and the substance becomes a solid.

- **Ice** - Water crystalizes when it freezes, which means that it actually expands when it freezes, making it less dense than liquid water. This is uncommon because solids are usually the most dense form of a substance because the atoms are more tightly compressed. That is why ice actually floats in liquid water, rather than sinks.
- **Water Vapor** – Water exists in gas form as it evaporates or boils. Water vapor exists in the air and is often referred to as humidity. There is always some moisture in the air, though as the temperatures drop or pressure changes, it will condense and become liquid water again. Just like all other gas forms, water vapor spreads out in its container and flows much like a liquid.
- **Liquid Water** – Liquid water is the most common form on Earth. Water is needed for life and makes up most of the matter in a human body. Liquid water follows all of the typical rules for liquids, including taking the shape of its container, but has a constant mass and volume.

Heat Transfer

Heat is a type of energy. Heat transfers from the hot object to the cold object through the three forms of heat transfer: conduction, convection, and radiation.

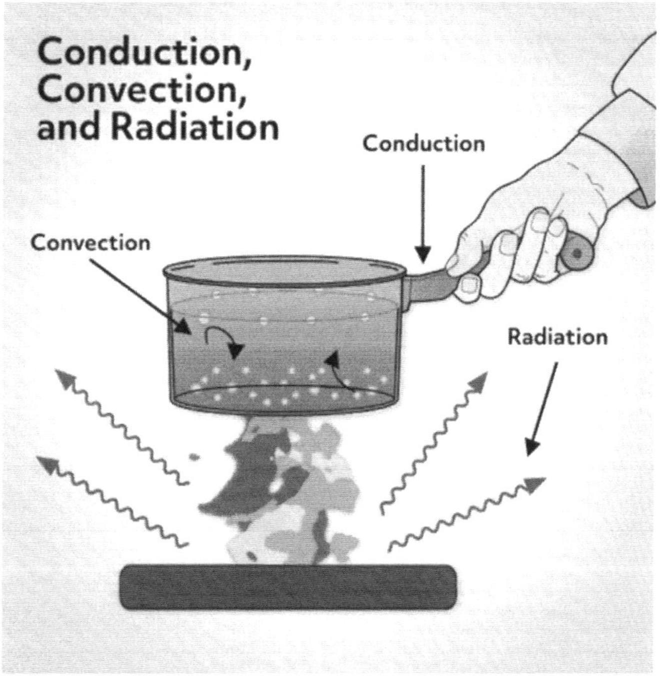

Conduction is the transfer of heat by physical contact. When you touch a hot pot, the pot transfers heat to your hand by conduction.

Convection is the transfer of heat by the movement of fluids. When you put your hand in steam, the steam transfers heat to your hand by convection.

Radiation is the transfer of heat by electromagnetic waves. When you put your hand near a campfire, the fire heats your hand by radiation.

Review Video: Heat Transfer
Visit mometrix.com/academy and enter code: 451646

Mixture, Solution, and Colloid

A **mixture** is made of two or more substances that are combined in various proportions. The exact proportion of the constituents is the defining characteristic of any mixture. There are two types of mixtures: homogeneous and heterogeneous. **Homogeneous** means that the mixture's composition and properties are uniform throughout. Conversely, **heterogeneous** means that the mixture's composition and properties are not uniform throughout.

Solutions and Solubility

A **solution** is a homogeneous mixture of substances that cannot be separated by filtration or centrifugation. Solutions are made by dissolving one or more solutes into a solvent. For example, in a solution of sugar and water, sugar is the solute and water is the solvent. If there is more than one liquid present in the solution, then the most prevalent liquid is considered the solvent. The exact mechanism of dissolving varies depending on the mixture, but the result is always individual solute ions or molecules surrounded by solvent molecules. The proportion of solute to solvent for a particular solution is its **concentration**. Not all materials are able to be dissolved. Sugar is considered **soluble** in water, but sand does not dissolve in water, so it is considered **insoluble** in water.

A **colloid** is a heterogeneous mixture in which small particles (<1 micrometer) are suspended, but not dissolved, in a liquid. As such, they can be separated by centrifugation. A commonplace example of a colloid is milk.

Physical Properties of Mixtures and Solutions

When making a mixture or solution of ingredients, a person is not making a chemical change to the ingredients. Since the original ingredients are still present, their **physical properties** are usually still observable in the final mixture. Take, for instance, a solution of salt and water. The salt dissolves completely in the water, but since the salt is still present, the solution then tastes salty. Other properties, such as magnetism, do not transfer to the whole mixture. If a person were to mix sand and iron filings, then wave a magnet over the mixture, the iron filings would separate out, leaving only sand behind.

Acids and Bases and Water

One property of matter is called its pH value, which determines if a chemical is an **acid** or a **base**. Acids, such as lemon juice, tend to taste sour, whereas bases, such as soap, tend to feel slippery and taste bitter. Some chemicals, such as water, are called **neutral** because they are neither an acid or a base. Just like with other mixtures of ingredients with different properties, an acid or a base can be mixed with water to change the strength of the property. Lemon juice is very strong and sour to the taste at full strength, but when mixed with water and sugar, it can be sweet instead of sour. To add water to reduce the strength of a solution is called **dilution.**

	Very Acidic			**Neutral**			**Very Basic**
pH value	0-2	2-4	5-7	7	7-9	10-12	12-14
	Hydrochloric Acid and Stomach Acid	Vinegar, Fruit Juice, and Sodas	Tomatoes and Bananas	Water	Eggs and Baking Soda	Soap and Ammonia	Bleach and Drain Cleaner

Law of Conservation of Energy

The **law of conservation of energy** states that in a closed system, energy cannot be created or destroyed but only changed from one form to another. This is also known as the first law of thermodynamics. Another way to state this is that the **total energy in an isolated system is constant**. Energy comes in many forms that may be transformed from one kind to another, but in a closed system, the total amount of energy is conserved or remains constant. For example, potential energy can be converted to kinetic energy, thermal energy, radiant energy, or mechanical energy. In an isolated chemical reaction, there can be no energy created or destroyed. The energy simply changes forms.

Types of Energy

Kinetic Energy

The **kinetic energy of an object** is that quality of its motion that can be related in a qualitative way to the amount of work performed on the object. Kinetic energy can be defined as $KE = mv^2/2$, in which m is the mass of an object and v is the magnitude of its velocity. Kinetic energy cannot be negative, since it depends on the square of velocity. Units for kinetic energy are the same as those for work: joules. Kinetic energy is a scalar quantity.

Changes in kinetic energy occur when a force does work on an object, such that the speed of the object is altered. This change in kinetic energy is equal to the amount of work that is done, and can be expressed as $W = KE_f - KE_i = \Delta KE$. This equation is commonly referred to as the work-kinetic energy theorem. If there are several different forces acting on the object, then W in this equation is simply the total work done by all the forces, or by the net force. This equation can be very helpful in solving some problems that would otherwise rely solely on Newton's laws of motion.

Potential Energy

Potential energy is the amount of energy that can be ascribed to a body or bodies based on configuration. There are a couple of different kinds of potential energy. **Gravitational potential energy** is the energy associated with the separation of bodies that are attracted to one another gravitationally. Any time you lift an object, you are increasing its gravitational potential energy. Gravitational potential energy can be found by the equation $PE = mgh$, where m is the mass of an object, g is the gravitational acceleration, and h is its height above a reference point, most often the ground.

Another kind of potential energy is **elastic potential energy**; elastic potential energy is associated with the compression or expansion of an elastic, or spring-like, object. Physicists will often refer to potential energy as being stored within a body, the implication being that it could emerge in the future.

Review Video: Potential and Kinetic Energy
Visit mometrix.com/academy and enter code: 491502

Mechanical Energy

Mechanical energy is the term for the total potential and kinetic energy of an object. Another way to say that is with the equation:

$$mechanical\ energy = potential\ energy + kinetic\ energy$$

Mechanical energy can be increased by increasing either the potential energy, the kinetic energy, or both. For example, lifting a block or squishing a spring increases potential energy. In contrast, throwing a ball or swinging a hammer increases kinetic energy. In each of those examples, mechanical energy is increased.

Thermal Energy

Thermal energy is energy that is produced when particles move and give off **heat**. The Sun is the main source of the thermal energy on Earth. Fire is another natural source of thermal energy. Many devices, such as hair dryers, can also produce thermal energy using parts that are designed to heat up when they are powered using electrical energy.

Electrical Energy

Electrical energy is energy that is produced when **electrons** or **electric charges** move from one place to another. Items that need **electricity**, such as lights and household appliances, use electrical energy.

Light and Sound Energy

Light travels in waves, and the light visible to humans is an example of **light energy**. Most of the light energy on Earth comes from sunlight or bulbs powered by electricity.

Sound energy is caused by **vibrations**. When something moves or has an electrical current moving through it, it will vibrate. This creates waves that move through the space around the object that is vibrating, and sound energy is generated as those waves move. The way the vibration sounds depends on characteristics of the wave. Machines such as alarm clocks or radios include parts that are designed to produce sound waves.

EXAMPLES OF ENERGY CONVERSIONS

The **law of conservation of energy** states that energy cannot be created nor destroyed; it can only be **converted,** or transformed from one form to another. In fact, many everyday actions require energy conversions. For example, batteries contain **chemical energy** in the form of charged materials. When you switch on a flashlight, it completes an electrical circuit, which converts the chemical energy from the battery into **electrical energy.** Then, the bulb on the flashlight converts this electrical energy into **light,** a form of **electromagnetic energy.** The human body also uses chemical energy by processing food to produce **mechanical energy** that can be used to move the muscles. Plugging in a space heater converts **electrical energy** into **thermal energy** or heat. Another example of energy conversion is a falling object. At its peak, an object has **gravitational potential energy**, or the potential to fall and gain speed. When an object is dropped, gravitational potential energy is converted into **kinetic energy**, the energy of motion. In some cases, it may seem like energy is being lost or destroyed, such as when a skateboarder slows down to a stop. However, in this case, the kinetic energy is instead being converted into thermal energy as a result of **friction**.

EXAMPLE

Which of these actions is an example of mechanical energy?

a. Warming your hands over a campfire
b. Using a lamp to read a book
c. Riding a bicycle
d. Listening to the radio

Choice A describes the transfer of heat from a fire to your hands. Heat is the movement of thermal energy, while mechanical energy is based on an object's motion or position. Choice A is not an example of mechanical energy.

Choice B involves a lamp, which converts electrical energy to produce light energy. Neither of these are examples of mechanical energy, so Choice B is not the answer.

Choice C involves someone applying a force to the pedals of a bicycle, causing the bicycle to move forward. Since mechanical energy has to do with the movement of an object, Choice C could be the answer.

Choice D describes a radio, which receives radio wave signals and converts them into sound energy. Sound energy does not involve the movement of an object, so Choice D is not the answer.

Choice C, riding a bicycle, is the only option that describes the energy of an object due to its motion or position, making it the correct answer.

Motion and Force

Sir Isaac Newton observed three major laws explaining how the motion of an object works. The term **motion** refers to the movement of an object and the term **force** refers to physical energy that is applied to an object. Newton also referred to objects that are not moving as being in a state of **rest**.

- **Newton's First Law of Motion** - a body will remain at **rest** or in **motion** until a **force** is applied to it.
  - A bowling ball continues to roll in the same direction it was thrown until friction eventually slows it down.
  - A ball sitting on the ground will not move unless a force is applied to it.
- **Newton's Second Law of Motion** -the amount of **acceleration** is determined by the amount of **force** and the **mass** of the object being moved.
  - A soccer ball will accelerate more if kicked harder.

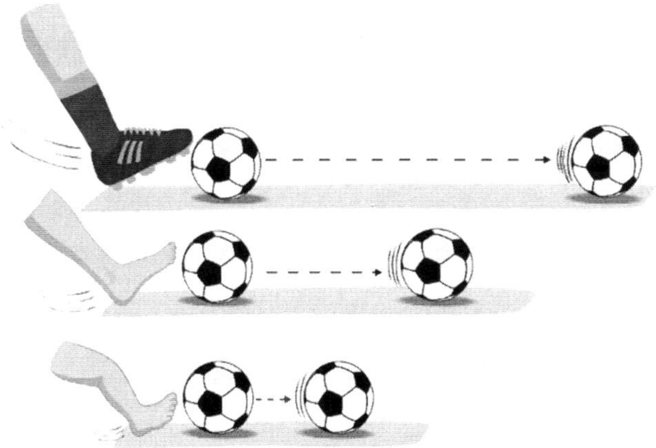

  - A shopping cart is much easier to push than a car because it is much less massive.

- **Newton's Third Law of Motion** – For every **action**, there is an equal and opposite **reaction**.
  - The floor applies force upward to hold up the weight of a person standing on it.
  - A dog pulls against a leash that his owner is holding.

Examples of Newton's Laws in the Real World

- **Vehicle restraints** – seat belts and air bags all work to slow down the acceleration applied to the body in a car wreck. When a car hits another car, it slows down almost immediately, but the body and objects inside have inertia of their own, so they want to continue moving forward. Acceleration is directly related to force, so stopping immediately with the car would be harmful. Instead, the safety features help slow down the acceleration to keep the people inside safe.
- **Amusement park rides** – Rollercoasters apply Newton's laws in many ways. Rollercoasters tend to go very fast, but before you see them do so, they often climb a tall hill before falling very fast. In this way, they use gravity to their advantage to gain as much speed as possible before performing stunts like loop-the-loops and twists. Rollercoasters and other rides seem to defy gravity sometimes, making people feel like they are floating when they are only falling slower than the rollercoaster itself. If a rollercoaster goes down quickly, the body tries to stay in the air, causing this type of effect.
- **Earth's tectonic activities** – The theory of plate tectonics says that there are moving layers of the Earth's crust called plates. These plates are very slow moving, but enormous. When these plates bump into each other or slide past each other, they cause massive amounts of force because of Newton's laws. Every action produces an equal and opposite reaction. This is the cause of earthquakes, mountain volcano formation, and some forms of tidal waves.
- **Rocket launches** – When rockets are launched, many forces are at play. The rockets are huge, and they require a great amount of force to lift them into the air and into space. To do so, the rockets ignite fuel underneath and push downwards to cause lift upwards. These forces must be carefully calculated, however, so that the rocket does not veer off in the wrong direction and so that the humans and cargo inside don't accelerate fast enough that they are harmed in the process.

Example

Newton's third law of motion states that forces come in pairs of equal size and opposite direction. In which of the following scenarios does an object move as a result of Newton's third law?

a. A soccer player kicks a ball with a force of 25 Newtons.
b. Someone pushes a car, but it does not move.
c. A rocket launches from Earth.
d. An astronaut can jump higher on the Moon.

Choice A describes a soccer player kicking a ball. The action force in this case is the player's foot kicking the ball. According to Newton's third law, the soccer ball exerts an equal and opposite force on the player's foot. This does not cause the player to move, so Choice A can be eliminated.

Choice B describes pushing a car that does not move. The action force in this scenario is the push applied to the car, while a reaction force is applied to the person. Neither the car nor the person moves, so Choice B can be eliminated.

Choice C describes a rocket being launched from Earth. When a rocket is launched, large amounts of hot gas are shot out from the bottom of the rocket. When the gases push the air molecules behind them, there is an equal and opposite reaction force that pushes back on the rocket and causes it to move. Choice C could be the answer.

Choice D has to do with an astronaut jumping higher on the Moon due to the Moon's lower gravity. In this case, the Moon exerts a gravitational force on the astronaut, which pulls the astronaut toward the Moon. The reaction force exerted by the astronaut does not cause the Moon to move, so Choice D can be eliminated.

Choice C is the best answer because it is the only situation in which a reaction force causes something to move.

Directions of Motion

Motion can be either linear, rotational, or oscillating.

- **Linear motion** - a single direction, like a bowling ball rolling down the lane or a train moving in one direction down its tracks.
- **Rotational motion** – rotating or spinning in a circular motion, such as a top spinning, a merry-go-round, or the Earth rotating around the Sun.
- **Oscillating motion** – bouncing up and down repeatedly, such as a yo-yo on a string or a spring. This also includes waves as they rise and fall.

Mass and Strength of Force

An object with a large mass can be moved by strong forces, but may not be moved by a weak force. However, a weak force may move an object with little mass very easily. In general, a strong force will have a greater effect on an object than a weak force will.

Gravity

Gravity is a force that exists between all objects with matter. **Gravity** is a pulling force between objects, meaning that the forces on the objects point toward the opposite object. Gravity as we experience it is the force that the Earth exerts on objects, pulling them downward toward the center of the Earth. When Newton's third law is applied to gravity, the force pairs from gravity are shown to be equal in magnitude and opposite in direction.

Technically, all matter pulls other matter. The more massive the object, the more it pulls. The Earth is seen as our center of gravity because it is the most massive object nearby. Gravity is also reason that the Earth and other planets revolve around the Sun. The Sun is so massive that the Earth and all of the other bodies within the solar system are drawn to it and revolve around it as a result.

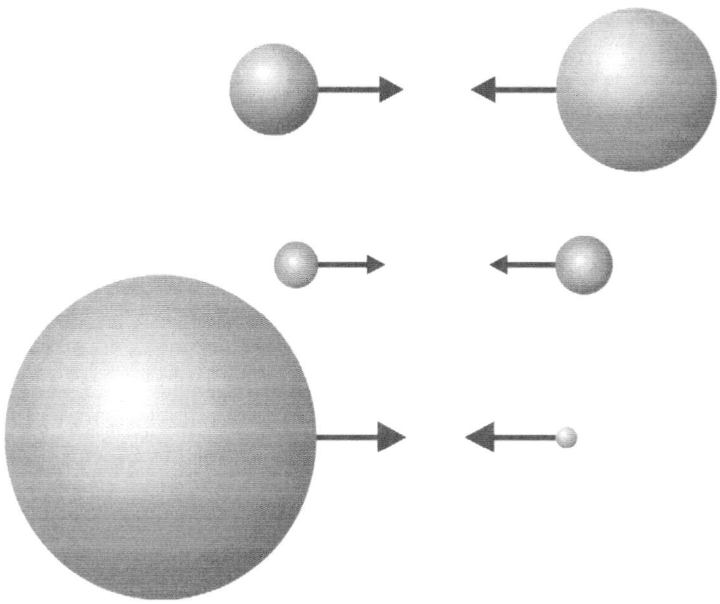

FRICTION

Friction is a resistance to motion between contacting surfaces. In order to illustrate the concept of friction, let us imagine a book resting on a table. As it sits, the force of its weight is equal to and opposite of the normal force. If, however, we were to exert a force on the book, attempting to push it to one side, a frictional force would arise, equal and opposite to our force. This kind of frictional force is known as static frictional force.

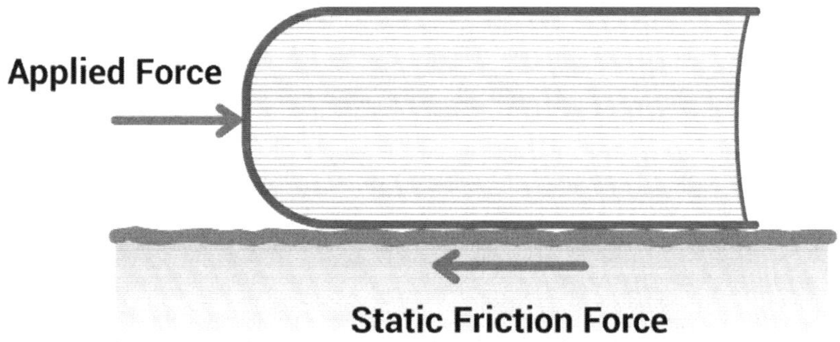

As we increase our force on the book, however, we will eventually cause it to accelerate in the direction of our force. At this point, the frictional force opposing us will be known as kinetic friction. For many combinations of surfaces, the magnitude of the kinetic frictional force is lower than that of the static frictional force, and consequently, the amount of force needed to maintain the movement of the book will be less than that needed to initiate the movement.

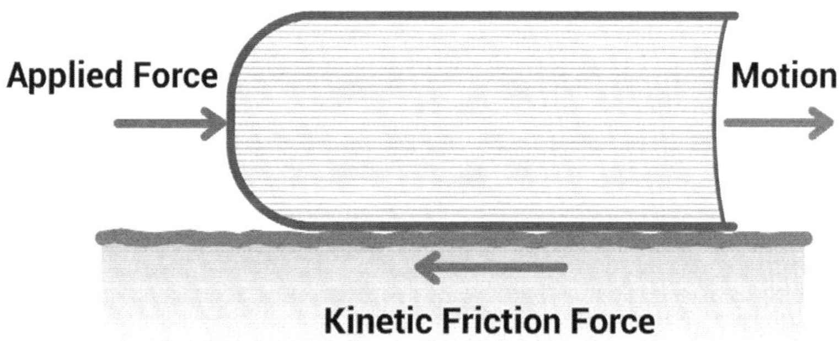

Review Video: Friction
Visit mometrix.com/academy and enter code: 716782

MAGNETISM

Magnetism is an **attraction** between opposite poles of **magnetic materials** and a **repulsion** between similar poles of magnetic materials. Magnetism can be natural or induced with the use of electric currents. Magnets almost always exist with two polar sides: north and south. A magnetic force exists between two poles on objects. Different poles attract each other. Like poles repel each other.

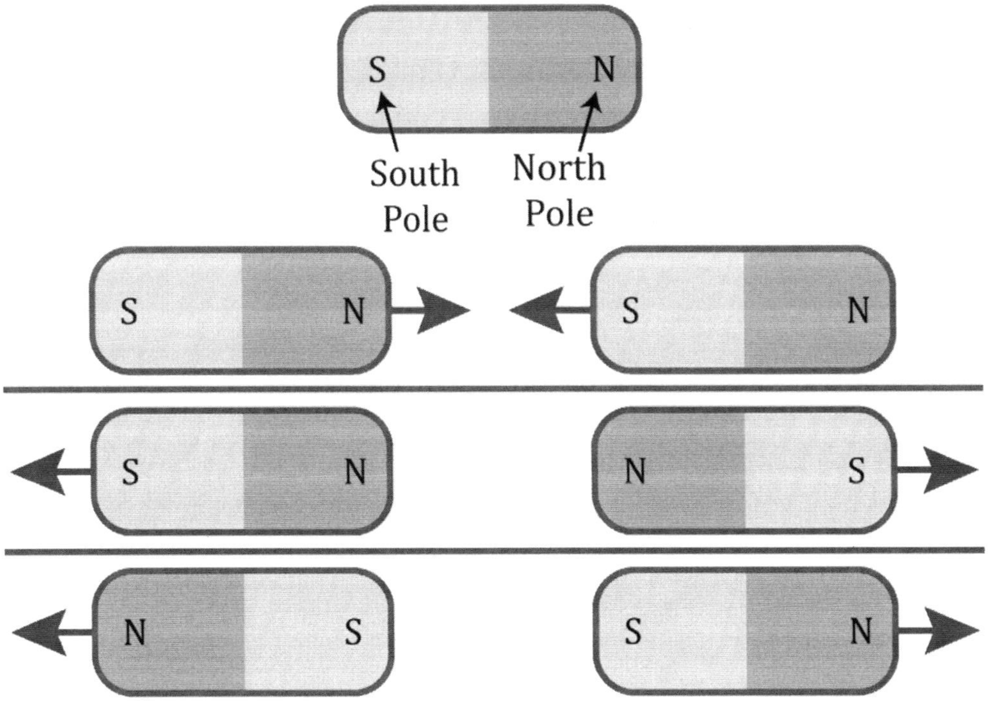

UNBALANCED FORCES AND SPEED AND VELOCITY

A **force** can cause an object to move and accelerate. **Newton's first law** of motion states that an object will not change its motion unless acted on by an unbalanced force. When forces of the same strength or magnitude are applied to the same object in opposite directions, they cancel out, resulting in a **balanced force**. When two people of the same size and strength pull on either end of a tug-of-war rope with the same force, this results in a balanced force, and neither the rope nor the people will move. An **unbalanced force** is one that is not fully canceled out by an opposing force. For example, if there are two people pulling on one end of the rope and only one person pulling on the other, the two people would most likely exert a stronger pulling force than the person pulling alone. In this example, the rope would move in the direction of the stronger force because the direction of motion is always the same as the direction of the unbalanced force.

EXAMPLE

A group of students in P.E. play tug-o-war. The group of students on the left side pulls with a force of 250 Newtons (N), while the group on the right pulls with a force of 200 Newtons. Which of the following accurately describes the size and direction of the net force?

a. 50 Newtons to the left
b. 50 Newtons to the right
c. 450 Newtons to the left
d. 450 Newtons to the right

Choice A: 50 Newtons to the left. The net force is the force left over when multiple forces are acting on an object and one force is bigger than the other. In this case, the group on the left side pulls the rope with more force (250 N) than the group on the right (200 N). To calculate net force, you can subtract the smaller force from the bigger force, resulting in a net force of 50 Newtons. The direction of the net force is the same as the direction of the bigger force. In this case, the direction of the net force is to the left. Thus, the net force is 50 Newtons to the left, making this answer correct.

Choice B: 50 Newtons to the right. This answer has the correct net force, 50 N, because the 200 N to the right cancels out part of the 250 N force to the left. However, the direction of the net force should be in the same direction as the larger force, which is to the left in this case. This answer is incorrect.

Choice C: 450 Newtons to the left. To calculate net force, it is important to keep in mind the direction of the forces at play. In this case, because the forces are in opposite directions, they partially cancel out and we can subtract one from the other. Forces are only added together if they are applied in the same direction, such as two people pushing an object together. This answer is incorrect.

Choice D: 450 Newtons to the right. This answer is incorrect because the size of the force should be 50, not 450. The direction is also incorrect because it should be in the direction of the larger force.

Choice A is the correct answer.

Speed and Velocity

Speed is a scalar quantity. That is, it has a **magnitude** but the **direction** does not matter. The formula for speed is the distance traveled within a certain amount of time. Velocity is a **vector quantity,** which means it has both magnitude and **direction**. For example, if you drive your car at a constant 70 kilometers per hour in any direction, you will be traveling at the **same speed**. Even if you drive around a curve and change your direction of travel, you are still traveling at the same speed as long as the car remains at 70 km/h. However, if you change your direction of travel, you have changed your velocity. **Velocity** is a specified speed in a specified direction. When you go around a corner in your car, even though you maintain the same speed, you have changed velocity because the direction has changed. Any change in velocity, such as a change in speed, direction, or both, constitutes acceleration and requires that a net unbalanced force act upon the moving system.

Acceleration

Acceleration is the **change in the velocity** of an object. Like velocity, acceleration may be computed as an average or an instantaneous quantity. To calculate average acceleration, we may use this simple equation: $a_{av} = \frac{v_f - v_i}{t_f - t_i}$, where the subscripts *i* and *f* denote the initial and final values of the velocity and time. The so-called instantaneous acceleration of an object can be found by reducing the time component to the limiting value until instantaneous velocity is approached. Acceleration will be expressed in units of distance divided by time squared; for instance, meters per second squared. Like position and velocity, acceleration is a vector quantity and will therefore have both magnitude and direction.

Examples of Newton's Laws in the Real World

- **Vehicle restraints** – seat belts and air bags all work to slow down the acceleration applied to the body in a car wreck. When a car hits another car, it slows down almost immediately, but the body and objects inside have inertia of their own, so they want to continue moving forward. Acceleration is directly related to force, so stopping immediately with the car would be harmful. Instead, the safety features help slow down the acceleration to keep the people inside safe.
- **Amusement park rides** – Rollercoasters apply Newton's laws in many ways. Rollercoasters tend to go very fast, but before you see them do so, they often climb a tall hill before falling very fast. In this way, they use gravity to their advantage to gain as much speed as possible before performing stunts like loop-the-loops and twists. Rollercoasters and other rides seem to defy gravity sometimes, making people feel like they are floating when they are only falling slower than the rollercoaster itself. If a rollercoaster goes down quickly, the body tries to stay in the air, causing this type of effect.
- **Earth's tectonic activities** – The theory of plate tectonics says that there are moving layers of the Earth's crust called plates. These plates are very slow moving, but enormous. When these plates bump into each other or slide past each other, they cause massive amounts of force because of Newton's laws. Every action produces an equal and opposite reaction. This is the cause of earthquakes, mountain volcano formation, and some forms of tidal waves.
- **Rocket launches** – When rockets are launched, many forces are at play. The rockets are huge, and they require a great amount of force to lift them into the air and into space. To do so, the rockets ignite fuel underneath and push downwards to cause lift upwards. These forces must be carefully calculated, however, so that the rocket does not veer off in the wrong direction and so that the humans and cargo inside don't accelerate fast enough that they are harmed in the process.

Properties of Light

Light is a type of **energy** that is on the **electromagnetic spectrum**. Light energy travels straight in one direction unless it touches another object that interferes with its path. Therefore, if a flashlight were turned on in space, the light could be seen on the other side of the galaxy, as long as it did not run into an object.

Light and Different Media

When talking about light, a **medium** is a substance through which light travels. There is no air in space, so there is no medium in space. This is why space is sometimes called a **vacuum**. On Earth, air and water are media through which light travels. Even though air is invisible, it slightly interferes with light. Air can cause light to **diffract**, or spread out. A flashlight does not shine in a perfectly straight line due to diffraction in air. Instead, it spreads out and gets weaker with distance from the light source.

Reflection

When light touches an object, it interacts with the object in one of three ways. On shiny objects, such as mirrors, metal, and glass, at least some of the light energy **reflects**, causing it to suddenly change directions. The light hits the object at one angle, then leaves the object at a different angle.

Refraction

When light moves through one medium and then moves through a different medium, the appearance of the light changes because the two media have different **densities**. The density of a medium will affect the properties of a light wave. Those properties control which direction the light travels. Water has a different density than air, so when a light wave enters water from the air, its angle changes. This is called **refraction**. Because human vision is dependent on light, refraction creates an optical illusion when objects are put in water. If you were to insert a pencil into a cup of water, it would appear to bend at the surface of the water. This is because the light waves that allow humans to see the pencil are being refracted.

Absorption

Not all objects reflect light well. When light touches an object that is not shiny, little energy is reflected. The energy is instead **absorbed**. When light is absorbed, the light energy is converted to **thermal energy**, causing the temperature of the object to increase.

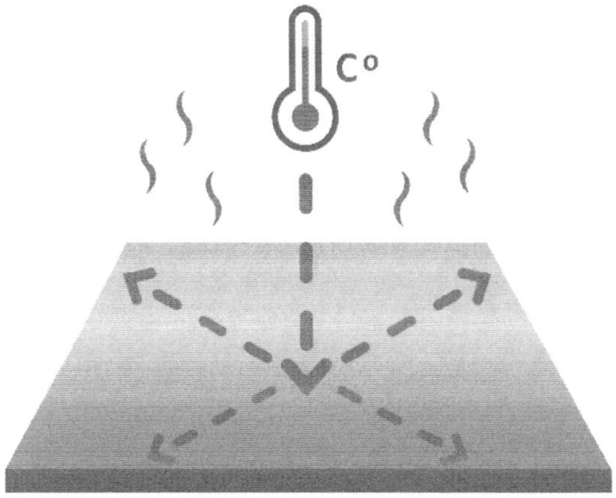

Example

In science class, a student aims a laser pointer at an angled mirror at the back of the classroom. The student observes that the laser beam is reflected at the same angle and notices a red dot on the wall beside her. Which of these statements describes the behavior of light in this scenario?

a. Light particles are carried by the air and disperse throughout a room.
b. The speed of light depends on the density of the surrounding air.
c. When light reaches an object, it moves in a curved line around the object.
d. Light travels in a straight line until it hits an object and changes direction.

Choice A states that light moves in particles that disperse similar to a gas. If this were the case, the light would not reflect off the mirror and would instead disperse in all directions from the laser. Choice A is incorrect.

Choice B states that the speed of light depends on the density of the surrounding air. The speed of light is constant and is not affected by the material it moves through, so this is incorrect.

Choice C proposes that light is able to curve around an object. If this were true, the laser would not reflect off the mirror and would instead curve around it. Choice C is incorrect.

Choice D states that light travels in a straight line, which matches the observation that the light traveled until it hit the mirror and then reflected from the mirror to the other side of the room. It also states that light changes direction when it hits an object like a mirror. Choice D could be the right answer.

Choice D is correct. Light always travels in a straight line until it hits an object where it can be absorbed, reflected, or go through the material.

Sound Waves

The **pitch of a sound** as it reaches one's ear is based on the frequency of the sound waves. A high-pitched sound has a higher frequency than a low-pitched sound. Like all waves, sound waves transmit energy. The rate at which this energy is transmitted is the sonic power. Loudness, or intensity of sound, is the sonic power received per unit area.

When a pair of sound waves with slightly different frequencies interfere with one another causing a periodic variation in sound intensity or a **beat**. The frequency of the variation, called the **beat frequency**, is equal to the difference between frequencies of the two sound waves. The phenomenon is used when tuning two instruments to one another. As the two pitches get closer, the beat frequency will become smaller and smaller until it disappears entirely, indicating that the instruments are in tune.

Review Video: Sound
Visit mometrix.com/academy and enter code: 562378

Types of Waves and their Characteristics

Transverse and Longitudinal Waves

Transverse waves have oscillations that are **perpendicular** to the direction of motion. A light wave is an example of a transverse wave. A group of light waves traveling in the same direction will be oscillating in several different planes. Light waves are said to be polarized when they are filtered such that only waves oscillating in a particular plane are allowed to pass, with the remainder being absorbed by the filter. If two such polarizing filters are employed successively and aligned to allow different planes of oscillation, they will block all light waves.

Longitudinal waves are waves that oscillate in the **same direction** as their primary motion. Their motion is restricted to a single axis, so they may not be polarized. A sound wave is an example of a longitudinal wave.

Velocity, Amplitude, Wavelength, and Frequency

The **velocity of a wave**, v, is the rate at which it travels in a given medium. It is defined in the same way that velocity of physical objects is defined, a change in position divided by a change in time. A single wave may have a different velocity for every medium in which it travels. Some types of waves, such as light waves, do not require a medium.

Amplitude, A, is one measure of a wave's strength. It is half the verticle distance between the highest and lowest points on the wave, the crest and trough, respectively. The vertical midpoint, halfway between the crest and trough, is sometimes called an equilibrium point, or a node.

The **wavelength**, λ, is the horizontal distance between successive crests or troughs, or the distance between the first and third of three successive nodes.

Frequency, f, is the number of crests or troughs that pass a particular point in a given period of time. It is the inverse of the period, the time required for the wave to cycle from one crest or trough to the next. Frequency is generally measured in hertz, or cycles per second.

Velocity, wavelength, and frequency are not independent quantities. They are related by the expression $v = \lambda f$. Note that amplitude, however, is independent from these quantities.

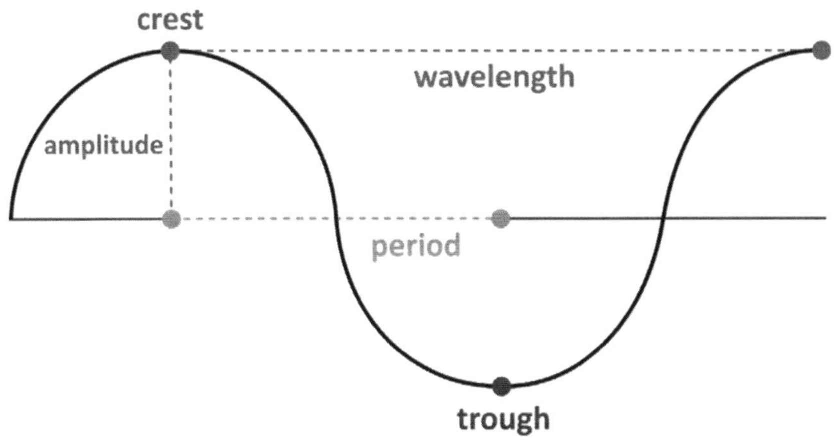

Electromagnetic Spectrum

Electromagnetic radiation is a form of energy that travels in waves. The **electromagnetic spectrum** is the range of all wavelengths and frequencies of known electromagnetic waves. Visible light occupies only a small portion of the electromagnetic spectrum. Some of the common classifications of electromagnetic waves are listed in the table below with their approximate frequency ranges.

Classification	Freq. (Hz)
Gamma Rays	$\sim 10^{19}$
X-Rays	$\sim 10^{17} - 10^{18}$
Ultraviolet	$\sim 10^{15} - 10^{16}$
Visible Light	$\sim 10^{14}$
Infra-red	$\sim 10^{11} - 10^{14}$
Microwaves	$\sim 10^{10} - 10^{11}$
Radio/TV	$\sim 10^{6} - 10^{9}$

Types of Electromagnetic Waves

- **Gamma rays** have the smallest wavelength, highest frequency, and highest energy of any type of electromagnetic radiation. Because of their small size, they can easily penetrate human skin, bones, and organs and alter DNA, making them more dangerous than other types of electromagnetic radiation. Gamma rays are produced by supernova explosions and anything traditionally known as "radioactive," such as uranium.
- **X-rays** have the second smallest wavelength, second highest frequency, and second highest amount of energy. They are used for medical imaging such as taking pictures to look at a broken bone, and they naturally occur when electrons move within an atom. X-rays can be dangerous in large amounts.
- **Ultraviolet radiation** is characterized by wavelengths larger than those of x-rays and gamma rays but smaller than those of visible light and all the other categories of electromagnetic radiation. This means that it has the third highest frequency and third highest amount of energy. Its frequency and energy can be categorized as moderate. Some species can see certain frequencies of ultraviolet light. Ultraviolet radiation most often comes from sunlight and can cause skin damage.

- **Visible light** possesses a range of moderate wavelengths, frequency, and energy levels. It falls right in the middle of the six other types of radiation. The visible light spectrum comprises approximately seven colors, with violet light having the shortest wavelength and highest frequency and red light having the longest wavelength and lowest frequency of the seven colors.
- **Infrared** waves have a larger wavelength and lower frequency than visible light and cannot be detected by human eyes. Infrared radiation is naturally produced by the Sun and by fire and causes objects it interacts with to heat up. Infrared radiation is used in thermal imaging and night vision technology.
- **Microwaves** have the second largest wavelength and the second lowest frequency and amount of energy. They are too large and lacking in energy to cause damage to human cells and have many uses, including microwave cooking.
- **Radio waves** have the largest wavelength on the spectrum along with the lowest frequency and energy. They are useful for transmitting information over large distances.

Review Video: Light
Visit mometrix.com/academy and enter code: 900556

Life Science

Organizational Hierarchy within Multicellular Organisms

Cell theory states that all organisms are made of cells, that cells are the basic unit of biological life, and that all cells arise from other cells. In **multicellular** organisms, cells combine to create different physiological structures with specific functions. There are four levels of organization in the human body: cells, tissues, organs, and organ systems. Different types of **cells** make up **tissues**. For example, muscle cells make up muscular tissue. Tissues make up **organs** with specific functions, such as the brain, heart, or liver. Organs work together as **organ systems**, such as the digestive system or the cardiovascular system. Organ systems are complex networks that achieve processes necessary to sustain life, such as breathing, moving, or eating.

Cells

Cells are the basic structural units of all living things. Cells are composed of various molecules including proteins, carbohydrates, lipids, and nucleic acids. All animal cells are eukaryotic and have a nucleus, cytoplasm, and a cell membrane. Organelles include mitochondria, ribosomes, endoplasmic reticulum, Golgi apparatuses, and vacuoles. Specialized cells are numerous, including but not limited to, various muscle cells, nerve cells, epithelial cells, bone cells, blood cells, and cartilage cells. Cells are grouped to together in tissues to perform specific functions.

Tissues

Tissues are groups of cells that work together to perform a specific function. Tissues can be grouped into four broad categories: muscle tissue, connective tissue, nerve tissue, and epithelial tissue. Muscle tissue is involved in body movement. **Muscle tissues** can be composed of skeletal muscle cells, cardiac muscle cells, or smooth muscle cells. Skeletal muscles include the muscles commonly called biceps, triceps, hamstrings, and quadriceps. Cardiac muscle tissue is found only in the heart. Smooth muscle tissue provides tension in the blood vessels, controls pupil dilation, and aids in peristalsis. **Connective tissues** include bone tissue, cartilage, tendons, ligaments, fat, blood, and lymph. **Nerve tissue** is located in the brain, spinal cord, and nerves. **Epithelial tissue** makes up the layers of the skin and various membranes. Tissues are grouped together as organs to perform specific functions.

Organs and Organ Systems

Organs are groups of tissues that work together to perform specific functions. **Organ systems** are groups of organs that work together to perform specific functions. Complex animals have several organs that are grouped together in multiple systems. In mammals, there are 11 major organ systems: integumentary system, respiratory system, circulatory system, endocrine system, nervous system, digestive system, excretory system, muscular system, skeletal system, reproductive system, and immune system.

1. **Integumentary system:** the protective barrier of the body, including skin, hair, and nails.
2. **Respiratory system:** responsible for allowing air to enter and exit the lungs to obtain oxygen and release carbon dioxide. The respiratory system consists of the nasal passages, pharynx, larynx, trachea, bronchial tubes, lungs, and diaphragm.
3. **Circulatory system:** includes the heart, blood, and blood vessels that carry blood through the body, delivering oxygen to tissues.

4. **Endocrine system:** manages and releases hormones responsible for bodily functions and behavior, including hunger, stress, sleep, and many others. The endocrine system consists of several ductless glands, which secrete hormones directly into the bloodstream.
5. **Nervous system:** includes your brain, spinal cord, sense organs, and nerves. The nervous system allows you to sense, process, and respond to external stimuli. It also helps regulate physiological and behavioral processes.
6. **Digestive system:** processes and extracts nutrients from food. The excretory system is responsible for removing waste following digestion. The digestive system includes the stomach, intestines, liver, gallbladder, pancreas, and anus.
7. **Excretory system:** metabolizes food, filters blood, and excretes waste. It includes the kidneys and bladder.
8. **Muscular system:** includes muscles that allow the body to move. The muscles work in combination with the skeletal system.
9. **Skeletal system:** includes the bones, joints, and cartilage that make up your skeleton.
10. **Reproductive system:** enables humans to produce offspring. It includes the external and internal reproductive organs.
11. **Immune System:** keeps a record of microbes to recognize and destroy the microbes that enter your body and make you feel sick. It includes white blood cells, antibodies, complement system, lymphatic system, spleen, bone marrow, and thymus.

Cells

PROKARYOTES AND EUKARYOTES

SIZES AND METABOLISM

Cells of the domains of Bacteria and Archaea are **prokaryotes**. Bacteria cells and Archaea cells are much smaller than cells of eukaryotes. Prokaryote cells are usually only 1 to 2 micrometers in diameter, but eukaryotic cells are usually at least 10 times and possibly 100 times larger than prokaryotic cells. Eukaryotic cells are usually 10 to 100 micrometers in diameter. Most prokaryotes are unicellular organisms, although some prokaryotes live in colonies. Because of their large surface-area-to-volume ratios, prokaryotes have a very high metabolic rate. **Eukaryotic cells** are much larger than prokaryotic cells. Due to their larger sizes, they have a much smaller surface-area-to-volume ratio and consequently have much lower metabolic rates.

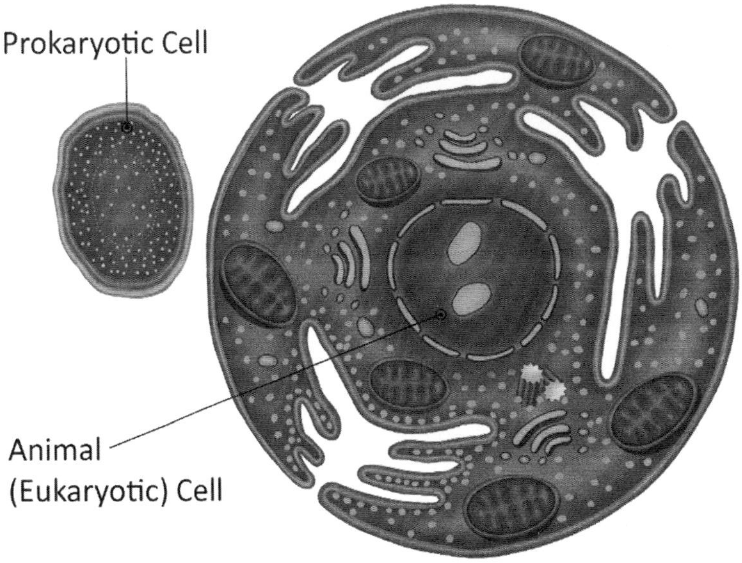

Review Video: Eukaryotic and Prokaryotic Cells
Visit mometrix.com/academy and enter code: 231438

Review Video: Cell Structure
Visit mometrix.com/academy and enter code: 591293

MEMBRANE-BOUND ORGANELLES

Prokaryotic cells are much simpler than eukaryotic cells. Prokaryote cells do not have a nucleus due to their small size and their DNA is located in the center of the cell in a region referred to as a **nucleoid**. Eukaryote cells have a **nucleus** bound by a double membrane. Eukaryotic cells typically have hundreds or thousands of additional **membrane-bound organelles** that are independent of the cell membrane. Prokaryotic cells do not have any membrane-bound organelles that are independent of the cell membrane. Once again, this is probably due to the much larger size of the eukaryotic cells. The organelles of eukaryotes give them much higher levels of intracellular division than is possible in prokaryotic cells.

Chromosome Structure

Prokaryote cells have DNA arranged in a **circular structure** that should not be referred to as a chromosome. Due to the small size of a prokaryote cell, the DNA material is simply located near the center of the cell in a region called the nucleoid. A prokaryotic cell may also contain tiny rings of DNA called plasmids. Prokaryote cells lack histone proteins, and therefore the DNA is not actually packaged into chromosomes. Prokaryotes reproduce by binary fission, while eukaryotes reproduce by mitosis with the help of **linear chromosomes** and histone proteins. During mitosis, the chromatin is tightly wound on the histone proteins and packaged as a chromosome. The DNA in a eukaryotic cell is located in the membrane-bound nucleus.

Cell Walls

Not all cells have cell walls, but most prokaryotes have cell walls. The cell walls of organisms from the domain Bacteria differ from the cell walls of the organisms from the domain Archaea. Some eukaryotes, such as some fungi, some algae, and plants, have cell walls that differ from the cell walls of the Bacteria and Archaea domains. The main difference between the cell walls of different domains or kingdoms is the composition of the cell walls. For example, most bacteria have cell walls outside of the plasma membrane that contains the molecule peptidoglycan. **Peptidoglycan** is a large polymer of amino acids and sugars. The peptidoglycan helps maintain the strength of the cell wall. Some of the Archaea cells have cell walls containing the molecule pseudopeptidoglycan, which differs in chemical structure from the peptidoglycan but basically provides the same strength to the cell wall. Some fungi cell walls contain **chitin**. The cell walls of diatoms, a type of yellow algae, contain silica. Plant cell walls contain cellulose, and woody plants are further strengthened by lignin. Some algae also contain lignin. Animal cells do not have cell walls.

Cells and Organelles of Plant Cells and Animal Cells

Plant cells and animal cells both have a nucleus, cytoplasm, cell membrane, ribosomes, mitochondria, endoplasmic reticulum, Golgi apparatus, and vacuoles. Plant cells have only one or two extremely large vacuoles. Animal cells typically have several small vacuoles. Plant cells have chloroplasts for photosynthesis and use this process to produce their own food, distinguishing plants as **autotrophs**. Animal cells do not have chloroplasts and therefore cannot use photosynthesis to produce their own food. Instead animal cells rely on other sources for food, which classifies them as **heterotrophs**. Animal cells have centrioles, which are used to help organize microtubules and in in cell division, but only some plant cells have centrioles. Additionally, plant cells have a rectangular and more rigid shape due to the cell wall, while animal cells have more of a circular shape because they lack a cell wall.

Review Video: Difference Between Plant and Animal Cells
Visit mometrix.com/academy and enter code: 115568

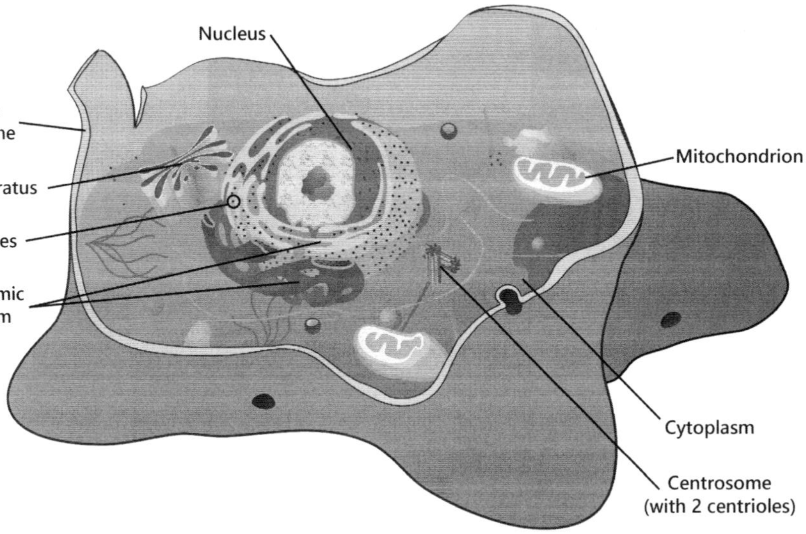

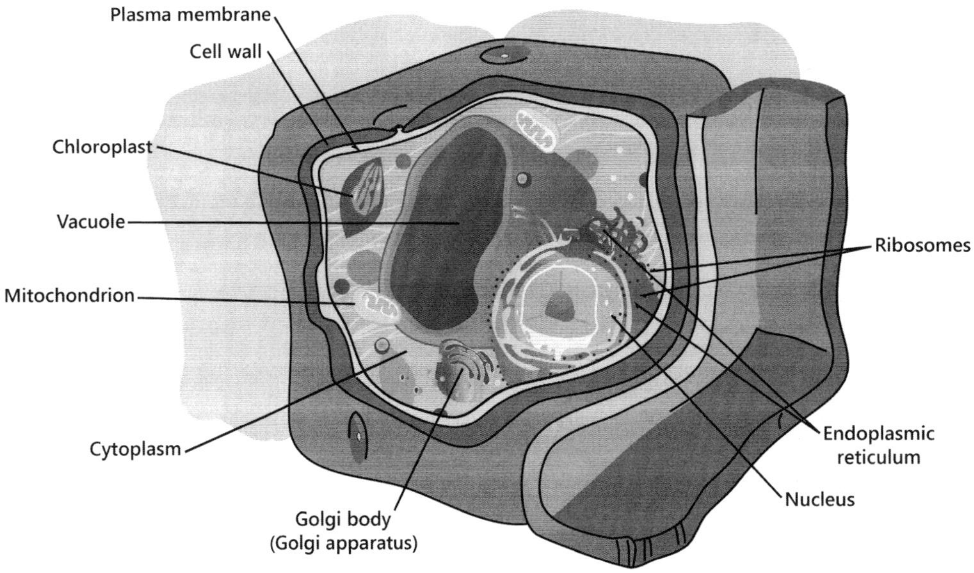

Cell Membranes

The **cell membrane**, also referred to as the plasma membrane, is a thin semipermeablė membrane of lipids and proteins. The cell membrane isolates the cell from its external environment while still enabling the cell to communicate with that outside environment. It consists of a phospholipid bilayer, or double layer, with the hydrophilic ("water-loving") ends of the outer layer facing the external environment, the inner layer facing the inside of the cell, and the hydrophobic ("water-fearing") ends facing each other. Cholesterol in the cell membrane adds stiffness and flexibility. Glycolipids help the cell to recognize other cells of the organisms. The proteins in the cell membrane help give the cells shape. Special proteins help the cell communicate with its external environment, while other proteins transport molecules across the cell membrane.

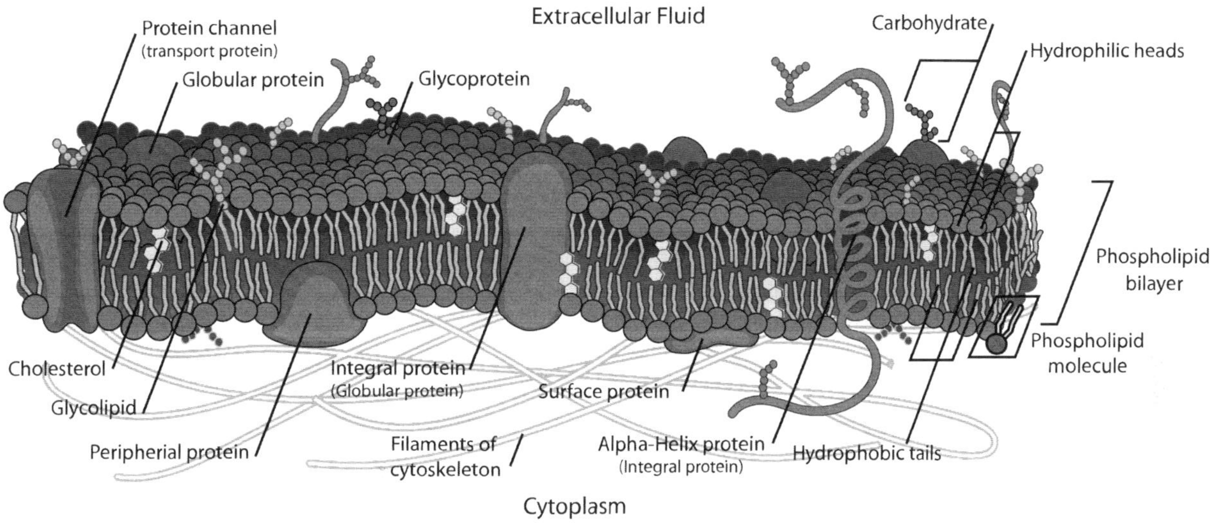

Review Video: Function of the Plasma Membrane
Visit mometrix.com/academy and enter code: 943095

Nucleus

Typically, a eukaryote has only one nucleus that takes up approximately 10% of the volume of the cell. Components of the nucleus include the nuclear envelope, nucleoplasm, chromatin, and nucleolus. The **nuclear envelope** is a double-layered membrane with the outer layer connected to the endoplasmic reticulum. The nucleus can communicate with the rest of the cell through several nuclear pores. The chromatin consists of deoxyribonucleic acid (DNA) and histones that are packaged into chromosomes during mitosis. The **nucleolus**, which is the dense central portion of the nucleus, produced and assembles ribosomes with the help of ribosomal RNA and proteins.

Functions of the nucleus include the storage of genetic material, production of ribosomes, and transcription of ribonucleic acid (RNA).

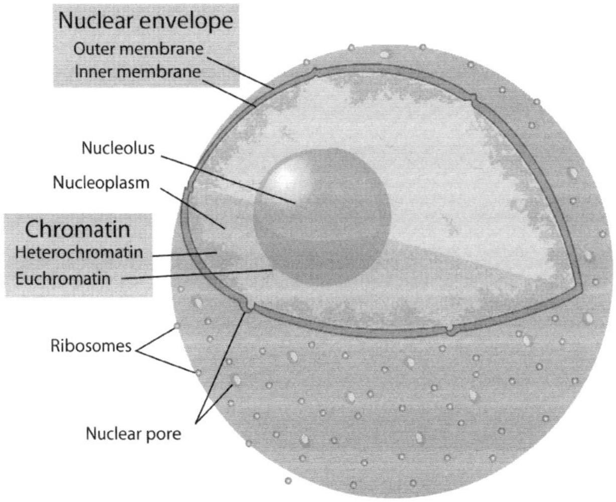

CHLOROPLASTS

Chloroplasts are large organelles that are enclosed in a double membrane. Just as cells contain a fluid called cytoplasm, chloroplasts contain a fluid called the **stroma**. Within the stroma, there are discs called **thylakoids**, which are arranged in stacks called grana (singular: granum). The thylakoids have chlorophyll molecules on their surfaces. **Stromal lamellae** separate the thylakoid stacks. Chloroplasts perform photosynthesis and make food (in the form of sugars) for the plant. The light reaction stage of photosynthesis occurs in the grana, and the dark reaction stage of photosynthesis occurs in the stroma. Sugars are formed in the stroma. Chloroplasts have their own DNA and can reproduce by fission independently.

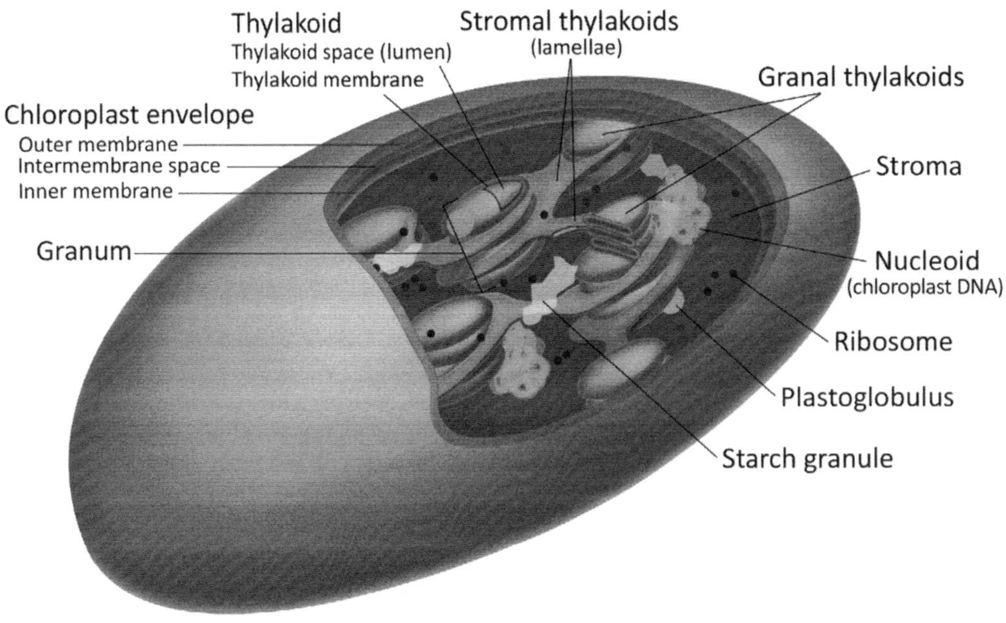

MITOCHONDRIA

Mitochondria break down sugar molecules and produce energy in the form of molecules of adenosine triphosphate (ATP). Both plant and animal cells contain mitochondria. Mitochondria are enclosed in a bilayer semi-membrane of phospholipids and proteins. The intermembrane space is the space between the two layers. The **outer membrane** has proteins called porins, which allow small molecules through. The **inner membrane** contains proteins that aid in the synthesis of ATP. The matrix consists of enzymes that help synthesize ATP. Mitochondria have their own DNA and can reproduce by fission independently. Mitochondria also help to maintain calcium concentrations, form blood components and hormones, and are involved in activating cell death pathways.

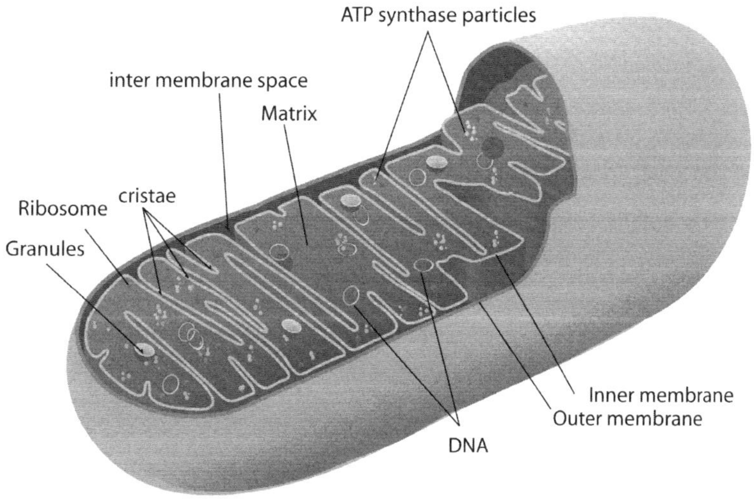

Review Video: Mitochondria
Visit mometrix.com/academy and enter code: 444287

Ribosomes

A **ribosome** consists of RNA and proteins. The RNA component of the ribosome is known as ribosomal RNA (rRNA). Ribosomes consist of two subunits, a large subunit and a small subunit. Few ribosomes are free in the cell. Most of the ribosomes in the cell are embedded in the rough endoplasmic reticulum located near the nucleus. Ribosomes are protein factories and translate the code of DNA into proteins by assembling long chains of amino acids. **Messenger RNA** (mRNA) is used by the ribosome to generate a specific protein sequence, while **transfer RNA** (tRNA) collects the needed amino acids and delivers them to the ribosome.

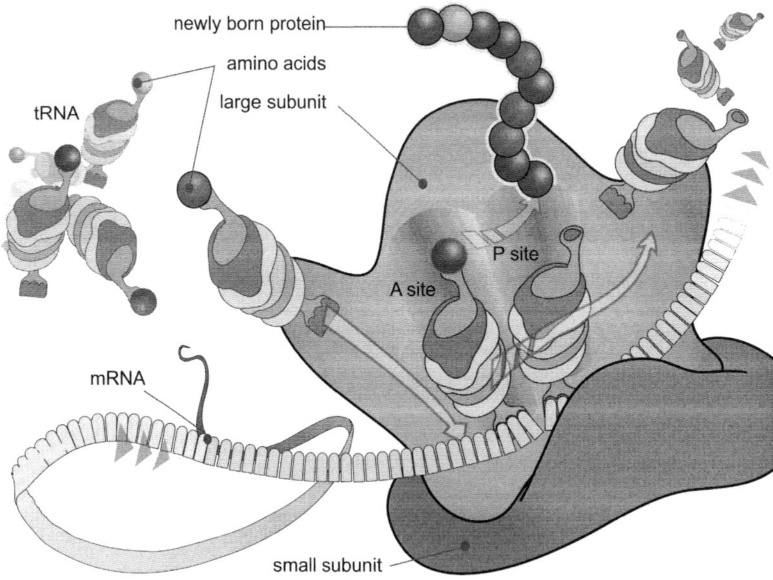

GOLGI APPARATUS

The **Golgi apparatus**, also called the Golgi body or Golgi complex, is a stack of flattened membranes called **cisternae** that package, ship, and distribute macromolecules such as carbohydrates, proteins, and lipids in shipping containers called **vesicles**. It also helps modify proteins and lipids before they are shipped. Most Golgi apparatuses have six to eight cisternae. Each Golgi apparatus has four regions: the cis region, the endo region, the medial region, and the trans region. Transfer vesicles from the rough endoplasmic reticulum (ER) enter at the cis region, and secretory vesicles leave the Golgi apparatus from the trans region.

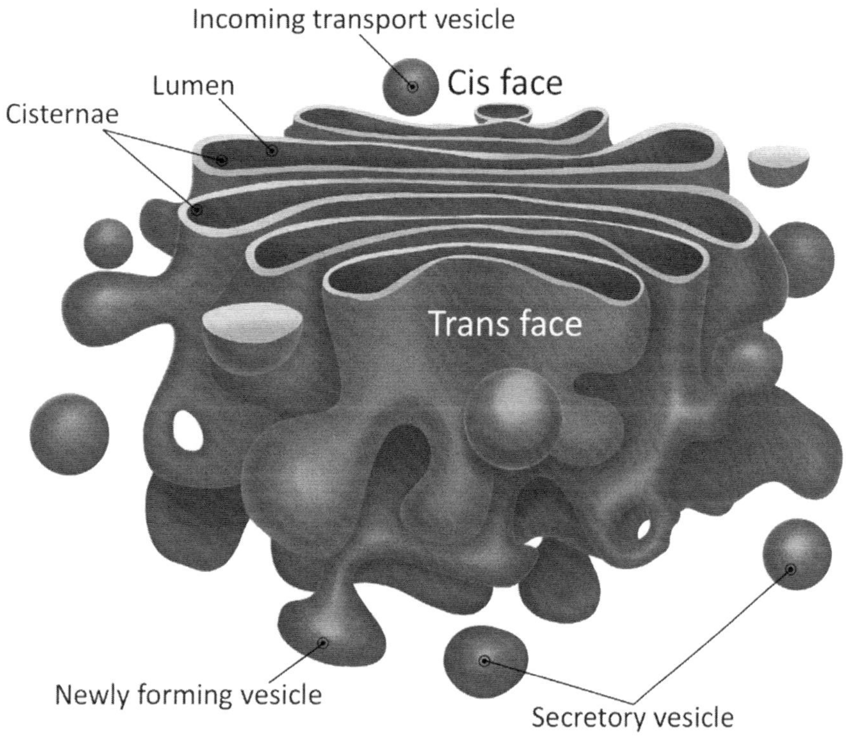

Cytoskeleton

The **cytoskeleton** is a scaffolding system located in the cytoplasm. The cytoskeleton consists of elongated organelles made of proteins called microtubules, microfilaments, and intermediate filaments. These organelles provide shape, support, and the ability to move. These structures also assist in moving the chromosomes during mitosis. Microtubules and microfilaments help transport materials throughout the cell and are the major components in cilia and flagella.

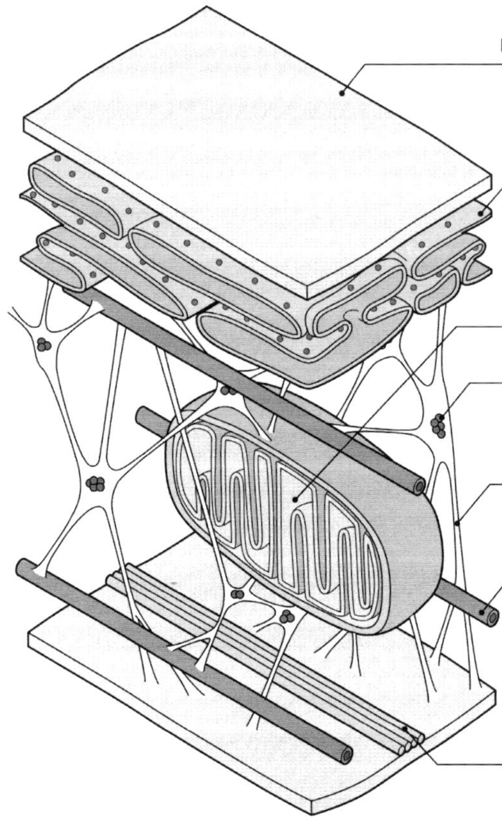

Plastids

Plastids are major organelles found in plants and algae that are used to synthesize and store food. Because plastids can differentiate, there are many forms of plastids. Specialized plastids can store pigments, starches, fats, or proteins. Two examples of plastids are amyloplasts and chloroplasts. **Amyloplasts** are the plastids that store the starch formed from long chains of glucose produced during photosynthesis. Amyloplasts synthesize and store the starch granules through the polymerization of glucose. When needed, amyloplasts also convert these starch granules back into sugar. Fruits and potato tubers have large numbers of amyloplasts. **Chloroplasts** can synthesize and store starch. Interestingly, amyloplasts can redifferentiate and transform into chloroplasts.

Infectious Agents

Viruses

Viruses are nonliving, infectious particles that act as parasites in living organisms. Viruses are acellular, which means that they lack cell structure. Viruses cannot reproduce outside of living cells. The structure of a virus is a nucleic acid genome, which may be either DNA or RNA, surrounded by a protective protein coat or **capsid**. In some viruses, the capsid may be surrounded by a lipid membrane or envelope. Viruses can contain up to 500 genes and have various shapes. They usually are too small to be seen without the aid of an electron microscope. Viruses can infect plants, animals, fungi, protists, and bacteria. Viruses can attack only specific types of cells that have specific receptors on their surfaces. Viruses do not divide or reproduce like living cells. Instead, they use the host cell they infect by "reprogramming" it, using the nucleic acid genome, to make more copies of the virus. The host cell usually bursts to release these copies.

Review Video: Viruses and Antiviral Drugs
Visit mometrix.com/academy and enter code: 984455

Bacteria

Bacteria are small, prokaryotic, single-celled organisms. Bacteria have a circular loop of DNA (plasmid) that is not contained within a nuclear membrane. Bacterial ribosomes are not bound to the endoplasmic reticulum, as in eukaryotes. A cell wall containing peptidoglycan surrounds the bacterial plasma membrane. Some bacteria such as pathogens are further encased in a gel-like, sticky layer called the **capsule**, which enhances their ability to cause disease. Bacteria can be autotrophs or heterotrophs. Some bacterial heterotrophs are saprophytes that function as decomposers in ecosystems. Many types of bacteria share commensal or mutualistic relationships with other organisms. Most bacteria reproduce asexually by binary fission. Two identical daughter cells are produced from one parent cell. Some bacteria can transfer genetic material to other bacteria through a process called conjugation, while some bacteria can incorporate DNA from the environment in a process called transformation.

Protists

Protists are small, eukaryotic, single-celled organisms. Although protists are small, they are much larger than prokaryotic bacteria. Protists have three general forms, which include plantlike protists, animal-like protists, and fungus-like protists. **Plantlike protists** are algae that contain chlorophyll and perform photosynthesis. Animal-like protists are **protozoa** with no cell walls that typically lack chlorophyll and are grouped by their method of locomotion, which may use flagella, cilia, or a different structure. **Fungus-like protists**, which do not have chitin in their cell walls, are generally grouped as either slime molds or water molds. Protists may be autotrophic or heterotrophic. Autotrophic protists include many species of algae, while heterotrophic protists include parasitic, commensal, and mutualistic protozoa. Slime molds are heterotrophic fungus-like protists, which consume microorganisms. Some protists reproduce sexually, but most reproduce asexually by binary fission. Some reproduce asexually by spores while others reproduce by alternation of generations and require two hosts in their life cycle.

Fungi

Fungi are nonmotile organisms with eukaryotic cells and contain chitin in their cell walls. Most fungi are multicellular, but a few including yeast are unicellular. Fungi have multicellular filaments called **hyphae** that are grouped together into the mycelium. Fungi do not perform photosynthesis and are considered heterotrophs. Fungi can be parasitic, mutualistic or free living. Free-living fungi include mushrooms and toadstools. Parasitic fungi include fungi responsible for ringworm and athlete's foot. Mycorrhizae are mutualistic fungi that live in or near plant roots increasing the roots' surface area of absorption. Almost all fungi reproduce asexually by spores, but most fungi also have a sexual phase in the production of spores. Some fungi reproduce by budding or fragmentation.

Parasites

Parasites are organisms that live on or inside another organism called a *host*. The parasite drains energy from the host and may release substances that harm it. Many parasites cause the host to get sick and eventually may even kill it. However, with parasites the host is not killed outright as with predation. Certain kinds of worms, mosquitoes, and ticks are examples of parasites.

Populations of Animals or Plants

A population consists of all of the organisms of a certain kind in a defined area, region, or habitat. It may be all the red foxes in a given national park, all the loblolly pines in Virginia (very hard to count), all the bullfrogs in a certain pond, or even all of the boxelder bugs on a single box elder tree. In the case of rare or endangered species it may be all of the individuals still living in the wild.

Several factors operate to keep animal and plant populations under control. Predation, grazing, disease, competition for limiting resources such as food or nutrients, water, habitat and living space, hunting and breeding territory, and sunlight for plants all play important roles. Even the size of the population can influence factors such as birth rate and severity of disease outbreaks or force individuals to migrate to other less crowded areas.

Abiotic and Biotic Factors

An ecosystem is a connected community of organisms that interact with one another as well as with their physical environment. Nonliving aspects of an organism's physical environment are called **abiotic factors**. Abiotic factors include things like water, air, soil, minerals, and sunlight. Animals drink water from sources such as streams and breathe in oxygen (O_2) from fresh air. Plants use their roots to obtain water and minerals from the soil. In addition, plants require sunlight and carbon dioxide (CO_2) from the air in order to carry out photosynthesis to live and grow. The living aspects of the ecosystem are called **biotic factors**. They include other organisms in that community, such as plants, animals, bacteria, fungi and protists.

Sources of Energy in Organisms

Energy flows in one direction: from the **sun**, through photosynthetic organisms such as green plants (producers) and algae (autotrophs), and then to herbivores, carnivores, and decomposers. **Autotrophs** are organisms capable of producing their own food. The organic molecules they produce are food for all other organisms (heterotrophs). **Producers** are green plants that manufacture food by photosynthesis. **Herbivores** are animals that eat only plants (deer, rabbits, etc.). Since they are the first animals to receive the energy captured by producers, herbivores are called primary consumers. **Carnivores**, or secondary consumers, are animals that eat the bodies of other animals for food. **Predators** (wolves, lions, etc.) kill other animals (prey), while scavengers consume animals that are already dead from predation or natural causes (buzzards). **Omnivores** are animals that eat both plants and other animals (humans). **Decomposers** include saprophytic fungi and bacteria that break down the complex structures of the bodies of living things into simpler forms that can be used by other living things. This recycling process releases energy from organic molecules.

Producers, Consumers, and Decomposers

Producers are organisms that can make their own food. Most producers are plants. Through photosynthesis plants make sugars that provide energy. Plants only need sunlight, water, and the proper minerals and other nutrients to live, grow, and reproduce themselves. **Consumers** are organisms that eat other organisms. Consumers are animals that eat plants or other animals that eat plants. **Decomposers** are organisms that feed on decaying plant and animal matter. Since decomposers cannot make their own food they are classified as consumers. Fungi such as mushrooms are *decomposers* that break down the tissues and wood of living or dead plants or the bodies of dead animals.

Mushrooms

Mushrooms are **fungi**, and most are **decomposers**, which is a special type of consumer. Fungi have no chlorophyll and cannot engage in photosynthesis. Therefore, they cannot produce their own food and must get it from other organisms. Mushrooms are the fruiting bodies of fungi which live in the ground or grow the roots or trunks of living or dead trees. Mushrooms produce spores, which like the seeds of plants produce new fungal colonies. Some fungi are parasites on plants or animals or even other fungi.

Herbivores, Carnivores, and Omnivores

Herbivores are animals that only eat plants. Examples are rabbits, deer, antelope, rhinoceroses and elephants. *Carnivores* are animals that only eat other animals, like lions, wolves, foxes, most bats, hawks and owls, insect-eating birds, snakes, and sharks. *Omnivores* are animals that eat both plants and other animals. Examples include bears, pigs, skunks, raccoons, birds like crows and ravens, and human beings.

Scavengers

Vultures are mostly *scavengers* that eat *carrion*— the dead and decaying flesh of animals. When an animal dies it immediately begins to decay or rot. Bacteria break down the dead tissues and release a foul smell that attracts scavengers like vultures, hyenas, crabs and lobsters, and certain flies that feed on decaying flesh. Many carnivores like coyotes, hyenas, opossums, hawks and eagles will also eat carrion in addition to catching live prey.

ENERGY PYRAMID

Energy flow through an ecosystem can be tracked through an energy pyramid. An **energy pyramid** shows how energy is transferred from one trophic level to another. **Producers** always form the base of an energy pyramid, and the consumers form successive levels above the producers. Producers only store about 1% of the solar energy they receive. Then, each successive level only uses about 10% of the energy of the previous level. That means that **primary consumers** use about 10% of the energy used by primary producers, such as grasses and trees. Next, **secondary consumers** use 10% of primary consumers' 10%, or 1% overall. This continues up for as many trophic levels as exist in a particular ecosystem.

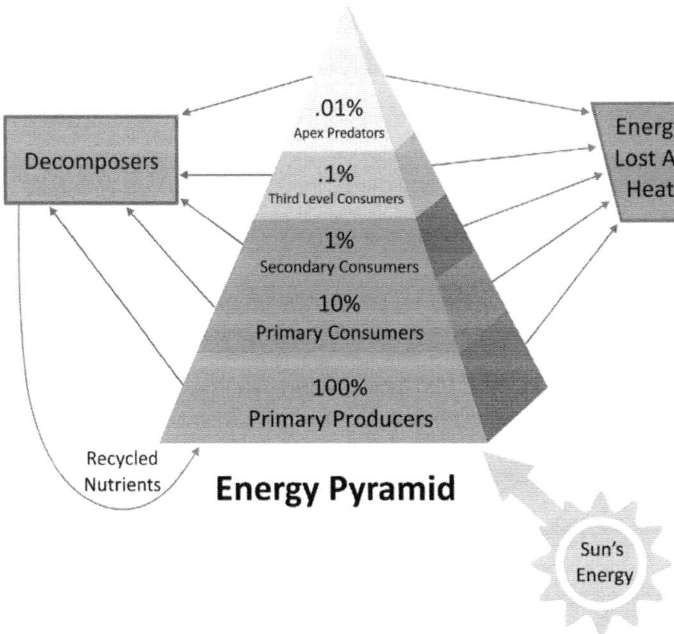

Food Web

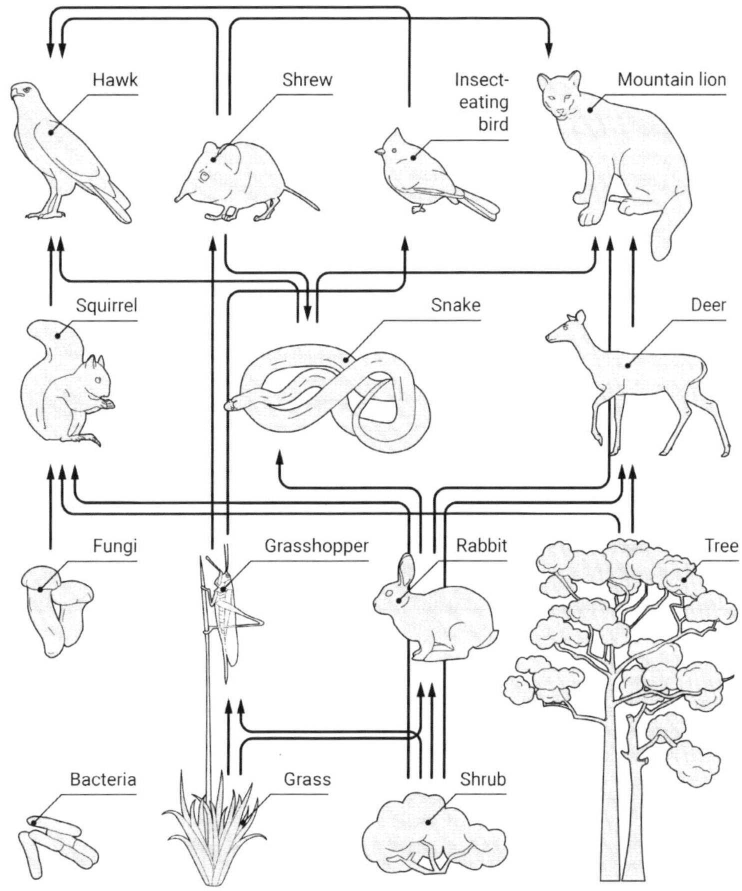

Energy flow through an ecosystem can be illustrated by a **food web**. Energy moves through the food web in the direction of the arrows. In the food web, **producers** such as grass, trees, and shrubs use energy from the Sun to produce food through photosynthesis. **Herbivores** or **primary consumers** such as squirrels, grasshoppers, and rabbits obtain energy by eating the producers. **Secondary consumers**, which are carnivores such as snakes and shrews, obtain energy by eating the primary consumers. **Tertiary consumers**, which are carnivores such as hawks and mountain lions, obtain energy by eating the secondary consumers.

Review Video: Food Webs
Visit mometrix.com/academy and enter code: 853254

Interdependence of the Food Web

Because each level of consumer is dependent on the previous level for food, the population of each level affects the other animal groups. For instance, if an ecosystem is made up of only grass, deer, and wolves, the grass are the producers, the deer eat the grass, and the wolves eat the deer. If deer are overhunted one year, the grass is given room to grow more because less of it is consumed, but the wolves will not have enough food, so the population will reduce size. Eventually, because of the abundance of grass and a reduced population of wolves, the deer may then have a surge of population. This example is an over-simplistic example, as there are usually many more producers, consumers, and predators within an ecosystem.

Food Web in a Pond

Sunlight allows green algae to photosynthesize and grow. The algae are fed upon by small animals like water fleas and copepods. In turn, these are eaten by small worms, mosquito larvae and other larval insects. These are then eaten by mosquito fish, which in turn are eaten by larger fishes like bluegills. The bluegills are preyed upon by even larger fishes like bass and by herons, egrets and raccoons (which also eat the bass). Then the animal waste and everything that dies and settles to the bottom is decomposed by bacteria and fungi.

Food Web in a Meadow

Sunlight allows grass and other plants to grow. These plants are eaten by a variety of *herbivores* like insects, rodents, and rabbits. Their seeds are consumed by various birds such as sparrows and quail. The insects are eaten by *carnivores*, including other kinds of birds, shrews, and bats. The rodents, rabbits, and some of the birds are then eaten by larger carnivores like weasels and foxes. Also, the quail, mice, rabbits and shrews are eaten by owls at night and by hawks during the day.

Relationships Between Organisms

Organisms can interact with one another in many ways. For example, **herbivores** eat plants, and **predators**, or **carnivores**, eat other animals. Organisms can also **compete** for biotic or abiotic resources in an ecosystem. In addition, organisms can rely on each other through **mutualism**, **commensalism**, and **parasitism**.

Symbiosis

Many species share a special nutritional relationship with another species, called **symbiosis**. The term symbiosis means "living together." In symbiosis, two organisms share a close physical relationship that can be helpful, harmful, or neutral for each organism. Three forms of symbiotic relationships are parasitism, commensalism, and mutualism. **Parasitism** is a relationship between two organisms in which one organism is the parasite, and the other organism is the host. The parasite benefits from the relationship because the parasite obtains its nutrition from the host. The host is harmed from the relationship because the parasite is using the host's energy and giving nothing in return. For example, a tick and a dog share a parasitic relationship in which the tick is the parasite, and the dog is the host. **Commensalism** is a relationship between two organisms in which one benefits, and the other is not affected. For example, a small fish called a remora can attach to the belly of a shark and ride along. The remora is safe under the shark, and the shark is not affected. **Mutualism** is a relationship between two organisms in which both organisms benefit. For example, a rhinoceros usually can be seen with a few tick birds perched on its back. The tick birds are helped by the easy food source of ticks, and the rhino benefits from the tick removal.

Review Video: Mutualism, Commensalism, and Parasitism
Visit mometrix.com/academy and enter code: 757249

Competition Between Different Organisms

Animals and plants have to compete with other species for food or nutrients, water, a place to live, nesting or breeding sites, sunlight in the case of plants, and other factors in the environment that may be scarce or limiting. Also, animals and plants of the same species have to compete with each other for the same things, as well in some cases for the right to breed and reproduce.

Plant Species Competing with Each Other

Creosote bush is the most widespread shrub in the deserts of the American Southwest where water can be very scarce for long periods. The roots of mature creosote bushes are extremely efficient and absorb all the water in the sandy soil around them. This creates very dry zones around each plant. The seeds of other plants cannot survive long enough to germinate. Therefore, the plants tend to be spaced far apart from each other.

Animals of the Same Species Competing with Each Other

Male elk known as bulls have large antlers, which they shed and regrow each year. Like their smaller deer cousins, bull elk engage in bugling contests and ritual combat (like the photo below) to dominate other males and win all the female (cow) elk in a harem.

Different species of animals often compete for food. The spotted hyena and the African lion shown here compete for prey like zebras and wildebeest. Both hyenas and lions run in groups. A larger pack of hyenas can drive a smaller pride of lions away from prey the lions have killed. However, one lion can easily kill one or more hyenas. They rarely tolerate each other as they seem to be doing below.

Historical and Current Kingdom Systems

In 1735 Carolus Linnaeus devised a two-kingdom classification system. He placed all living things into either the *Animalia* kingdom or the *Plantae* kingdom. Fungi and algae were classified as plants. Also, Linnaeus developed the binomial nomenclature system that is still used today. In 1866, Ernst Haeckel introduced a three-kingdom classification system, adding the *Protista* kingdom to Linnaeus's animal and plant kingdoms. Bacteria were classified as protists and cyanobacteria were still classified as plants. In 1938, Herbert Copeland introduced a four-kingdom classification system in which bacteria and cyanobacteria were moved to the *Monera* kingdom. In 1969, Robert Whittaker introduced a five-kingdom system that moved fungi from the plant kingdom to the *Fungi* kingdom. Some algae were still classified as plants. In 1977, Carl Woese introduced a six-kingdom system in which in the *Monera* kingdom was replaced with the *Eubacteria* kingdom and the *Archaebacteria* kingdom.

Domain Classification System

In 1990, Carl Woese introduced his domain classification system. **Domains** are broader groupings above the kingdom level. This system consists of three domains- *Archaea*, *Bacteria*, and *Eukarya*. All eukaryotes such as plants, animals, fungi, and protists are classified in the *Eukarya* domain. The *Bacteria* and *Archaea* domains consist of prokaryotes. Organisms previously classified in the *Monera* kingdom are now classified into either the *Bacteria* or *Archaea* domain based on their ribosomal RNA structure. Members of the *Archaea* domain often live in extremely harsh environments.

Review Video: Biological Classification Systems
Visit mometrix.com/academy and enter code: 736052

Taxonomies

A **taxonomy** is a classification system that helps sort out different groups of something. A strong example of a taxonomy is the classification system for animals. The animal kingdom is often depicted as a pyramid showing different levels of the taxonomy. The lower down the pyramid, the more specific the definition. For instance, an animal's Class identifies whether it is a fish, reptile, amphibian, bird, or mammal.

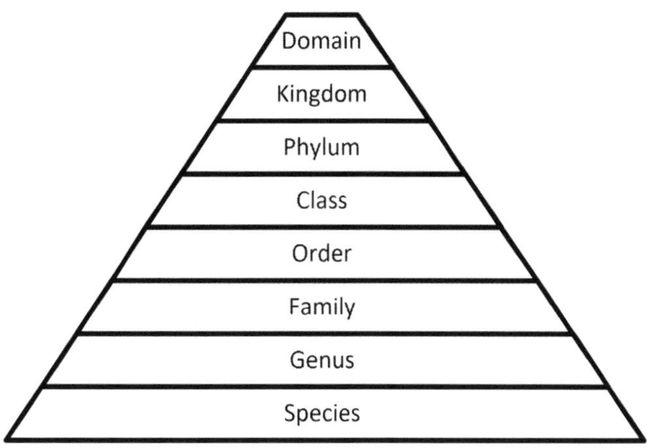

Dichotomous Keys

Dichotomous keys are an important tool for identifying and distinguishing different types of organisms or objects in a taxonomy. For instance, to identify an animal's class, we ask a series of questions that help sort out what category it belongs in. We might ask what type of animal a frog is. If you follow the dichotomous key example below, you will find that frogs do not have fur or hair, so they are not mammals. They do not have feathers, so they are not birds. Frogs have moist skin, so they are not reptiles, and they do not have scales, so they are amphibians and not fish.

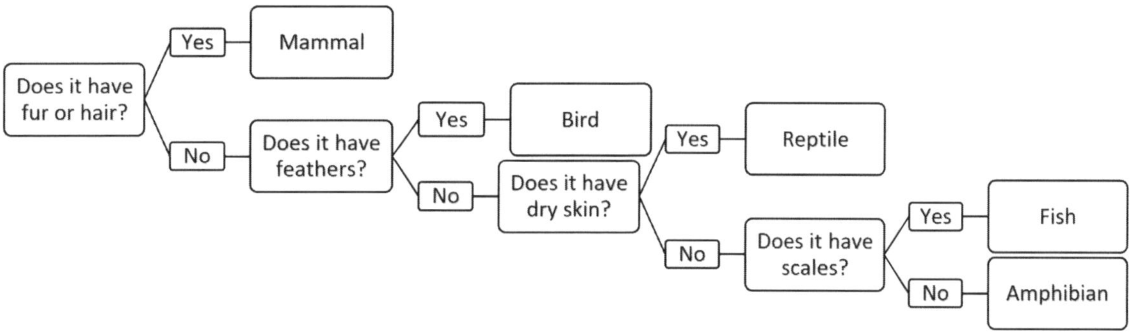

Evolution

Evolution is the process whereby organisms pass certain acquired traits to successive generations, affecting the attributes of later organisms and even leading to the creation of new species. Charles Darwin is the name often associated with the formulation of natural selection, a vital component of evolution as it is known today. **Natural selection** states that members of a species are not identical—due to their respective genetic make-ups, each individual will possess traits which make it stronger or weaker and more or less able to adapt. The other tenet of natural selection is that members of a species will always have to compete for scarce resources to survive. Therefore, organisms with traits which will help them survive are more likely to do so and produce offspring, passing along the "desirable" traits. Darwin suggested that this process, by creating groups of a species with increasingly different characteristics, would eventually lead to the formation of **a new species**.

Significant Events Leading to Evolution of Man

The **origination of life** is the most fundamental development in the history of life on Earth. Prokaryotic microfossils, the earliest fossils identified by paleontologists, are dated to near 3.5 billion years ago. However, the presence of large amounts of certain carbon and oxygen isotopes in sedimentary rocks dated at about 3.8 billion years ago may indicate the presence of organic material. The next significant event suggested by a drastic change in the fossil record is the huge diversification of species which occurred approximately 543 million years ago, near the end of the Precambrian eon and the beginning of the Phanerozoic. This theoretical evolutionary stage included higher-level tissue organization in multicellular organisms, the development of predator-prey relationships, and, most importantly, the development of skeletons. The final critical step toward the evolution of man is the emergence of life on land about 418 million years ago. This necessitated the evolution of structures which could breathe air, obtain and retain water on land, and support its own weight out of water.

Natural and Artificial Selection

Natural selection and artificial selection are both mechanisms of evolution. **Natural selection** is a process of nature in which a population can change over generations. Every population has variations in individual heritable traits and organisms best suited for survival typically reproduce and pass on those genetic traits to offspring to increase the likelihood of them surviving. Typically, the more advantageous a trait is, the more common that trait becomes in a population. Natural selection brings about evolutionary **adaptations** and is responsible for biological diversity. Artificial selection is another mechanism of evolution. **Artificial selection** is a process brought about by humans. Artificial selection is the selective breeding of domesticated animals and plants such as when farmers choose animals or plants with desirable traits to reproduce. Artificial selection has led to the evolution of farm stock and crops. For example, cauliflower, broccoli, and cabbage all evolved due to artificial selection of the wild mustard plant.

Example of Natural Selection

One of the most famous examples of natural selection is that of the Galapagos Medium Ground Finch. This bird populates the Galapagos islands, a small group of islands containing birds clearly related, but with distinctive traits, such as small and large beaks, specialized to eat food available on the island it lives in.

Darwin's Contributions to the Theory of Evolution

Charles Darwin's theory of evolution by natural selection is the unifying concept in biology today. From 1831 to 1836, Darwin traveled as a naturalist on a five-year voyage on the *H.M.S. Beagle* around the tip of South America and to the Galápagos Islands. He studied finches, took copious amounts of meticulous notes, and collected thousands of plant and animal specimens. He collected 13 species of finches each with a unique bill for a distinct food source, which led him to believe, due to similarities between the finches, that the finches shared a common ancestor. The similarities and differences of fossils of extinct rodents and modern mammal fossils led him to believe that the mammals had changed over time. Darwin believed that these changes were the result of random genetic changes called mutations. He believed that mutations could be beneficial and eventually result in a different organism over time. In 1859, in his first book, *On the Origin of Species*, Darwin proposed that natural selection was the means by which adaptations would arise over time. He coined the term "natural selection" and said that it is the mechanism of evolution. Because variety exists among individuals of a species, he stated that those individuals must compete for the same limited resources. Some would die, and others would survive. According to Darwin, evolution is a slow, gradual process. In 1871, Darwin published his second book, *Descent of Man, and Selection in Relation to Sex*, in which he discussed the evolution of man.

HOMOLOGY

Homology is the similarity of structures of different species based on a similar anatomy in a common evolutionary ancestor. For instance, the forelimbs of humans, dogs, birds, and whales all have the same basic pattern of the bones. Specifically, all of these organisms have a humerus, radius, and ulna. They are all modifications of the same basic evolutionary structure from a common ancestor. Tetrapods resemble the fossils of extinct transitional animal called the *Eusthenopteron*. This would seem to indicate that evolution primarily modifies preexisting structures.

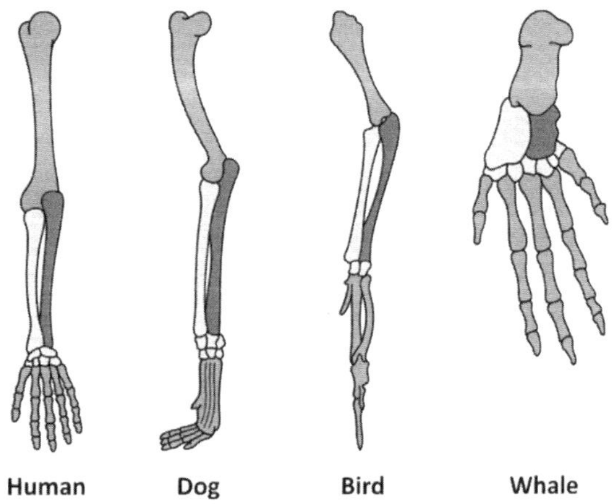

Organisms and Adapted Environment

Animals and plants are adapted to live in their environments in many special ways. For example, polar bears have white fur as camouflage which helps them blend in with their icy and snowy background. This makes it easier to sneak up on the seals on which they prey. They also have thick fur and a thick layer of blubber to help keep them warm in their frigid environment.

GENETICS AND HEREDITY

Genetics is the study of biological inheritance in organisms. Animals generally reproduce with a mother and a father, which both contribute their **genetic** information to offspring. The passing along of genetic traits is also known as **heredity**. The offspring of a mother with red hair and blue eyes with a father who has brown hair and brown eyes may receive any combination of those traits. Another example may be a red fox mating with a brown fox; the offspring may have either brown fur or red fur, and a pack of siblings may have a mixture of inherited traits. This type of inheritance can also be seen in plant life, as pink and white flowered plants may breed together to produce either pink or white flowered offspring, or even special hybrids with blended colors.

Innate Behaviors

Similar to genetics, there are some behaviors that are innate, or instinctual. Instinctive behaviors are actions that are automatic in an animal and do not have to be taught or learned. Many animals do not nurture their young, but instead, the newborn creatures are capable of fending for themselves. Below are some examples of innate behaviors that are not learned or taught.

- Birds migrate from North to South for the winter to protect themselves from the cold.
- Salmon swim upstream to nesting grounds.
- Some insects migrate and form cocoons to metamorphose.
- Rattlesnakes shake their rattles to warn other animals.
- Newly hatched sea turtles automatically crawl across the beach towards the ocean with no mother around to show them what to do.
- Tree squirrels automatically store acorns and nuts during the summer in order to have food in the coming winter.
- Salmon automatically return from the ocean to the freshwater river where they hatched in order to spawn.

Learned Behaviors

Some behaviors and traits may be inherited, but many behaviors must be taught by the parents or pack to the young. Below are some examples of learned or taught behaviors.

- A wolf pack teaches the young wolves how to hunt effectively as a group.
- Some primates use sticks as tools to gather food.
- Dogs learn tricks and commands from their owners.
- Pelicans learn to hunt for fish in groups.
- Humans teach their children words and how to read.

Camouflage and Mimicry

Generally speaking, *camouflage* is when an organism blends in with its surroundings in a way that it cannot be seen as in the case of the flounder blending in with the gravel on the bottom of a lake (Fig. B). *Mimicry* is when an organism resembles something else, like the leaf insect in Fig. A. In these two examples each animal is able to avoid being seen and eaten by a predator. However, sometimes it is the predator that is camouflaged or a mimic which enables it to pounce on its unsuspecting prey.

Warning Coloration

Dangerously venomous or poisonous animals often are brightly colored to warn predators that they are best left alone. This is called aposematic coloration. The deadly venomous coral snake (Fig. A.) has bright red, yellow and black bands that circle its body. The harmless milk snake (Fig. B) mimics the dangerous coral snake which fools predators to leave them alone, too.

Adaptation to Environment

Organisms must be able to adapt to their environment in order to thrive or survive. Individuals must be able to recognize stimuli in their surroundings and adapt quickly. For example, an individual euglena can sense light and respond by moving toward the light. Individual organisms must also be able to adapt to changes in the environment on a larger scale. For example, plants must be able to respond to the change in the length of the day to flower at the correct time. Populations must also be able to adapt to a changing environment. Evolution by **natural selection** is the process by which populations change over many generations to become better adapted to their environment, thus surviving longer and reproducing more successfully. For example, wooly mammoths were unable to adapt to a warming climate and are now extinct, but many species of deer did adapt and are abundant today.

Extinction of Species

Causes of Extinction of Species

Lack of Genetic Diversity

Genetic diversity provides a mechanism for populations to adapt to changing environments or even human impacts. With a diverse genome, individuals possessing genes making them better suited for the environment are more likely to exist. Without genetic diversity, populations cannot develop adaptations. Populations cannot resist diseases or adapt to changes in the habitat. As the populations of endangered species decrease, genetic diversity decreases even further. Normally, specific genes that resist disease or help the organism to adapt to changes in the habitat and therefore increase survivability are passed on to future generations. However, if those genes have drifted out of the population, the population cannot evolve with their changing environment and may become extinct. A small gene pool does not provide much variety for selection. For example, tigers in India are now in danger of extinction. Studies show that more than 90% of the genome has been lost largely due to a period when tigers were heavily killed by British officials and Indian royalty. With fewer than 2,000 tigers in the world and these in small populations, the genetic diversity can continue to decrease, possibly leading to extinction if much effort is not made to preserve the remaining genetic diversity.

Environmental Pressures

A changing environment may lead to the extinction of a species. If an animal has a small tolerance range to food sources and habitat needs or if a population is small, it is less likely to adapt to changes in the environment. For example, the giant panda feeds almost exclusively on bamboo. Bamboo is being threatened by global warming. Due to the dwindling of their food source, giant pandas are less able to adapt to a changing environment. **Climate change** and global warming can affect an ecosystem and some species may not be able to adapt to even seemingly minor temperature changes especially if their populations are small. If possible, animals needing cooler climates may need to move to cooler habitats. Melting ice caps and glaciers and rising sea levels can seriously disrupt many ecosystems and affect numerous species. For example, the polar bear may become extinct due to global warming as the polar bears' habitat is destroyed. Sea turtles may become extinct as the rising sea levels destroy the beaches needed for laying eggs. Even if the beaches are not destroyed, increasing temperatures affect the incubation process and the number of offspring being produced.

Human Impacts

Humans are responsible for impacting the environment in such a way as to endanger or harm species that may even lead to extinction. Humans destroy habitats directly through deforestation and clearing land for agriculture, logging, mining, and urbanization. Humans also threaten or endanger species through overfishing and overhunting. Pollution can destroy a habitat, and if a species is unable to relocate, this can eventually cause extinction if the effects cause drastic impacts. The intentional or unintentional introduction of an invasive species, allows a new predator or competitor into the ecosystem, and can threaten native species in that specific ecosystem if they cannot outcompete the invasive species. An example of human impacts leading to the extinction of a species is the case of the passenger pigeon. Millions of passenger pigeons were killed for meat from around 1850 to 1880. Because passenger pigeons only laid one egg at a time, huge flocks were destroyed. The last passenger pigeon died in 1914.

Interspecific Competition

Interspecific competition is competition between individuals of different species for the same limited resources such as food, water, sunlight, and living space. This is especially threatening if the two species share a limiting resource and that resource is not in abundant supply. Interspecific competition can limit the population size of a species. With reduced population size, there is less genetic variation. The species may not be able to adapt to environmental changes. For example, firs and spruces compete for resources in coniferous forests. Cheetahs and lions compete for prey in savannas.

Heredity and Reproduction

Genetics, Genes, and Chromosomes

Genetics is the science devoted to the study of how characteristics are transmitted from one generation to another. In the 1800s, Gregor Mendel outlined the three laws of heredity that explain how genetics works. Genes are the hereditary units of material that are transmitted from one generation to the next. They are capable of undergoing mutations, can be recombined with other genes, and can determine the nature of an organism, including its color, shape, and size. **Genotype** is the genetic makeup of an individual based on one or more characteristics, while phenotype is the external manifestation of the genotype. For example, genotype determines hair color genes, whereas phenotype is the actual color of the hair observed. **Chromosomes** are the structures inside the nucleus of a cell made up primarily of deoxyribonucleic acid (DNA) and proteins. The chromosomes carry the genes. The numbers vary according to the species, but they are always the same for each species. For example, the human has 46 chromosomes, and the water lily has 112.

Review Video: Chromosomes
Visit mometrix.com/academy and enter code: 132083

Review Video: DNA
Visit mometrix.com/academy and enter code: 639552

Review Video: Genotype vs Phenotype
Visit mometrix.com/academy and enter code: 922853

Mendel's Contributions to Genetics

Johann Gregor Mendel is known as the father of **genetics**. Mendel was an Austrian monk who performed thousands of experiments involving the breeding of the common pea plant in the garden of his monastery. Mendel kept detailed records including seed color, pod color, seed type, flower color, and plant height for eight years and published his work in 1865. Unfortunately, his work was largely ignored until the early 1900s. Mendel's work showed that genes come in pairs and that dominant and recessive traits are inherited independently of each other. His work established the law of segregation, the law of independent assortment, and the law of dominance.

Contribution to Genetics Made by Alfred Hershey and Martha Chase

Alfred Hershey and Martha Chase did a series of experiments in 1952 known as the **Hershey-Chase experiments**. These experiments showed that deoxyribonucleic acid (DNA), not protein, is the genetic material that transfers information for inheritance. The Hershey-Chase experiments used a bacteriophage, a virus that infects bacteria, to infect the bacteria *Escherichia coli.* The bacteriophage T2 is basically a small piece of DNA enclosed in a protein coating. The DNA contains phosphorus, and the protein coating contains sulfur. In the first set of experiments, the T2 was marked with radioactive phosphorus-32. In the second set of experiments, the T2 was marked with radioactive sulfur-35. For both sets of experiments, after the *E. coli* was infected by the T2, the *E. coli* was isolated using a centrifuge. In the first set of experiments, the radioactive isotope (P-32) was found in the *E. coli*, showing that the genetic information was transferred by the DNA. In the second set of experiments, the radioactive isotope (S-35) was not found in the *E. coli*, showing that the genetic information was not transferred by the protein as was previously thought. Hershey and Chase conducted further experiments allowing the bacteria from the first set of experiments to reproduce, and the offspring was also found to contain the radioactive isotope (P-32) further confirming that the DNA transferred the genetic material.

MODES OF REPRODUCTION

Animals can reproduce sexually or asexually. Most animals reproduce sexually. In **sexual reproduction**, males and females have different reproductive organs that produce **gametes**. Males have testes that produce sperm, and females have ovaries that produce eggs. During fertilization, a sperm cell unites with an egg cell, forming a **zygote**. Fertilization can occur internally such as in most mammals and birds or externally such as aquatic animals such as fish and frogs. The zygote undergoes cell division, which develops into an embryo and eventually develops into an adult organism. Some embryos develop in eggs such as in fish, amphibians, reptiles, and birds. Some mammals are **oviparous** meaning that they lay eggs, but most are **viviparous** meaning they have a uterus in which the embryo develops. One particular type of mammal called **marsupials** give birth to an immature fetus that finishes development in a pouch. However, there are some animals reproduce **asexually**. For example, hydras reproduce by budding, and starfish and planarians can reproduce by fragmentation and regeneration. Some fish, frogs, and insects can even reproduce by parthenogenesis, which is a type of self-reproduction without fertilization.

EFFECTS OF THE MODES OF REPRODUCTION ON OFFSPRING

With **asexual reproduction**, an organism provides all of the **genes** to its offspring, making it like a **clone**, or exactly like the parent in its genetic makeup. This means that the offspring will be very similar to the parent unless there is a random mutation that causes a change. This means that the offspring will be very uniform to each other. In **sexual reproduction**, both parents provide genetic information that can be inherited, causing much more variety in the offspring from generation to generation. This more aggressive variation means that natural selection and adaptation is more likely to make a difference for the species in the long-term.

Due to mutations over long periods, genes come in alternate forms, called **alleles**, that determine how a **trait** will be represented in the offspring. Different alleles govern many different traits. Sexual reproduction makes new combinations of existing alleles. These new combinations lead to variations in physical and behavioral traits that lead to adaptation and selection, which are key components of evolution.

MITOSIS

Eukaryotic cells divide into two genetically identical daughter cells in a process called mitosis. Meiosis is another form of cell division that produces haploid gametes for sexual reproduction. At the beginning of mitosis, DNA chromatin condenses into chromosomes, which replicate themselves forming two sister chromatids joined by a centromere. These chromosomes line up along an equatorial plate in the center of the cell, the centromere divides, and each of the two paired chromatids is pulled to opposites sides of the cell by microtubules attached to the centromere and the star-shaped centrosome. The cytoplasm then divides in a process called cytokinesis. At the end of mitosis, the diploid ($2n$) genome of the original cell, the entirety of the parent cell's DNA, is passed on to each daughter cell.

MEIOSIS

Sexual reproduction in eukaryotic organisms involves a form of cell division known as meiosis, in which a diploid ($2n$) primary germ cell gives rise to haploid (n) gametes or spores. The diploid germ cell contains two exact copies of each chromosome (known as a homologous pair) in its genome, one from each parent. As in mitosis, meiosis begins by DNA replication and the doubling of each chromosome into two sister chromatids. The homologous pairs then come together along the equatorial plate and usually exchange fragments from one chromosome to the other—known as crossing over or recombination. Thus, genetic material from the paternal and maternal chromosomes are exchanged. The reshuffled homologous pairs are pulled to opposite poles of the cell and the cell divides to produce two 2*n* daughter cells that are genetically different from the parent cell (meiosis I). A second division (meiosis II) occurs next resulting in four haploid (*n*) gametes or spores. When two gametes combine during fertilization, a diploid zygote is formed.

Dominant and Recessive Genes

Gene traits are represented in pairs with an uppercase letter for the **dominant trait** (A) and a lowercase letter for the **recessive trait** (a). Genes occur in pairs (AA, Aa, or aa). There is one gene on each chromosome half supplied by each parent organism. Since half the genetic material is from each parent, the offspring's traits are represented as a combination of these. A dominant trait only requires one gene of a gene pair for it to be expressed in a phenotype, whereas a recessive requires both genes in order to be manifested. For example, if the mother's genotype is Dd and the father's is dd, the possible combinations are Dd and dd. The dominant trait will be manifested if the genotype is DD or Dd. The recessive trait will be manifested if the genotype is dd. Both DD and dd are **homozygous** pairs. Dd is **heterozygous**.

Punnett Squares

Punnett squares are used to show all of the possible gene combinations for specific traits between two animals. To complete a Punnett square, you must be able to identify the trait and the alleles that the animal has for that trait. This is best illustrated with an example.

Homozygous Father with Red Hair	Heterozygous Mother with Black Hair	**B**	**b**
	b	Bb	bb
	b	Bb	bb

In this example, a female cow that is heterozygous for black hair is crossed with a male cow that is homozygous for red hair. Half of the offspring could be expected to have black hair; half could be expected to have red hair from this cross.

For two-factor crosses, use the genotypes to create the possible gene combinations for each parent, and plug them into a two-factor square.

Homozygous Red Bull with Horns (bbPp)	Heterozygous Black Polled Cow (Bbpp)	**Bp**	**bp**	**Bp**	**bp**
	bP	BbPp	bbPp	BbPp	bbPp
	bp	Bbpp	bbpp	Bbpp	Bbpp
	bP	BbPp	bbPp	BbPp	bbPp
	bp	Bbpp	bbpp	Bbpp	bbpp

In this example, we have crossed a heterozygous black, polled cow with a homozygous red, horned bull. The Punnett square shows you an expected ratio of animals based on the hair color and the presence of horns from this cross.

Phenotype and Genotype of Animals

The **phenotype** refers to the appearance of an animal. Phenotypes are traits that can be seen or measured. Examples of phenotypes would be hair color, height, weaning weight, or the possession of horns or being polled. **Genotype** tells the genes that the animal has. Phenotypes can give you clues about the genotypes that the animal has. The genotype will tell the actual alleles that the animal has for a certain trait. It will show whether the animal is homozygous or heterozygous for a trait. It will also show whether the alleles are dominant or recessive. An example of this can be seen with polled animals. Being polled is recessive, so an animal that is polled would have a genotype of hh. A horned animal would have a genotype of either HH or Hh because being horned is a dominant trait. Genotypes are used to complete Punnett squares and predict the traits of potential offspring.

Review Video: Genotype vs Phenotype
Visit mometrix.com/academy and enter code: 922853

Pedigree

Pedigree analysis is a type of genetic analysis in which an inherited trait is studied and traced through several generations of a family to determine how that trait is inherited. A **pedigree** is a chart arranged as a type of family tree using symbols for people and lines to represent the relationships between those people. Squares usually represent males, and circles represent females. Horizontal lines represent a male and female mating, and the vertical lines beneath them represent their children. Usually, family members who possess the trait are fully shaded and those who only carry the trait are half-shaded. Genotypes and phenotypes are determined for each individual if possible. The pedigree below shows the family tree of a family in which the first male who was red-green color blind mated with the first female who was unaffected. They had five children. The three sons were unaffected, and the two daughters were carriers.

Inheritance of Red-Green Color Blindness: an X-linked Recessive Trait

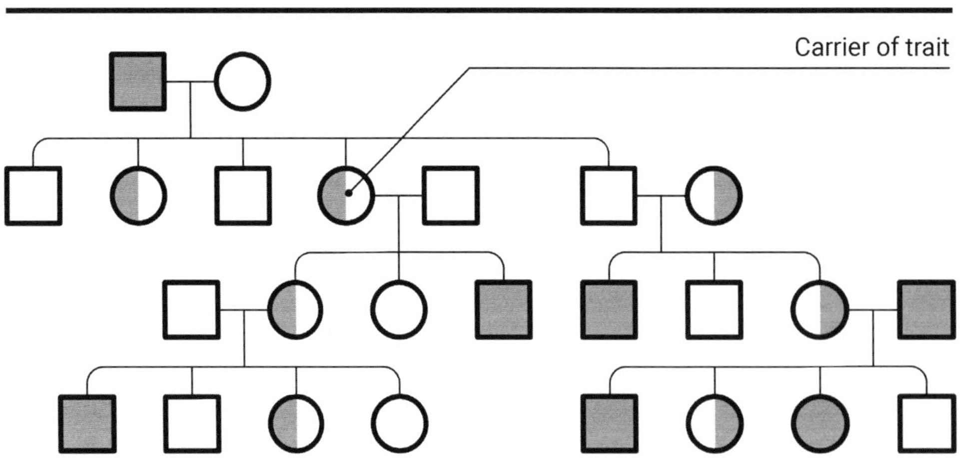

Plants

Plants are multicellular organisms with eukaryotic cells containing cellulose in their cell walls. Plant cells have chlorophyll and perform photosynthesis. Plants can be vascular or nonvascular. **Vascular plants** have true leaves, stems, and roots that contain xylem and phloem. **Nonvascular plants** lack true leaves, stems and roots and do not have any true vascular tissue but instead rely on diffusion and osmosis to transport most of materials or resources needed to survive. Almost all plants are autotrophic, relying on photosynthesis for food. A small number do not have chlorophyll and are parasitic, but these are extremely rare. Plants can reproduce sexually or asexually. Many plants reproduce by seeds produced in the fruits of the plants, while some plants reproduce by seeds on cones. One type of plant, ferns, reproduce by a different system that utilizes spores. Some plants can even reproduce asexually by vegetative reproduction.

Review Video: Kingdom Plantae
Visit mometrix.com/academy and enter code: 710084

Major Plant Processes

There are three key processes that plants need to survive: photosynthesis, respiration, and transpiration. **Photosynthesis** is the process that plants use to create food. Photosynthesis requires water, carbon dioxide, and sunlight. Photosynthesis creates glucose molecules that can be broken down and used as energy for the plant. The cellular **respiration** process breaks glucose molecules into usable energy for the cell. Respiration requires oxygen to take place, so the plants take in oxygen. **Transpiration** is the process of plants losing water through their leaves. Plants can control the amount of water lost through their leaves. Water is lost through stomata on the underside of the leaves. Stomata can be opened and closed by guard cells.

Net Equation for Photosynthesis

Photosynthesis is the food-making process in green plants. Photosynthesis occurs in the chloroplasts of cells in the presence of light and chlorophyll. The reactants are **carbon dioxide** and **water**. The energy from the sunlight is absorbed and stored in the glucose molecules. The net equation for photosynthesis can be represented by the following equations:

$$\text{carbon dioxide} + \text{water} + \text{light} \xrightarrow{\text{chlorophyll}} \text{glucose} + \text{oxygen}$$

$$6CO_2 + 6H_2O + \text{light} \xrightarrow{\text{chlorophyll}} C_6H_{12}O_6 + 6O_2$$

The products of photosynthesis are glucose and oxygen gas.

Respiration

Cellular respiration is the process in which energy is released from glucose in the form of adenosine triphosphate (ATP). **Cellular respiration** is the reverse process of photosynthesis. In cellular respiration, glucose is burned or combined with oxygen as shown in the following equations:

$$\text{glucose} + \text{oxygen} \rightarrow \text{carbon dioxide} + \text{water} + \text{ATP}$$

$$C_6H_{12}O_6 + 6O_2 \rightarrow 6CO_2 + 6H_2O$$

The products of cellular respiration are carbon dioxide and water. Energy is released from glucose in the form of ATP.

TRANSPIRATION

Transpiration is the mechanism by which water evaporates into the atmosphere from the leaves or stems of plants. Plants absorb water into their roots through osmosis. Then, as explained by **cohesion-tension theory**, water moves upward from the roots of a plant to its leaves. Some transpiration occurs directly through surface cells on the stem of a plant. More often, however, water escapes through pores in its leaves called **stomates**. Water droplets on the exterior surface of the leaves (usually on the bottom of the leaves) are consequently subjected to the process of evaporation. The process of transpiration enables **photosynthesis**, which in turn releases vital oxygen into Earth's atmosphere. Transpiration also has a cooling effect on the surface and air around the plant.

CARBON CYCLE

Carbon drives photosynthesis; is a major component in nutrients such as fat, protein and carbohydrates; and provides energy in the form of hydrocarbons. All of these characteristics make it imperative to understanding the **carbon cycle**. Carbon is involved in a multitude of processes and steadily moves through the carbon cycle. In the atmosphere, carbon attaches to oxygen to create carbon dioxide. Plants breathe in carbon dioxide and use it during photosynthesis to create a carbon-containing molecule called glucose. The carbon becomes part of the plant. Animals consume the plant, consuming the carbon. Dead organisms and waste materials containing carbon decompose and become part of the soil, eventually creating carbon-containing fossil fuels. When we burn fossil fuels, carbon is released into the atmosphere. Carbon is also released into the atmosphere by animal respiration, plant respiration, and even root respiration.

Practice Test #1

1. Karen bought two pens of the same kind and wants to see if writing in cursive makes the ink run out faster. She uses one pen to write a word in cursive, and she uses the other pen to write the same word in print. Then she makes marks on the ink to show how much is used every day. What is the test variable or independent variable in Karen's experiment?

a. The type of pen used
b. How many words she writes
c. Whether she writes in cursive or print
d. The amount of ink that is used

2. Students are working in groups to complete an experiment their teacher assigned. The steps for the experiment are listed below.

Experiment Steps
1. Pour $\frac{1}{2}$ cup of hydrogen peroxide into an empty water bottle.
2. Add 1 teaspoon of dish soap to the water bottle.
3. Swirl the water bottle to mix the liquids.
4. In a small glass, mix 1 tablespoon of yeast and 3 tablespoons of warm water.
5. Pour the yeast mixture into the water bottle containing the hydrogen peroxide and dish soap.
6. Place your hand right above the water bottle and notice the heat coming from it.
7. Notice the foam rises in the water bottle and begins to overflow.

Which step above suggests that a chemical reaction occurred during the experiment?

a. Step 2: add 1 teaspoon of dish soap to the water bottle.
b. Step 3: swirl the water bottle to mix the liquids.
c. Step 5: pour the yeast mixture into the water bottle containing the hydrogen peroxide and dish soap.
d. Step 6: place your hand right above the water bottle and notice the heat coming from it.

3. Silver (Ag) is one of the best conductors of heat and electricity. What other element would be a great conductor of heat and electricity like silver?

a. Hydrogen (H)
b. Phosphorus (P)
c. Krypton (Kr)
d. Copper (Cu)

4. Using the table below, which student is likely to receive a 100% for the fourth quarter should this trend continue?

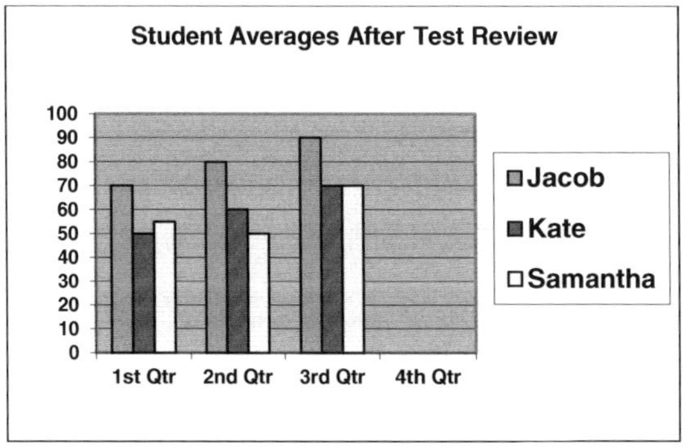

a. Jacob
b. Kate
c. Samantha
d. None of them

5. The students were asked to identify an unknown cell from the image below.

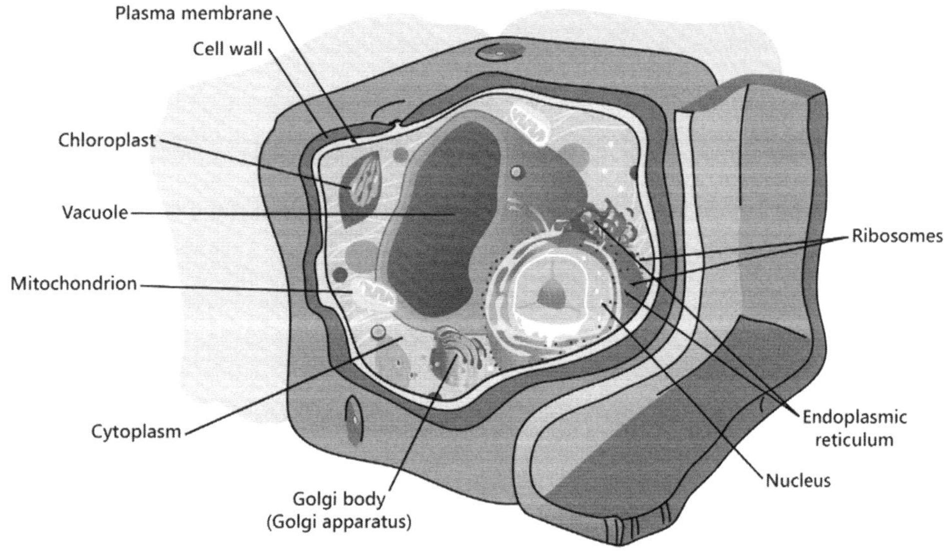

The table below shows the argument each student made about his or her determination. Which argument is correct?

Argument 1	The cell is an animal cell because it has mitochondria. The mitochondria in animal cells produce food. Plants don't have mitochondria because they make their own food.
Argument 2	The cell is a plant cell because it has a large vacuole, a cell wall, and chloroplasts.
Argument 3	The cell is an animal cell because it has a cell wall and mitochondria, which are only present in animal cells.
Argument 4	The cell is a plant cell because it has a plasma membrane, which is only present in plant cells. The nucleus is small, which is also a characteristic of plant cells.

a. Argument 1
b. Argument 2
c. Argument 3
d. Argument 4

6. In your garden, you noticed that the tomato plants did better on the North side of your house than the West side and you decided to figure out why. They are both planted with the same soil that provides adequate nutrients to the plant, and they are watered at the same time during the week. Over the course of a week, you begin to measure the amount of sunlight that hits each side of the house and determine that the North side gets more light because the sunlight is blocked by the house's shadow on the West side. What is the name of the factor in your observations that affected the tomato plants growth?

a. The control
b. The independent variable
c. The dependent variable
d. The conclusion

7. Many homeowners are adding solar panels to the roofs of their homes to help lower their electricity bills. In the home below, the family uses solar panels to help provide power for appliances like their oven.

How is energy being transformed in the home of the family described above?

a. Light energy from the Sun is converted by the solar panels to mechanical energy to power the oven and then converted to thermal energy to cook the food.
b. Thermal energy from the Sun is converted by the solar panels to mechanical energy to power the oven and then converted to light energy to cook food.
c. Light energy from the Sun is converted by the solar panels to electrical energy to power the oven and then converted into thermal energy to cook the food.
d. Chemical energy from the Sun is converted by the solar panels to electrical energy to power the oven and then converted into light energy to cook food.

8. A group of researchers in Antarctica discovered an organism belonging to an undiscovered species. Below are some characteristics of the organism.

Characteristics:

- Has many cells
- Has no cell wall
- Is heterotrophic

To which kingdom does the organism belong?

a. Bacteria
b. Protista
c. Fungi
d. Animalia

9. A ball is thrown and the distance it traveled is measured. Which data set corresponds to the graph below?

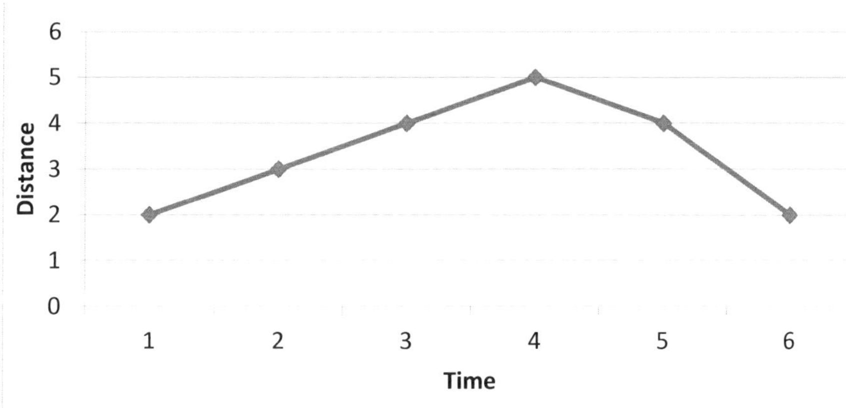

a.

Time	Distance
1	2
2	4
3	6
4	8
5	9

b.

Time	Distance
1	2
3	4
5	6
7	8
9	9

c.

Time	Distance
2	0
4	1
6	3
8	5
9	7

d.

Time	Distance
1	2
2	3
3	4
4	5
5	4
6	2

10. Which of the following descriptions concerning air masses is true?

a. Maritime tropical air masses bring warm, dry weather.
b. Continental polar air masses bring warm, moist weather.
c. Continental tropical air masses bring cold, dry weather.
d. Maritime polar air masses bring cold, moist weather.

11. In 1912, Alfred Wegener proposed that:

a. The earth's magnetic poles have reversed several times throughout history
b. Tectonic plates move because of convection currents in the mantle
c. Mountains are formed by tectonic plates pushing against one another
d. The continents once formed a single land mass, but have since drifted apart

12. A scientist who has been studying a certain species of plant believed that this species only flowers during the summer. As the climate changes, the area where the plants grow has become hotter. The plants have begun to flower in the autumn and spring as well. How should the scientist respond?

a. She should investigate the change in plant behavior.
b. She should change her old work because she made a mistake.
c. She should assume that climate change prompted the plants to flower at different times.
d. She should presume that there was a change in the soil composition.

13. The Hertzsprung–Russell diagram was created to help scientists organize stars by temperature and luminosity. Fill in the bubbles to match the descriptions below with their correct placement on the Hertzsprung–Russell diagram.

a. A white dwarf star that is hotter and less bright than the Sun

b. A supergiant that is cooler than the Sun but has more luminosity

c. A main sequence star that is both brighter and hotter than the Sun

d. A main sequence star that is cooler and dimmer than the Sun

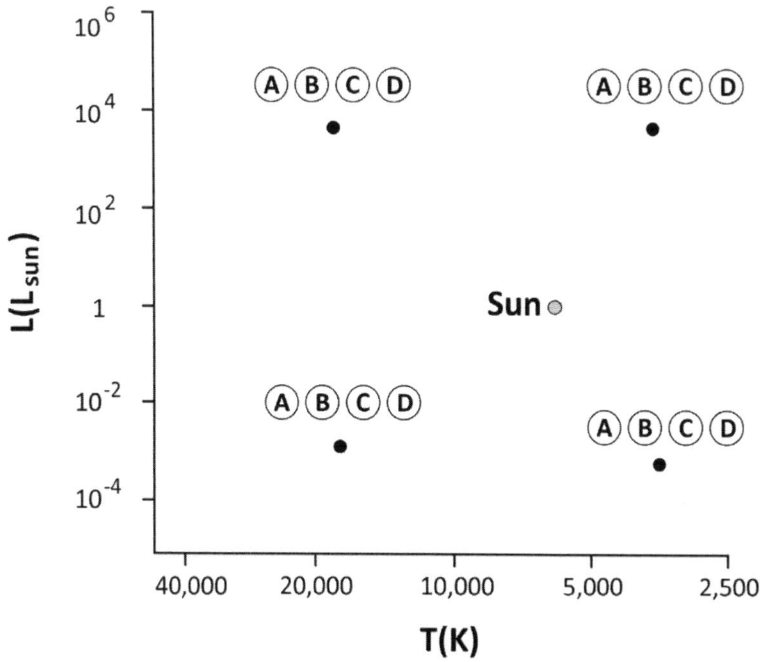

14. Amber is working on her science fair project. She completed an experiment in which she is trying to determine the dishwashing detergent that gets dishes the cleanest without prewashing. After testing 3 different types of dishwashing detergent and recording her findings, Amber decided to complete the experiment again. Why do scientists often repeat the procedures of their experiments?

a. Scientists often repeat experiments because they are enjoyable to complete.
b. Repeating experiments leads to more reliable results.
c. Experiments are repeated so different variables can be added to make the experiment more diverse.
d. When experiments are repeated carefully, different materials are often used.

15. Which one of the following examples would represent a scientific theory?

a. A scientist notices that objects do not start moving unless acted on by an outside force.
b. A scientist hypothesizes that the universe began after a large explosion event.
c. A scientist observes that objects in the universe are attracted to each other depending on how large and close they are.
d. A scientist discovers that the mass of water does not change as the water changes states from liquid to solid to gas.

16. All living things have:

a. Organelles
b. Cells
c. Tissues
d. Cell walls

17. The Gulf Oil Spill of 2010 deposited millions of gallons of crude oil into the wetlands of Louisiana, and many people in the area suffered. Which of the factors below was not among those drastically affected by the oil spill?

a. Water quality
b. Water temperature
c. Air quality
d. Presence of fish

18. What is the name of the process by which plants generate their own food source using sunlight, carbon dioxide, and water?

a. Photoemission
b. Chemotherapy
c. Chemosynthesis
d. Photosynthesis

19. In the marine waters, there is a beautiful, orange clown fish that lives closely with a sea anemone. This sea anemone can sting its prey with poisonous venom before devouring it; however, the clown fish is not affected by the sea anemone at all. The clown fish is only safe when hiding within the sea anemone's poisonous tentacles and protects the hiding spot from a certain type of fish who tries to eat the sea anemone. This is an example of what type of relationship?

a. Commensalism
b. Mutualism
c. Parasitism
d. None of the above

20. The sun provides a source of light for our planet, but it also plays an important role by heating the air and water, in turn causing atmospheric winds and ocean currents. The sun heats the air and water by ________.

a. Conduction
b. Radiation
c. Convection
d. None of the above

21. Which of the following is the most likely explanation for the reason finches on separate islands within an archipelago have differently shaped beaks?

a. Each bird evolved from a pre-existing ancestor on each island
b. The finches spread among the islands, but in small numbers, so genetic drift caused beak shape to change
c. Natural selection shaped the beaks in accordance with food availability on each island
d. The different finches were introduced by ancient humans

22. Genetics is the study of:

a. Anatomy
b. Physiology
c. Heredity
d. Science

23. Which of the following situations would result in the generation of new crust?

a. Two crustal plates converge
b. Two crustal plates move apart
c. Two crustal plates slide past one another
d. A crustal plate is pushed down into the mantle

24. 100 g of ethanol C_2H_6O is dissolved in 100 g of water. The final solution has a volume of 0.2 L. What is the density of the resulting solution?

a. 10,000 g/mL
b. 10 g/mL
c. 0.1 g/mL
d. 1 g/mL

25. The moon plays an important role in which of the following earth events?

a. Tides
b. Earthquakes
c. Earth's orbit
d. Northern Lights

26. The average distance from the earth to the sun is equal to one:

a. Astronomical unit
b. Light year
c. Parsec
d. Arcsecond

27. On your way to school you are carrying a book bag full of academic supplies, books, and lunch. What is causing the book bag to begin to feel very heavy as you walk to school?

a. The mass of the book bag
b. The weight of the book bag
c. The volume of the book bag
d. The size of the book bag

28. Cells are the smallest unit of a living organism; therefore, atoms would be the smallest unit of _____.

a. Matter
b. Mass
c. Weight
d. Periodic Table

29. The reason for seasonal changes on earth is because of the earth's revolution around the sun and which unique aspect of the earth?

a. The earth rotates around the moon
b. The earth is tilted at its equator
c. The earth is tilted at its axis
d. None of these

30. What are the three main sections of the Periodic Table?

a. Metals, nonmetals, and gases
b. Metals, metalloids, and gases
c. Metals, nonmetals, and metalloids
d. Nonmetals, metalloids, and gases

31. The brain is part of the:

a. Integumentary system
b. Nervous system
c. Endocrine system
d. Respiratory system

32. Which of the following is an example of an unbalanced force?

a. A book resting on a table.
b. Two football players of equal size and strength pushing each other from opposite directions.
c. A soccer player kicking the ball.
d. Two equal teams playing tug of war with a rope.

Answer Key and Explanations for Test #1

1. C: SC.8.N.1.1

The test variable, or independent variable, is the variable the researcher changes in an experiment. Changing the independent variable results in change to the outcome variable, or dependent variable. In this case, Karen uses the same type of pen but changes the style of writing from cursive to print to see how it affects the amount of ink used, which is the dependent variable. Answer choice A is incorrect because Karen uses the same kind of pen throughout the experiment. Answer choice B is incorrect because Karen writes the same number of words with each pen. Answer choice D is incorrect because the amount of ink used is the outcome variable, or dependent variable.

2. D: SC.8.P.9.2

Step 6 of the experiment states the ingredients in the bottle are producing heat, which is a temperature change. A temperature change is a sign that a chemical reaction has happened. Adding dish soap, mixing the liquids, and combining mixtures do not, on their own, suggest a chemical reaction has occurred.

3. D: SC.8.P.8.4

Silver is a great conductor of heat and electricity because it is made of metal. The only other listed element that is in the metal group on the periodic table is copper. Hydrogen (A), phosphorus (B), and krypton (C) are all nonmetals.

4. A: SC.6.N.1.1

According to the table, Jacob started with a 70% and has consistently moved up 10% with each quarter, as has Kate, but she started at 60%. Samantha started at 55% and has not always increased her scores. Should this trend continue, Jacob will most likely earn a 100%.

5. B: SC.6.L.14.4

Argument 2 is correct because only plant cells have a cell wall, chloroplasts, and large vacuole. Argument 1 is incorrect because the cell is a plant cell, and plant cells also have mitochondria. Argument 3 is incorrect because only plant cells have a cell wall, and both plant and animal cells have mitochondria. Argument 4 is incorrect because neither statement is true about plant cells.

6. B: SC.7.N.1.4

The conclusion was that the amount of sunlight received by the plants was affecting their growth. The independent variable was the amount of light that was given to the plants and could have been manipulated by the experimenter by moving the plants or adding equal parts of light. No control was used in this experiment.

7. C: SC.7.P.11.2

The solar panels are powered by the light energy of the Sun. The solar panels convert the light energy into electrical energy that provides power to the home. The oven converts electrical energy into thermal energy to cook the food. Although the Sun does provide thermal energy, the solar panels are not powered by heat. The Sun does not provide chemical energy. The home is powered by electrical energy, in the form of electricity, and not mechanical energy. Although an oven may have a light source, thermal energy is needed to cook the food.

8. D: SC.6.L.15.1

The organism must be an animal belonging to kingdom Animalia, as organisms in this kingdom are heterotrophic and have many cells, none of which have cell walls. Choices A and B are incorrect because organisms in kingdoms Bacteria and Protista only have one cell. Choice C is incorrect because organisms in kingdom Fungi have cells with cell walls.

9. D: SC.6.P.12.1

The graph represents a set of data. The line graph increases in distance from 1 second to 4 seconds and then begins decreasing. The only data set that shows distance increasing and then decreasing is set D.

10. D: SC.6.E.7.5

Air masses are named for the areas over which they form. Since maritime polar air masses form over oceans in frigid regions, they bring cold, moist weather. Since maritime tropical air masses form over oceans in warmer regions, they bring warm, moist weather. Since continental polar air masses form over northern Canada or Alaska, they bring cold, dry weather. Since continental tropical air masses form over deserts, they bring warm, dry weather.

11. D: SC.7.E.6.5

In 1912, Alfred Wegener proposed that the continents once formed a single land mass called Pangaea, but have since drifted apart. Theories about the earth's magnetic fields and plate tectonics did not emerge until years later. Once they did, they helped produce evidence to support Wegener's theory.

12. A: SC.6.N.2.2

Answer choice A is correct because when scientists receive information that challenges their original theories or research, they do not throw away their research or make assumptions but, instead, investigate the change to refine their work. In this case, the scientist believed that the plant species she studies flowered during one specific time of year, but now they have started flowering at another time. The scientist should investigate why the flowers have begun to flower differently than expected. Answer choice B is incorrect because the scientist did not make a mistake in her previous work and should not change her work. If scientists change their old work because something changed or was discovered, there would be no record of the way life used to be. Answer choice C is incorrect because, without further study, the scientist cannot know if climate change is the reason for the plants' change in behavior. Instead of assuming, she should run an experiment or perform research. Answer choice D is incorrect because the scientist has not tested the soil composition, and assuming an answer without research is not part of the scientific method.

13. SC.8.E.5.5

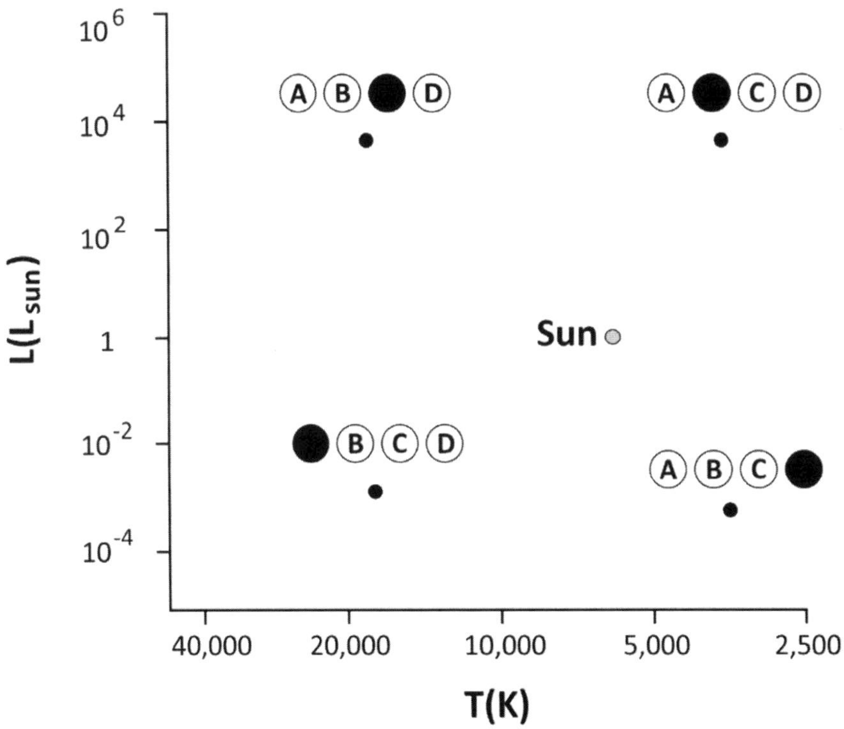

On the Hertzsprung–Russell diagram, a white dwarf that is hotter and less bright than the Sun would be located to the left and below the Sun. A supergiant that is cooler and has more luminosity would be located to the right and above the Sun. A main sequence star that is brighter and hotter than the Sun would be located above and to the left of the Sun. A main sequence star that is cooler and dimmer would be located to the right and below the Sun.

14. B: SC.

When experiments are repeated, the results are more reliable because they have been repeated several times. Scientists do not repeat experiments just for fun. Adding different variables when repeating an experiment would create less reliable results. If the experiment is repeated carefully, the same materials should be used.

15. B: SC.7.N.3.1

A law describes something that scientists have observed, but it does not offer an explanation as to why the observed phenomenon occurs. Theories, on the other hand, are attempts to explain why a certain phenomenon occurs. The scientist in answer choice B is attempting to understand why and how the universe came to be but does not offer an observation, making this a theory. Answer choice A reflects a law because the scientist notices something about the universe but does not explain why it occurs. Answer choice C also describes a scientist who observes the phenomenon of gravity in the universe but does not attempt to explain why gravity exists or its effects. Similarly, the scientist in answer choice D observes that the mass of water does not change, but the scientist does not attempt to explain why this is so, meaning this answer choice also reflects a law.

16. B: SC.6.L.14.2

Cells are the basic units of life, and all organisms have them. Some organisms like bacteria have just a single cell, while complex organisms like humans have hundreds of trillions. Prokaryotes do not have organelles Not all organisms have tissues, groups of cells that make up connective tissue, muscle tissue, etc. Finally, only some types of cells, including plant cells, have cell walls d.

17. B: SC.7.E.6.6

All of the factors above were drastically affected by the oil spill except the temperature of the water. Oil did not significantly impact the temperature of the water. The spill did impact the water quality and air quality by the introduction of oil and other chemicals from the cleanup into the water and air. The presence of the oil also killed or drove away many of the fish that would otherwise have been near the gulf coast.

18. D: SC.8.L.18.1

Photosynthesis is the process by which plants generate their own food (glucose), using sunlight, water, and carbon dioxide. Oxygen is also generated as a byproduct.

19. B: SC.7.17.2

The relationship between the clown fish and the sea anemone is an example of mutualism - because both organisms are benefitting from the relationship. The Clown fish gains the protection from the anemone while offering protection to the anemone from being eaten by a certain type of fish.

20. B: SC.6.E.7.1

Radiation is the heat energy that is transferred from electromagnetic waves such as the sun. Convection is the transfer of heat energy within a gas or liquid substance because of circulation. Conduction is the transfer of heat by direct contact. Once the air and water have been heated, they move and circulate because of the difference in the density of hot and cold water and of hot and cold air.

21. C: SC.7.L.15.1

Finches with beaks well-suited for the types of food available on an island had an evolutionary advantage. As a result, these finches survived and reproduced, a phenomenon known as natural selection. The finches share a common ancestor, regardless of the island on which they now live. Genetic drift refers to genetic changes that occur due to random chance; this would not account for different beaks on different islands. Introduction by humans would not account for different beaks, since phenotypes change over time.

22. C: SC.7.L.16.1

Genetics is the study of heredity.

23. B: SC.7.E.6.2

When two crustal plates move apart, magma welling up could result in the formation of new crust. This has been shown to be occurring on the ocean floor where places of the crust are weaker. The crust spreads apart at these trenches, pushing outward and erupting at the ridges. When two crustal plates converge, sublimation occurs as one plate runs under another pushing it up. Two crustal plates slide past one another, is an example of a transform fault, which does not create new crust. A crustal plate is pushed down into the mantle, does not form new crust but perhaps recycles the old one.

24. D: SC.8.P.8.3

Density is determined by dividing the mass of the solution by its volume. The mass is 200 g, and the total volume is 0.2 L, or 200 mL. So 200 g/200 mL = 1 g/mL.

25. A: SC.8.E.5.9

The moon's gravitational pull against the earth causes the earth's oceans to bulge out at the points nearest to and farthest from the moon, causing the displacement of water that occurs twice a day, known as high and low tide.

26. A: SC.8.E.5.1

The average distance from the earth to the sun is equal to one astronomical unit (AU). An AU is equal to 93 million miles, and is far smaller than a light year or a parsec. A light year is defined as the distance light can travel in a vacuum in one year, and is equal to roughly 64,341 AU. A parsec is the parallax of one arcsecond, and is equal to $206.26 \times 10^{\wedge 3}$ astronomical units.

27. B: SC.8.P.8.2

Weight and mass are very similar but differ in that mass is the amount of matter something contains and can be measured in grams and weight is affected by the gravitational pull of the object. Weight is the answer because gravity is pulling on the book bag, making it feel heavier than it really is.

28. A: SC.8.P.8.7

Atoms are the smallest and most basic unit of matter. When combined, they form elements just as cells of the same type form tissues.

29. C: SC.8.E.5.9

The earth experiences seasons because it revolves around the sun while tilted on its axis, exposing one hemisphere to the sun more than the other hemisphere. The hemisphere closest to the sun will be experiencing summer, while the other hemisphere has winter. The Northern Hemisphere and Southern Hemisphere experience opposite seasons all year long.

30. C: SC.8.P.8.6

The Periodic Table systematically arranges elements according to their properties, and many of the properties are more reactive than others. The most reactive are the metals, which are found on the left side of the table. The least reactive are the nonmetals, found on the right. In between the metals and nonmetals are the metalloids, which share some of the properties of both groups.

31. B: SC.6.L.14.5

The brain is part of the nervous system.

32. C: SC.6.P.13.3

An unbalanced force is where one force overcomes another force to create movement. The soccer player applied a greater force by kicking the ball which causes the ball to move. A balanced force is one that has no net force being applied to an object; therefore, it does not move.

Practice Test #2

1. Which of the following answer choices does NOT give an example of the Law of Conservation of Mass?

a. When wood burns, it turns into ash, heat, and gases with the same mass as the original wood.
b. 100 grams of ice becomes 100 grams of liquid water.
c. When two hydrogens and one oxygen combine, they become one water molecule (H2O) composed of two hydrogens and one oxygen.
d. Water from the ocean evaporates into the atmosphere.

2. The category of elements that contains most of the semiconductors is called?

a. Metals
b. Metalloids
c. Nonmetals
d. Noble gases

3. What other planet in the solar system experiences a greenhouse effect similar to that observed on Earth?

a. Mercury
b. Venus
c. Neptune
d. Saturn

4. Once a hypothesis has been verified and accepted, it becomes which of the following?

a. A fact
b. A law
c. A conclusion
d. A theory

5. A student was given a solid object and made observations about it. Based on the observations provided, classify the solid as a metal or metalloid, and determine if this object conducts electricity.

Classification	Conductivity	Observation 1	Observation 2	Observation 3
____________	____________	Not malleable & broke easily when hammered	Shiny, reflective luster	High melting point

Match the correct response to the location in the table. Not all options will be used.

Metalloid	Metal
Conductor	Does not conduct electricity
Semiconductor	

6. Evidence of a chemical reaction can be determined by all of the following except?

a. Modifying the arrangement of atoms
b. Endothermic and exothermic reactions
c. Equal masses of reactants and products
d. No change in energy

7. Which trait of a child is NOT a trait that would be stored in the genes within the chromosomes of the parents?

a. The child is tall and has brown hair like his father.
b. The child is color blind like her mom and dad.
c. The child speaks Spanish like her mother.
d. The child has many freckles on her face like her dad.

8. Which of the following is an example of a chemical change?

a. Salt dissolving in water
b. Water evaporating
c. Silver tarnishing
d. Dry ice sublimating

9. Which of the following devices changes chemical energy into electrical energy?

a. Battery
b. Closed electric circuit
c. Generator
d. Transformer

10. Which of the following is a star with an absolute magnitude of +10 and a temperature of 25,000K?

a. Main Sequence
b. Super Giant
c. Giant
d. White Dwarf

11. You are watching the Olympic ice skating championships and see the pairs are up next. They begin their routine facing each other with their palms up and against each other. When the music starts they push themselves apart with their palms. What type of force is this?

a. Magnetic
b. Balanced
c. Action and reaction force
d. Centripetal force

12. Two rabbits are getting ready to jump across the field away from a predator. One of the rabbits is about twice the size of the other. As they bound away, which of the rabbits will have to exert more force on its jumps and why?

a. The smaller rabbit, because its legs are shorter
b. The smaller rabbit, because it will have to take more jumps to escape the predator
c. The larger rabbit, because it has more mass that must overcome gravity and accelerate
d. The larger rabbit, because it has more air resistance to deal with

13. Which statement below correctly explains the cause of wind?

a. Wind is produced when the temperatures in the ocean change quickly.
b. Cold air moves across the ocean creating high wind as it progresses.
c. The Sun heats the Earth unevenly, which powers convection and leads to wind.
d. An increase in clouds creates wind as the atmosphere is fuller.

14. Which of the following answer choices describes the repetition of a scientific experiment?

a. Jessica's friend does the same experiment that Jessica did and gets the same results.
b. Jessica discovers that plants release oxygen in her experiment.
c. Jessica does the same experiment three times.
d. Jessica tells her teacher the results of her experiment and discusses what they mean.

15. Kamal makes a scale model that shows the orbit of planets in the solar system. If she wants to compare the orbital size of Earth and Neptune, how does her model help?

a. It displays a phenomenon that is too big to be seen.
b. It shows how far apart the planets are.
c. It slows down a process that takes seconds.
d. It details how fast the planets are moving.

16. Which of the following is NOT a characteristic of scientific inquiry?

a. continual posing of questions and testing of hypotheses
b. objective analysis of experimental data
c. ongoing peer review of shared information
d. the assumption that published literature is accurate and unbiased

17. Amir decides to make a scale model of the solar system. If the Earth is represented by a medium-sized rice grain, which of the answer choices best represents the size of the Sun?

a. A soccer ball
b. A golf ball
c. A marble
d. A baseball

18. Scientists believe that the southern part of Florida was underwater during the Jurassic period. What evidence would best support this?

a. The southern part of Florida is covered by sea.
b. Scientists discover erosion in the area.
c. *Tyrannosaurus rex* fossils are not discovered in the area.
d. Scientists discover fossils of aquatic species in the area.

19. The cryosphere and geosphere often interact, and this influences Earth's structure. Which of the following answer choices best reflects this effect?

a. Glaciers eroding soil
b. Rocks eroding glaciers
c. Acid rain damaging a mountain
d. Soil storing groundwater

20. Which of the following answer choices is at the lowest level of structural organization in the human body?

a. The urinary system
b. A kidney cell
c. A kidney tissue
d. A kidney

21. A student is trying to determine if an organism should be classified in the domain Eukarya, Bacteria, or Archaea. Which of the following characteristics would result in its classification in the domain Archaea?

a. The organism lives in extreme environments.
b. The cells have nuclei.
c. The organism is microscopic.
d. It does not photosynthesize.

22. Which of the following below is not considered evidence of plate tectonics?

a. The shape of continents fits together like a puzzle
b. Fossil comparisons exist along where the continents would fit together
c. The Mid-Atlantic Ridge shows where new crust is formed
d. There is a large amount of inland seismic activity

23. Earth's oceans have many little waves that are caused by the various wind speeds around the globe. However, one type of wave is caused by a celestial body. Which celestial body causes this wave?

a. Sun
b. Stars
c. Planets
d. Moon

24. Mrs. Jones's class conducted an experiment on the effects of sugar and artificial sweetener on the cookie recipe's overall color when baked. What would be the independent variable in the cookie experiment?

a. The students should use the same ingredients in both recipes, but bake the cookies with sugar at 450 degrees and those with artificial sweetener at 475 degrees. They should increase the baking time on the artificial sweetener cookies, since the package instructs them to do so
b. The students should use the same ingredients in both recipes, but increase the baking time on the artificial sweetener cookies, since the package instructs them to do so
c. The students should only vary the sugar or sweetener and otherwise use the same ingredients, same baking temperatures, and same baking times for both recipes
d. The students should use the same ingredients and baking times in both recipes, but bake the cookies with sugar at 450 degrees and the artificial sweetener cookies at 475 degrees

25. The part of the human excretory system most responsible for maintaining normal body temperature is the:

a. Kidney
b. Bladder
c. Liver
d. Sweat glands

26. A tapeworm lives within another organism and feeds off the nutrients that are ingested by that organism. At times, this can cause the organism to experience malnutrition or death. This is an example of what type of relationship?

a. Predator/prey
b. Symbiosis
c. Parasite/host
d. Producer/consumer

27. Which answer below represents the first steps in the scientific investigation process?

a. Construct a hypothesis and test with experiment
b. Analyze results and draw conclusions
c. Report results
d. Ask a question about a problem and do background research

28. In Lake Erie, a species of fish called the Blue Pike was overfished one year. The following year, there was a pollution incident that killed off another large portion of the population. These events, combined with the previous year's overfishing of adult fish, led to the extinction of the Blue Pike species—none of the other species were affected. What happened to other fish species in the lake over time after the Blue Pike became extinct?

a. They became extinct
b. They were not affected by the other species' fate
c. Their numbers increased due to lack of competition
d. Their numbers decreased due to lack of competition

29. Of the following, which is the most basic unit of matter?

a. A helium atom
b. A sodium ion
c. A proton
d. An oxygen molecule

30. A local lake is home to many kinds of fish that require a high amount of oxygen in the water, but it has recently become polluted. The pollution level has reduced the water oxygen level. What is the most likely result?

a. The fish will learn how to survive with less oxygen.
b. Many of the fish will die because they lack oxygen.
c. A new species of fish will be born.
d. The fish will choke on the plastic.

31. Which of the following is NOT true for all cells?

a. All eukaryotic cells have a nucleus.
b. Cells can only reproduce from existing cells.
c. Cells are the basic structures of any organism.
d. All cells have chloroplast.

32. Which moon phase is the opposite moon phase of a new moon?

a. New moon
b. Last moon
c. Full moon
d. First quarter moon

Answer Key and Explanations for Test #2

1. D: SC.8.L.18.4

The Law of Conservation of Mass states that mass can be neither created nor destroyed, only changed. While answer choice D does mention the state of water changing, it does not mention the mass. This example would instead demonstrate a state change from liquid to gas. Choice A is an example of the Law of Conservation of Mass because it demonstrates that the mass of wood before a fire would be the same as the emissions of ash, heat, and gas when the fire burns through the wood. Similarly, answer choice B explains that in a state change, the mass of solid water is the same as the liquid water it becomes. Answer choice C describes how during the forming of a new molecule, mass does not change. As the two hydrogens and one oxygen become water, their mass is maintained in the new structure (H2O), which is composed of one oxygen and two hydrogens.

2. B: SC.8.P.8.6

An element that has semi-conductive properties would be a metalloid. Metals are good conductors of electricity and heat. In contrast, nonmetals and the noble gases are not good conductors of electricity and heat. A semi-conductor is one that will conduct electricity under some conditions, but not others.

3. B: SC.8.E.5.7

Venus experiences a greenhouse effect similar to that observed on Earth as its dense atmosphere traps the solar radiation and creates a greenhouse effect. The greenhouse gases, including ozone, carbon dioxide, water vapor, and methane, trap infrared radiation that is reflected back toward the atmosphere. While both Venus and Earth experience the greenhouse effect, Venus's greenhouse effect is much more severe. Earth, on the other hand, has many more natural convective processes that help move carbon and other gases around, tempering the effect some. Human activity produces byproducts that contribute to the greenhouse effect. Some practices that increase the amount of greenhouse gases are burning natural gas and oil; farming, which leads to more methane and nitrous oxide; deforestation, which decreases the amount of offset oxygen; and population growth in general, which increases the volume of greenhouse gases. Increased gases mean more infrared radiation is trapped. While the greenhouse effect is not itself debated, the long-term effects tend to be hotly debated among scientists and in political agendas.

4. D: SC.7.N.3.1

Once a hypothesis has been verified and accepted, it becomes a theory. A theory is a generally accepted explanation that has been highly developed and tested. A theory can explain data and be expected to predict outcomes of tests. A fact is considered to be an objective and verifiable observation, whereas a scientific theory is a greater body of accepted knowledge, principles, or relationships that might explain a fact. A law is an explanation of events for which the outcome is always the same. A conclusion is more of an opinion and could be based on observation, evidence, fact, laws, or even beliefs.

5. SC.8.P.8.4

Classification	Conductivity	Observation 1	Observation 2	Observation 3
Metalloid	**Semiconductor**	**Not malleable & broke easily when hammered**	**Shiny, reflective luster**	**High melting point**

Since the object was not malleable, it cannot be a metal. Shiny luster and a high melting point are characteristics that both a metal and a metalloid can have. Metalloids are semiconductors of electricity, and metals are better conductors of electricity.

6. D: SC.8.P.9.1

A chemical reaction will always have an endothermic (absorb energy) or exothermic (release energy) reaction, and a chemical formula must always be balanced. Therefore, the masses of the reactants and products will always be equal, resulting in the modification of the atoms arrangement and a change in energy.

7. C: SC.7.L.16.1

Speaking Spanish is a skill that is not genetic, as it is learned, and would therefore not be stored in the genes within the chromosomes of the parents. Height, hair color, freckles, and color blindness are all genetic traits children can inherit from their parents.

8. C: SC.8.P.9.2

A chemical change involves a chemical reaction where new products are formed. When silver tarnishes, a thin layer of corrosion is formed, indicating a chemical change. A physical change does not produce new substances. Phase changes such as evaporation and sublimation are examples of physical changes. Salt dissolving in water is also a physical change because the ions just separate, and no new substances are formed.

9. A: SC.7.P.11.2

In a Zn-Cu battery, the zinc terminal has a higher concentration of electrons than the copper terminal, so there is a potential difference between the locations of the two terminals. This is a form of electrical energy brought about by the chemical interactions between the metals and the electrolyte the battery uses. Creating a circuit and causing a current to flow will transform the electrical energy into heat energy, mechanical energy, or another form of electrical energy, depending on the devices in the circuit. A generator transforms mechanical energy into electrical energy, and a transformer changes the electrical properties of a form of electrical energy.

10. D: SC.8.E.5.5

White Dwarf stars are found at the lower left-hand corner of the Hertzsprung-Russell diagram and can be plotted by following the 10+ magnitude and a temperature of 25,000K until the two points meet.

11. C: SC.6.P.13.1

The ice skaters are applying Newton's Third Law to create an equal and opposite reaction force, causing both partners to move. Although each skater is pushing the other, there is another force that must be considered in that they moved as well.

12. C: SC.6.P.13.2

The larger rabbit, because it has more mass that must overcome gravity and accelerate. Newton's Second Law states that the force required to accelerate a body is directly proportional to its mass. Thus, the larger rabbit will have to exert more force on the ground to achieve the same level of acceleration as the smaller rabbit.

13. C: SC.6.E.7.5

Wind is produced by convection, the process of warm, less dense air rising and cold, more dense air sinking. Convection is powered by the Sun. The change in ocean temperature alone does not create wind. Cold air moving across the ocean is wind and is not the cause of wind. Clouds do not produce wind.

14. C: SC.7.N.1.2

Repetition is when a scientist runs many trials of the same experiment to see if the results were random or repeatable. Because Jessica ran the same experiment three times, she has demonstrated repetition. Answer choice A is incorrect because Jessica's friend performed the experiment. When another scientist does the same experiment as the first, this is known as replication. Answer choice B is incorrect because it describes a discovery that Jessica made but does not mention that she ran the experiment more than once. Answer choice D is incorrect because it describes the communication of results and does not mention that Jessica ran the experiment more than once.

15. A: SC.7.N.1.5

Models can simplify concepts and display concepts that do not exist or that are too big or small for people to see. A scale model of the solar system would show how the planets move in orbit. For Neptune, a full orbit of the Sun takes around 165 Earth years and covers 2.8 billion miles. Since this amount of distance and time are not possible for a person to see and can be difficult to conceptualize, a scale model is helpful as a demonstration. Answer choice B is incorrect because, while the model would show how far apart the planets are, the student wants to compare the orbits of Earth and Neptune, which is a different concept. Answer choice C is incorrect because the orbit around the Sun takes Earth one year and Neptune 165 Earth years, so the process takes a long time. Answer choice D is incorrect because the model may not show how fast the planets are moving. Furthermore, this would not answer the student's question because she wants to know the size of the planets' orbits.

16. D: SC.6.N.2.2

Not all scientific literature is reliable. Students must learn to distinguish between sources that are consistent with experimental evidence and those that are biased or misleading in their conclusions. Scientists study one another's work to direct and support original research, but they recognize that interpretations of data may vary and that existing theories are always subject to testing and revision.

17. A: SC.8.E.5.3

The diameter of the Sun is about 109 times as long as that of the Earth. The diameter of a rice grain is about two mm long, and that of a soccer ball is around 200 mm. The best way to understand the answer to this question, though, is not to know the lengths or diameters of random objects but to understand the scale. Imagine 109 rice grains side by side. When considering this image, answer choices B and C could not possibly be the right answers. A golf ball and a marble are not large enough to match the scale of the Sun to Earth. Answer choice D, a baseball, is a little closer to the correct size, but a baseball's diameter is still far from 109 times that of a rice grain. Using deductive reasoning, answer choice A would be the only object that comes close to the right size.

18. D: SC.7.E.6.4

The best evidence to support the theory that Florida was once underwater would be fossils of aquatic species. If the state was underwater during the Jurassic period, animal and/or plant remnants from that era would be proof of this. Fossils of aquatic species would show the changes that have occurred to the environment over time. Answer choice A is incorrect because the southern part of Florida being covered in the present would not be evidence of whether Florida was underwater in the past. Answer choice B is incorrect because the erosion could have been caused by any number of things, including rain, wind, ancient glaciers, or flowing water in the present day. Answer choice C is incorrect because finding no evidence of one type of land dinosaur in the area does not mean that area was underwater. Instead of trying to explain why evidence is not present, scientists usually make conclusions based on evidence at hand. Therefore, finding evidence of aquatic animals is more convincing than not finding evidence of a land-dwelling animal.

19. A: SC.6.E.7.4

The cryosphere refers to the ice on Earth. The geosphere refers to the planet's soil, rocks, etc.—in other words, the earth parts of the Earth. Glaciers are a part of the cryosphere, and they eroded the soil (which is a part of the geosphere) around two million years ago by scraping or picking up rocks from the ground. Answer choice B is incorrect because erosion is a process that only affects the geosphere. Answer choice C is incorrect because rain is part of the hydrosphere, not the cryosphere. Answer choice D is incorrect because soil storing groundwater is an interaction between the geosphere and hydrosphere.

20. B: SC.6.L.14.1

Among the answer choices, choice B, a kidney cell, is the lowest level of structural organization. The lowest level of structural organization is the atom, but the cell is the lowest of the answer options that are given. Atoms make up cells, which make up tissues. A collection of tissues makes up an organ. A collection of organs makes up a system, and systems make up bodies. Answer choice A is incorrect because a system would be the highest level of structural organization out of these answer choices. Answer choice C is incorrect because cells make up tissues, making a cell a lower level of organization out of the two. Answer choice D is incorrect because the kidney is an organ, which is at the higher end of the structural organization.

21. A: SC.6.L.15.1

Organisms in the domain Archaea are known for living in extreme environments that those in Bacteria and Eukarya cannot live in. Answer choice B is incorrect because organisms in the domain Eukarya (eukaryotes) have nuclei, not those in Archaea. Answer choice C is incorrect because both organisms classified as Bacteria and Archaea are microscopic; therefore, the student would not be able to determine which domain the organism belongs to just by its microscopic size. Answer choice D is incorrect because many organisms in Archaea, Bacteria, and Eukarya do not photosynthesize, so it would be impossible to determine which domain the organism belongs to with only this information.

22. D: SC.7.E.6.5

Evidence of plate tectonics is based on the shapes of the continents, which seem to fit together like a puzzle, as well as the fossils found along these edges. The Mid-Atlantic Ridge is the birthplace of new crust that is then destroyed in the subduction zones in the Pacific Ring of Fire, where most seismic activity takes place.

23. D: SC.8.E.5.9

Although all of the answers are celestial bodies, natural bodies outside of the earth's atmosphere, only one influences the earth's tides. The moon's gravitational pull on the earth causes the seas to rise and fall as one large wave, known as a tide, with a very large wavelength as compared to waves formed by wind.

24. C: SC.7.N.1.4

The independent variable is the variable that is changed in the experiment in order to determine its effect on the dependent variable or the outcome of the experiment. The dependent variable results from the experimenter making only one change to an experiment that can be repeated with the same results. Mrs. Jones's class was comparing the effects of sugar and artificial sweetener on the overall color of cookies once they are baked; thus, the one thing that should be changed in the experiment is the sugar and artificial sweetener in the recipe. All of the other ingredients stay the same. For the experiment to be valid and not influenced by any other variables, the students should keep the temperature and baking time the same, as these could affect the color of the cookies as well.

25. D: SC.6.L.14.5

Blood is cooled as it passes through capillaries surrounding the sweat glands. Heat is absorbed along with excess salt and water and transferred to the glands as sweat. Droplets of sweat then evaporate from the skin surface to dissipate heat and cool the body. The kidney, bladder, and liver are not involved in regulating body temperature.

26. C: SC.7.L.17.2

A parasite is an organism that feeds off the nutritional assets of another living thing called the host, which can lead to the host becoming malnourished or dying. Symbiosis occurs when there is a benefit to both organisms. A predator eats its prey. A producer produces food in the form of plant material that is eaten by a consumer.

27. D: SC.8.N.1.1

The first steps in a scientific investigation process involve asking a question about a problem and doing background research in order to determine if there is a valid reason for the question and whether it has been previously tested.

28. C: SC.7.L.17.3

In an ecosystem, when one species is affected by overfishing or pollution, other species will either thrive due to a lack of competition or become extinct for the same reasons. The question states that the other species were not impacted by the overfishing or pollution. Thus, their populations would not have decreased for those reasons. Once extinct, the other species were no longer the potential prey of the Blue Pike or competing against them for similar food sources and so had the opportunity to increase their population numbers.

29. C: SC.8.P.8.7

The most basic units of matter are protons, electrons, and neutrons. Protons are found in the nucleus, and have a positive charge. They are one of the three components of a helium atom a. When atoms have positive or negative charges, they are known as ions b. Molecules of oxygen, water, etc. d. are even more complex, consisting of one or more atoms held together by bonds.

30. B: SC.7.L.15.2

The fish will not be able to survive without high oxygen levels in the lake. Answer choice A is incorrect because animals do not learn how to use less oxygen, just as people could not learn to breathe less. In the best-case scenario, some fish will have been born with a mutation that would allow them to survive the change in condition. Answer choice C is incorrect because a new species will not be "born". The process of speciation takes a lot of time. It typically takes more than two million years. Answer choice D is incorrect because, although the fish may choke on plastic, the question did not specify what kind of pollution has affected the lake.

31. D: SC.6.L.14.4

Only plant cells have chloroplast. All eukaryotic cells do have a nucleus. Cells can only reproduce from other existing cells. Cells are the basic structures of any organism.

32. C: SC.8.E.5.9

The opposite moon phase of a new moon is a full moon. A new moon is the first moon phase, followed by the first quarter and then the full moon. The last moon is not a moon phase.

How to Overcome Test Anxiety

Just the thought of taking a test is enough to make most people a little nervous. A test is an important event that can have a long-term impact on your future, so it's important to take it seriously and it's natural to feel anxious about performing well. But just because anxiety is normal, that doesn't mean that it's helpful in test taking, or that you should simply accept it as part of your life. Anxiety can have a variety of effects. These effects can be mild, like making you feel slightly nervous, or severe, like blocking your ability to focus or remember even a simple detail.

If you experience test anxiety—whether severe or mild—it's important to know how to beat it. To discover this, first you need to understand what causes test anxiety.

Causes of Test Anxiety

While we often think of anxiety as an uncontrollable emotional state, it can actually be caused by simple, practical things. One of the most common causes of test anxiety is that a person does not feel adequately prepared for their test. This feeling can be the result of many different issues such as poor study habits or lack of organization, but the most common culprit is time management. Starting to study too late, failing to organize your study time to cover all of the material, or being distracted while you study will mean that you're not well prepared for the test. This may lead to cramming the night before, which will cause you to be physically and mentally exhausted for the test. Poor time management also contributes to feelings of stress, fear, and hopelessness as you realize you are not well prepared but don't know what to do about it.

Other times, test anxiety is not related to your preparation for the test but comes from unresolved fear. This may be a past failure on a test, or poor performance on tests in general. It may come from comparing yourself to others who seem to be performing better or from the stress of living up to expectations. Anxiety may be driven by fears of the future—how failure on this test would affect your educational and career goals. These fears are often completely irrational, but they can still negatively impact your test performance.

Elements of Test Anxiety

As mentioned earlier, test anxiety is considered to be an emotional state, but it has physical and mental components as well. Sometimes you may not even realize that you are suffering from test anxiety until you notice the physical symptoms. These can include trembling hands, rapid heartbeat, sweating, nausea, and tense muscles. Extreme anxiety may lead to fainting or vomiting. Obviously, any of these symptoms can have a negative impact on testing. It is important to recognize them as soon as they begin to occur so that you can address the problem before it damages your performance.

The mental components of test anxiety include trouble focusing and inability to remember learned information. During a test, your mind is on high alert, which can help you recall information and stay focused for an extended period of time. However, anxiety interferes with your mind's natural processes, causing you to blank out, even on the questions you know well. The strain of testing during anxiety makes it difficult to stay focused, especially on a test that may take several hours. Extreme anxiety can take a huge mental toll, making it difficult not only to recall test information but even to understand the test questions or pull your thoughts together.

Effects of Test Anxiety

Test anxiety is like a disease—if left untreated, it will get progressively worse. Anxiety leads to poor performance, and this reinforces the feelings of fear and failure, which in turn lead to poor performances on subsequent tests. It can grow from a mild nervousness to a crippling condition. If allowed to progress, test anxiety can have a big impact on your schooling, and consequently on your future.

Test anxiety can spread to other parts of your life. Anxiety on tests can become anxiety in any stressful situation, and blanking on a test can turn into panicking in a job situation. But fortunately, you don't have to let anxiety rule your testing and determine your grades. There are a number of relatively simple steps you can take to move past anxiety and function normally on a test and in the rest of life.

Physical Steps for Beating Test Anxiety

While test anxiety is a serious problem, the good news is that it can be overcome. It doesn't have to control your ability to think and remember information. While it may take time, you can begin taking steps today to beat anxiety.

Just as your first hint that you may be struggling with anxiety comes from the physical symptoms, the first step to treating it is also physical. Rest is crucial for having a clear, strong mind. If you are tired, it is much easier to give in to anxiety. But if you establish good sleep habits, your body and mind will be ready to perform optimally, without the strain of exhaustion. Additionally, sleeping well helps you to retain information better, so you're more likely to recall the answers when you see the test questions.

Getting good sleep means more than going to bed on time. It's important to allow your brain time to relax. Take study breaks from time to time so it doesn't get overworked, and don't study right before bed. Take time to rest your mind before trying to rest your body, or you may find it difficult to fall asleep.

Along with sleep, other aspects of physical health are important in preparing for a test. Good nutrition is vital for good brain function. Sugary foods and drinks may give a burst of energy but this burst is followed by a crash, both physically and emotionally. Instead, fuel your body with protein and vitamin-rich foods.

Also, drink plenty of water. Dehydration can lead to headaches and exhaustion, especially if your brain is already under stress from the rigors of the test. Particularly if your test is a long one, drink water during the breaks. And if possible, take an energy-boosting snack to eat between sections.

Along with sleep and diet, a third important part of physical health is exercise. Maintaining a steady workout schedule is helpful, but even taking 5-minute study breaks to walk can help get your blood pumping faster and clear your head. Exercise also releases endorphins, which contribute to a positive feeling and can help combat test anxiety.

When you nurture your physical health, you are also contributing to your mental health. If your body is healthy, your mind is much more likely to be healthy as well. So take time to rest, nourish your body with healthy food and water, and get moving as much as possible. Taking these physical steps will make you stronger and more able to take the mental steps necessary to overcome test anxiety.

Mental Steps for Beating Test Anxiety

Working on the mental side of test anxiety can be more challenging, but as with the physical side, there are clear steps you can take to overcome it. As mentioned earlier, test anxiety often stems from lack of preparation, so the obvious solution is to prepare for the test. Effective studying may be the most important weapon you have for beating test anxiety, but you can and should employ several other mental tools to combat fear.

First, boost your confidence by reminding yourself of past success—tests or projects that you aced. If you're putting as much effort into preparing for this test as you did for those, there's no reason you should expect to fail here. Work hard to prepare; then trust your preparation.

Second, surround yourself with encouraging people. It can be helpful to find a study group, but be sure that the people you're around will encourage a positive attitude. If you spend time with others who are anxious or cynical, this will only contribute to your own anxiety. Look for others who are motivated to study hard from a desire to succeed, not from a fear of failure.

Third, reward yourself. A test is physically and mentally tiring, even without anxiety, and it can be helpful to have something to look forward to. Plan an activity following the test, regardless of the outcome, such as going to a movie or getting ice cream.

When you are taking the test, if you find yourself beginning to feel anxious, remind yourself that you know the material. Visualize successfully completing the test. Then take a few deep, relaxing breaths and return to it. Work through the questions carefully but with confidence, knowing that you are capable of succeeding.

Developing a healthy mental approach to test taking will also aid in other areas of life. Test anxiety affects more than just the actual test—it can be damaging to your mental health and even contribute to depression. It's important to beat test anxiety before it becomes a problem for more than testing.

Study Strategy

Being prepared for the test is necessary to combat anxiety, but what does being prepared look like? You may study for hours on end and still not feel prepared. What you need is a strategy for test prep. The next few pages outline our recommended steps to help you plan out and conquer the challenge of preparation.

Step 1: Scope Out the Test

Learn everything you can about the format (multiple choice, essay, etc.) and what will be on the test. Gather any study materials, course outlines, or sample exams that may be available. Not only will this help you to prepare, but knowing what to expect can help to alleviate test anxiety.

Step 2: Map Out the Material

Look through the textbook or study guide and make note of how many chapters or sections it has. Then divide these over the time you have. For example, if a book has 15 chapters and you have five days to study, you need to cover three chapters each day. Even better, if you have the time, leave an extra day at the end for overall review after you have gone through the material in depth.

If time is limited, you may need to prioritize the material. Look through it and make note of which sections you think you already have a good grasp on, and which need review. While you are studying, skim quickly through the familiar sections and take more time on the challenging parts.

Write out your plan so you don't get lost as you go. Having a written plan also helps you feel more in control of the study, so anxiety is less likely to arise from feeling overwhelmed at the amount to cover.

Step 3: Gather Your Tools

Decide what study method works best for you. Do you prefer to highlight in the book as you study and then go back over the highlighted portions? Or do you type out notes of the important information? Or is it helpful to make flashcards that you can carry with you? Assemble the pens, index cards, highlighters, post-it notes, and any other materials you may need so you won't be distracted by getting up to find things while you study.

If you're having a hard time retaining the information or organizing your notes, experiment with different methods. For example, try color-coding by subject with colored pens, highlighters, or post-it notes. If you learn better by hearing, try recording yourself reading your notes so you can listen while in the car, working out, or simply sitting at your desk. Ask a friend to quiz you from your flashcards, or try teaching someone the material to solidify it in your mind.

Step 4: Create Your Environment

It's important to avoid distractions while you study. This includes both the obvious distractions like visitors and the subtle distractions like an uncomfortable chair (or a too-comfortable couch that makes you want to fall asleep). Set up the best study environment possible: good lighting and a comfortable work area. If background music helps you focus, you may want to turn it on, but otherwise keep the room quiet. If you are using a computer to take notes, be sure you don't have any other windows open, especially applications like social media, games, or anything else that could distract you. Silence your phone and turn off notifications. Be sure to keep water close by so you stay hydrated while you study (but avoid unhealthy drinks and snacks).

Also, take into account the best time of day to study. Are you freshest first thing in the morning? Try to set aside some time then to work through the material. Is your mind clearer in the afternoon or evening? Schedule your study session then. Another method is to study at the same time of day that you will take the test, so that your brain gets used to working on the material at that time and will be ready to focus at test time.

Step 5: Study!

Once you have done all the study preparation, it's time to settle into the actual studying. Sit down, take a few moments to settle your mind so you can focus, and begin to follow your study plan. Don't give in to distractions or let yourself procrastinate. This is your time to prepare so you'll be ready to fearlessly approach the test. Make the most of the time and stay focused.

Of course, you don't want to burn out. If you study too long you may find that you're not retaining the information very well. Take regular study breaks. For example, taking five minutes out of every hour to walk briskly, breathing deeply and swinging your arms, can help your mind stay fresh.

As you get to the end of each chapter or section, it's a good idea to do a quick review. Remind yourself of what you learned and work on any difficult parts. When you feel that you've mastered the material, move on to the next part. At the end of your study session, briefly skim through your notes again.

But while review is helpful, cramming last minute is NOT. If at all possible, work ahead so that you won't need to fit all your study into the last day. Cramming overloads your brain with more information than it can process and retain, and your tired mind may struggle to recall even previously learned information when it is overwhelmed with last-minute study. Also, the urgent nature of cramming and the stress placed on your brain contribute to anxiety. You'll be more likely to go to the test feeling unprepared and having trouble thinking clearly.

So don't cram, and don't stay up late before the test, even just to review your notes at a leisurely pace. Your brain needs rest more than it needs to go over the information again. In fact, plan to finish your studies by noon or early afternoon the day before the test. Give your brain the rest of the day to relax or focus on other things, and get a good night's sleep. Then you will be fresh for the test and better able to recall what you've studied.

Step 6: Take a Practice Test

Many courses offer sample tests, either online or in the study materials. This is an excellent resource to check whether you have mastered the material, as well as to prepare for the test format and environment.

Check the test format ahead of time: the number of questions, the type (multiple choice, free response, etc.), and the time limit. Then create a plan for working through them. For example, if you have 30 minutes to take a 60-question test, your limit is 30 seconds per question. Spend less time on the questions you know well so that you can take more time on the difficult ones.

If you have time to take several practice tests, take the first one open book, with no time limit. Work through the questions at your own pace and make sure you fully understand them. Gradually work up to taking a test under test conditions: sit at a desk with all study materials put away and set a timer. Pace yourself to make sure you finish the test with time to spare and go back to check your answers if you have time.

After each test, check your answers. On the questions you missed, be sure you understand why you missed them. Did you misread the question (tests can use tricky wording)? Did you forget the information? Or was it something you hadn't learned? Go back and study any shaky areas that the practice tests reveal.

Taking these tests not only helps with your grade, but also aids in combating test anxiety. If you're already used to the test conditions, you're less likely to worry about it, and working through tests until you're scoring well gives you a confidence boost. Go through the practice tests until you feel comfortable, and then you can go into the test knowing that you're ready for it.

Test Tips

On test day, you should be confident, knowing that you've prepared well and are ready to answer the questions. But aside from preparation, there are several test day strategies you can employ to maximize your performance.

First, as stated before, get a good night's sleep the night before the test (and for several nights before that, if possible). Go into the test with a fresh, alert mind rather than staying up late to study.

Try not to change too much about your normal routine on the day of the test. It's important to eat a nutritious breakfast, but if you normally don't eat breakfast at all, consider eating just a protein bar. If you're a coffee drinker, go ahead and have your normal coffee. Just make sure you time it so that the caffeine doesn't wear off right in the middle of your test. Avoid sugary beverages, and drink enough water to stay hydrated but not so much that you need a restroom break 10 minutes into the test. If your test isn't first thing in the morning, consider going for a walk or doing a light workout before the test to get your blood flowing.

Allow yourself enough time to get ready, and leave for the test with plenty of time to spare so you won't have the anxiety of scrambling to arrive in time. Another reason to be early is to select a good seat. It's helpful to sit away from doors and windows, which can be distracting. Find a good seat, get out your supplies, and settle your mind before the test begins.

When the test begins, start by going over the instructions carefully, even if you already know what to expect. Make sure you avoid any careless mistakes by following the directions.

Then begin working through the questions, pacing yourself as you've practiced. If you're not sure on an answer, don't spend too much time on it, and don't let it shake your confidence. Either skip it and come back later, or eliminate as many wrong answers as possible and guess among the remaining ones. Don't dwell on these questions as you continue—put them out of your mind and focus on what lies ahead.

Be sure to read all of the answer choices, even if you're sure the first one is the right answer. Sometimes you'll find a better one if you keep reading. But don't second-guess yourself if you do immediately know the answer. Your gut instinct is usually right. Don't let test anxiety rob you of the information you know.

If you have time at the end of the test (and if the test format allows), go back and review your answers. Be cautious about changing any, since your first instinct tends to be correct, but make sure you didn't misread any of the questions or accidentally mark the wrong answer choice. Look over any you skipped and make an educated guess.

At the end, leave the test feeling confident. You've done your best, so don't waste time worrying about your performance or wishing you could change anything. Instead, celebrate the successful completion of this test. And finally, use this test to learn how to deal with anxiety even better next time.

Review Video: Test Anxiety
Visit mometrix.com/academy and enter code: 100340

Important Qualification

Not all anxiety is created equal. If your test anxiety is causing major issues in your life beyond the classroom or testing center, or if you are experiencing troubling physical symptoms related to your anxiety, it may be a sign of a serious physiological or psychological condition. If this sounds like your situation, we strongly encourage you to seek professional help.

Online Resources

Due to our efforts to try to keep this book to a manageable length, we've created a link that will give you access to all of your online resources:

mometrix.com/resources719/flg8sci

It's Your Moment, Let's Celebrate It!

Share your story @mometrixtestpreparation